Jeremy Hooker grew up in Warsash near Southampton and at Pennington, on the edge of the New Forest, and the landscapes of this region have remained an important source of inspiration. Many of his poems were written in Wales, where he has lived for long periods. His academic career has taken him to universities in England, the Netherlands, and the USA. He is now Emeritus Professor of the University of South Wales. As well as for the eleven collections of poetry represented in *The Cut of the Light* (Enitharmon, 2006), Jeremy is well known as a critic and has published selections of writings by Edward Thomas and Richard Jefferies, and studies of David Jones and John Cowper Powys, all of them important to his own creative life. Other critical works include *Writers in a Landscape* (University of Wales Press, 1996) and *Imagining Wales* (University of Wales Press, 2001); his features for BBC Radio 3 include *A Map of David Jones*. Jeremy's most recent books are *Diary of a Stroke* (Shearsman, 2016) and two new collection of poems, *Scattered Light* (Enitharmon, 2015) and *Ancestral Lines* (Shearsman, 2016). He is a Fellow of the Welsh Academy and a Fellow of the Learned Society of Wales.

Also by Jeremy Hooker:

Poetry

The Elements
Soliloquies of a Chalk Giant
Landscape of the Daylight Moon
Solent Shore
Englishman's Road
A View from the Source: Selected Poems
Itchen Water (with Norman Ackroyd)
Their Silence a Language (with Lee Grandjean)
Master of the Leaping Figures
Groundwork (with Lee Grandjean)
Adamah
Our Lady of Europe
Arnolds Wood
The Cut of the Light. Poems 1965–2005
Scattered Light
Ancestral Lines

Prose

John Cowper Powys
David Jones: An Exploratory Study of the Writings
John Cowper Powys and David Jones: A Comparative Study
Poetry of Place: Essays and Reviews 1970–1981
The Presence of the Past: Essays on Modern British and American Poetry
Writers in a Landscape
Imagining Wales: A View of Modern Welsh Writing in English
Welsh Journal
Upstate: A North American Journal
Openings: A European Journal
Diary of a Stroke

Editions

Selected Poems of Alun Lewis (with Gweno Lewis)
Selected Stories by Frances Bellerby
Inwards Where All the Battle Is: A Selection of Alun Lewis's Writings from India
At Home on the Earth: A New Selection of the Later Writings of Richard Jefferies
The Ship of Swallows: A Selection of Short Stories by Edward Thomas
Mapping Golgotha: Letters & Poems of Wilfred Owen

Ditch Vision

Essays on Poetry, Nature, and Place

Jeremy Hooker

AWEN
Stroud

First published in 2017 by Awen Publications
12 Belle Vue Close, Stroud GL5 1ND, England
www.awenpublications.co.uk

Copyright © 2017 Jeremy Hooker

Jeremy Hooker has asserted his right in accordance with the Copyright, Designs and Patents Act 1988 to be identified as the author of this book

Front cover image: *Brief Sun (November)* by David Tress
© David Tress 2010
David Tress is represented internationally by Messum's Fine Art Ltd, London

Cover design: Kirsty Hartsiotis
Editing: Anthony Nanson
Proofreading: Richard Selby

ISBN 978-1-906900-51-9

Contents

Introduction	vii
Ditch Vision	1
Richard Jefferies: A Personal Discovery	17
Versions of Freedom: Nicolai Berdyaev and John Cowper Powys	36
Alone in Life: The Friendship of Robert Frost and Edward Thomas	52
The Bounded and the Wild	64
Alun Lewis: 'The Tragic Condition'	82
Mary Butts and Her English Landscape	88
Frances Bellerby, Poet	107
Three 'Powys Poems' with a Commentary on Each	116
Notes on 'Poetic Vision'	124
Water over Stone: Reflections on Poetry and Spirit	133
'Tending Words and Sheep': The Poetry of Les Arnold	154
Reflections on 'Ground'	163
Reflections on the Lyric 'I'	173
Revisiting 'God's Houses'	180
Mystery at the Heart of Things: An Interview with Jeremy Hooker (by Fiona Owen)	194
Land and Sea and Sky	207
Acknowledgements	217
Index	218

Introduction

Poetry and nature have been closely associated in my mind since I was a boy, and both have been connected with place. For some fifty years, in both my poetry and criticism, I have been writing about these subjects and their interrelationships. I have devised and taught university courses on writing and place, and on British and American poets and novelists for whom a sense of locality is integral to their vision of reality. My previous writings on the subjects include the books *Poetry of Place* (1982) and *Writers in a Landscape* (1997). At the same time, in my poetry and journals, I have been engaged with my personal apprehension of nature and place. This book both extends and deepens my thinking on these subjects and is part of a continuing process.

    Critical and poetic thinking are not the same, but in the life of a writer who is both poet and critic they work together and are mutually stimulating and illuminating. My writings move between the poles of critical exposition and poetic exploration, and between formal and informal modes, and they belong together as different approaches to the same related subjects. Poetry, nature, and place are vitally important to me, but their significance is far more than personal in a world threatened by placelessness and environmental ruin.

    This book consists in part of essays concerned with nature writing and the ecological imagination, and contrasts ideas of the wild or wilderness in British and American poetry and prose. I also consider poets and prose writers whose work makes imaginative use of landscape and myth. Robinson Jeffers and Richard Jefferies are among the contrasting figures I discuss, while in writing about Edward Thomas and Robert Frost my concern is rather with their affinities. Together with my other critical and expository writings, I think of these essays as inherently exploratory. By this I mean that it is my intention to examine the work in depth and to make it more available to other readers. As in all my criticism, I aim at objectivity, and to open the work of writers whose importance has not been fully recognized, such as John Cowper Powys and Mary Butts. In these and other writers, the use of nature informs a mythological imagination, and a sense of the sacred distinguishes their work within a mainly secular culture. This too is important to me as a poet, since, as my poetry has developed, my focus on place has become associated with ideas of the sacred and with the concept of 'ground' in a spiritual sense. In various ways, the writers I discuss have a poetic vision that challenges narrow ideas of the material world.

The connection between poetry and nature, and the writers who make the connection matter a great deal to me. I have been reading Richard Jefferies since boyhood, and I discovered other writers such as Edward Thomas and the Powys brothers as a young man. Much of the poetry I discuss has been part of my life for many years. It was natural, therefore, that I should include in this book essays about the development of my own work as poet, which owes so much to the tradition I describe as 'ditch vision'.

Several of the essays in this book are previously unpublished, others have appeared only in specialist journals, and all have been revised, some substantially. Together, they constitute my most important explorations of poetry, nature, and place, and associated subjects such as landscape, the meaning of 'ground', uses of myth, and 'green' or ecological poetic vision. There is necessarily some overlap of material, since certain themes and figures recur. I think of these as rich returns rather than repetitions, since they show a developing engagement with matters central to my making as poet and critic.

Ditch Vision

'The comfort we need is inhuman.' These words, with which Bill McKibben concludes *The End of Nature* (1990), echo Robinson Jeffers's 'inhumanism' and accord with McKibben's belief that 'we can no longer imagine that we are part of something larger than ourselves'.[1] The connection between 'something larger' and the American passion for wilderness is the starting point for this essay, since it calls up, by contrast, a quite different sense of the wild in the English tradition of natural vision, from Gilbert White to the present day. That is the sense that I call 'ditch vision' – a description based on a passage from a Richard Jefferies essay to be discussed later – and it consists of a number of different strands.

After visiting the Lake District in 1855, Nathaniel Hawthorne wrote,

> On the rudest surface of English earth, there is seen the effect of centuries of civilization, so that you do not quite get at naked Nature anywhere. And then every point of beauty is so well known, and has been described so much, that one must needs look through other people's eyes, and feel as if he were seeing a picture rather than a reality.[2]

This is a distinctively American way of seeing 'English earth'; a sense of 'naked Nature' belongs to 'the image of a wild, untrammelled nature ... deeply etched on the American consciousness'.[3] In the original sense of the word (*wild-deor-ness*, 'the place of wild beasts'), there has been no wilderness in the British Isles since the Middle Ages; even in the sense of the word given by Dr Johnson in his *Dictionary* ('a desert; a tract of solitude and strangeness'), wilderness is nowhere to be found upon an American scale in these islands. Hawthorne was right, of course, in claiming that the soil of England has been extensively cultivated since early times, so that, as Oliver Rackham says, 'our great wildwoods passed away in prehistory'.[4] Hawthorne was also aware that, following the vogue for the picturesque in the eighteenth century, the wilder areas have been among the most visited, pictured, and written about. The evidence of the English nature writing tradition suggests, however, that no English writer or painter has wanted 'to get at naked Nature' in the American way.

The wild, however, is not determined by the presence of wild beasts. Nor is it a feature of scale only. Gilbert White, with his 'parochial history', *The Natural History and Antiquities of Selborne* (1789), demonstrated that the study of a relatively small area can serve as a microcosm of the natural world. He wrote of finding that, 'in zoology as it is in botany: all nature is so full, that that district produces the greatest variety which is the most examined'. In examining the entire life of a district, White considered the human (including antiquities) and nature where he found them, side by side; he did not need to go beyond the bounds of his parish to find the fullness of nature.

White's combination of scientific curiosity and observation with a sense of wonder at God's creation was continued by his successors in the nineteenth century, though the religious sense frequently took less orthodox, and in some cases non-Christian, forms. Other writers in the English tradition of nature writing added aesthetic and political concerns to a focus upon locality or region. John Clare, in his letters and prose descriptions as well as his poems, showed that he knew his district as intimately as White knew Selborne. But Clare burns with an anger at the political system that enclosed common land and displaced him from his boyhood village which is quite different from anything we find in the pious and urbane Gilbert White. Political anger is a force motivating William Cobbett also when, on his travels on horseback through the southern shires in the 1820s, gathering material for *Rural Rides* (1830), he observes the pauperization of rural labourers. Cobbett is sensitive to natural beauty, which he perceives as a *common* right. Thus he reflects that 'the English Ploughman' could once hear birds singing 'without the sorrowful reflection that he himself was a *pauper* ... Shall he never have the due reward of his labour!'[5] Cobbett undertook his explorations to report on what was then a relatively unknown England, where even a native not far from home could still get benighted and lost. In considering the wild in a small country, we have to bear in mind the fact of distance relative to modes of transport. In *The Mayor of Casterbridge* (1886), Thomas Hardy wrote about the England of country people in the 1830s: 'To the liege subjects of Labour, the England of those days was a continent, and a mile a geographical degree.' Distance from centres of power facilitates the marginalization and exploitation that Cobbett and writers who follow him condemn.

Ideas of nature's fullness in English writing – whether owing to focus upon a particular locality or to a sense of geographical distance relative to means of transport and communication – ensure that a humanized nature takes the place wilderness holds in America. In England, however, it is a humanized nature within which wildness or the non-human is discoverable. Another element crucial to our understanding of this is the role played by childhood, since English writers frequently find the wild upon home ground, in the territory first known intimately. It is here that they have perceived the boundless in the bounded; found creative power in minute particulars; seen visions in ditches.

George Eliot was a writer who well understood that childhood forms a bond between person and place and induces a feeling that earth is sacred. 'We could never have loved the earth so well if we had had no childhood in it,' she wrote in *The Mill on the Floss* (1860). She described 'familiar' things – flowers, birdsong, sky, fields – as 'the mother-tongue of our imagination, the language that is laden with all the subtle inextricable associations the fleeting hours of our childhood left behind them'.

This love for familiar elemental and natural things was strongly influenced by *Lyrical Ballads* (1798) and Wordsworth's revolutionary choice of 'incidents and situations from common life', in which he finds 'the essential passions of the heart'. We should be aware, moreover, that both Wordsworth and Coleridge were influenced in their seeing by Dorothy Wordsworth, and so there is a link between her mode of perception and George Eliot's concept of the imagination's mother-tongue.

Dorothy Wordsworth's influence was partly a matter of sympathy – Edward Thomas went so far as to say that 'she sympathises where Wordsworth contemplates'.[6] But Dorothy Wordsworth's vision had other qualities, too. With an eye that, as Coleridge said, is 'watchful in minutest observation', she sees an animate nature – for example, water running, flowers growing – and she herself is energetic, walking through a world of living forces. Far from being passively receptive, she partly constructs scenes, forming aesthetic images, as when, in the *Alfoxden Journal*, she describes 'the young wheat streaked by silver lines of water' and 'the shafts of the trees ... like the columns of a ruin'. Reading her, we are made aware of how complicated 'observation' is – in the influence upon her of the picturesque, for example, and her use of personification, rising at times to a mythic mode of perception (the moon conceived as 'she').

Original vision and traditional influences are confluent in Dorothy Wordsworth's seeing. She combines scientific objectivity with aesthetic images and personal responses. Looking through her eyes, we see nature, and at the same time watch a human mind making itself at home in the world. Her vision is in part anthropomorphic, but she seems instinctively to assume equality between humans and non-human things, and she is alive to the independent life of nature. Thus, in *The Grasmere Journals*, she describes the Coniston Fells rising 'in their own shape and colour. Not Man's hills but all for themselves the sky and the clouds and a few wild creatures.'

Other writers have conveyed Dorothy Wordsworth's significance for them by naturalizing her, emphasizing her 'wildness'. To Thomas De Quincey, she was 'the very wildest (in the sense of the most natural) person I have ever known'.[7] Her brother William, in 'Lines Written a Few Miles Above Tintern Abbey', spoke of her 'wild eyes', her 'wild ecstasies', and saw her as a nature spirit: 'Her voice was like a hidden Bird that sang.' Her twentieth-century editor Helen Darbishire carries on this habit, speaking of 'phrases ... which seem to slip from her pen as easily as a raindrop slides from a leaf', likening her prose to a mountain stream and saying, 'we listen to what she tells us as we might listen to a thrush singing'.

The myth of the writer or literary work as a 'voice' of nature or of place recurs in the English nature writing tradition. Other instances include Charlotte Brontë's description of *Wuthering Heights*

(1847) as 'moorish, and wild, and knotty as the root of heath', Gerard Manley Hopkins's appreciation of William Barnes – 'it is as if Dorset life and Dorset landscape had taken flesh and tongue in the man' – Edward Thomas's image of Richard Jefferies as 'the genius, the human expression, of this country, emerging from it, not to be detached from it any more than the curves of some statues from their maternal stone', and his idea of Jefferies as an 'earth spirit'. When Geoffrey Grigson, in his poem 'To Wystan Auden', wrote that W. H. Auden 'emerged out/of England's life, and her centuries, out of Long Mynd/and her midlands', he too was expressing the strong need there has been in England from the Romantic period until modern times to naturalize writers and writing and to identify them, as if they were 'wild', with the soil of particular regions or places.

The myth that sees writers as 'wild', as 'voices' of nature, or as primitives 'rooted' in place, may be seen as largely compensatory and as an English equivalent to the American need for actual wilderness. It is a myth born of loss, of alienation, which arose as an ideal of participation within a changing, unsettling society, an increasingly industrial and urban world, in which nature was marginalized and the feeling of being at home was difficult to sustain. In face of social revolution and the breakdown of old ways of life and traditional beliefs, the idea of belonging, whether to nature or place, became associated with the past, with childhood, with the myth of a Golden Age.

The process receives poignant expression in John Clare's 'The Nightingale's Nest'. Here the poet invites the reader to accompany him as he moves deeper into the wood:

> Laughing and creeping through the mossy rails
> There have I hunted like a very boy
> Creeping on hands and knees through matted thorns
> To find her nest and see her feed her young
> And vainly did I many hours employ
> All seemed as hidden as a thought unborn
> And where these crimping fern leaves ramp among
> The hazels under boughs – Ive nestled down
> And watched her while she sung

The venture into the wood is a journey back to boyhood, an imagined creeping close to the ground, in which the poet identifies with the bird – as a man who also 'sings', and as one in search of home. 'Nestled', he watches the bird at her nest. Clare's descriptions are based on detailed knowledge and depict the nightingale's otherness, but he also renders the bird's meaning to him. He is a poet who has known security in his home life as a boy, and a man faced with insecurity, who returns to the past:

> nature is the builder and contrives
> Homes for her childrens comfort even here
> Where solitudes deciples spend their lives
> Unseen save when a wanderer passes near
> That loves such pleasant places – deep adown
> The nest is made an hermits mossy cell

Becoming a boy again, getting back close to the earth, native to hidden places, Clare recaptures his sense of being at home, a solitary in his society, but one who belongs, like the bird in its 'hermits mossy cell'. In sharing the experience with the reader he restores an idea of wild England, safe from the changes transforming the actual countryside during his time. Even now, in a transformed England, a reader can find in the poem an equivalent sense of coming home to nature.

Restoration of 'Wild England', the alternative title of Richard Jefferies' novel *After London* (1885), was both a primary aim of Jefferies and central to 'ditch vision' as a mode of perception among other writers, too. His importance in the present context is immediately evident from the opening of his essay 'The Pageant of Summer' (1883):

> Green rushes, long and thick, standing up above the edge of the ditch, told the hour of the year as distinctly as the shadow on the dial the hour of the day. Green and thick and sappy to the touch, they felt like summer, soft and elastic, as if full of life, mere rushes though they were. On the fingers they left a green scent; rushes have a separate scent of green, so, too,

have ferns, very different to that of grass or leaves. Rising from brown sheaths, the tall stems enlarged a little in the middle, like classical columns, and heavy with their sap and freshness, leaned against the hawthorn sprays. From the earth they had drawn its moisture, and made the ditch dry; some of the sweetness of the air had entered into their fibres, and the rushes – the common rushes – were full of beautiful summer.

Whether consciously or not, Jefferies is here writing in the tradition of *Lyrical Ballads*, but with a microscopic observation that is closer to Dorothy Wordsworth. The writing is charged with love of its subject. It is also a kind of writing with which Jefferies made a living, from its appeal to a largely urban, middle-class readership nostalgic for news of nature and the life of the countryside.

Jefferies emphasizes the supreme value of the 'common rushes', as if for the instruction of a reader who may overlook it, or the refreshment of a reader starved of the proximity of a flowering ditch. His style is pictorial, yet he uses it not to indulge in word painting but to render the life of the rushes and their interaction with the environment. The simile likening rushes to 'classical columns' may remind us of Dorothy Wordsworth's Gothic images. Jefferies, however, is not a picturesque writer; his figure ennobles the rushes, reinforcing our sense of their importance as conduits of life and objects of beauty. Later in the essay he argues that 'the whole office of Matter is to feed life'. Hence the magnitude of the rushes' importance: 'so much greater is this green and common rush than all the Alps'.

In 'The Pageant of Summer' Jefferies characteristically proceeds to work his imagined way into the undergrowth, pushing through grasses and hedges that partially hide the abundance of life. He reveals nature in and beyond the ditch to be an arena of innumerable ceaseless activities. It has unfathomable depth. The grass and leaves are 'endless'; the oak has 'immense strength'. Whereas Gilbert White shows the fullness of nature in a district, Jefferies reveals it, here, in a ditch. The effect of his vision, therefore, is to show that there is a vast hidden life in even a small area of the countryside. Wild England survives alongside the highway, in and among and behind the ditch full of common rushes. And here, we may feel, through the vision he has created, Jefferies is at home again. He is the boy and young man who roamed the fields and poked about in hedges and ditches on and around the family smallholding at Coate in Wiltshire, not the journalist who has moved away in order to make a living, and is now a sick man.

Jefferies' mysticism, which he expresses and treats philosophically in *The Story of My Heart* (1883), had its origins in his boyhood sense of participation in the universe, in the experience he ascribes to the boy Bevis in the novel of that name (1882):

> There was magic in everything, blades of grass and stars, the sun and the stones upon the ground.
>
> The green path by the strawberries was the centre of the world, and round about it by day *and* night the sun circled in a magical golden ring.

In his later writing, Jefferies developed a social and moral vision, with which he exposed 'the realities of rural life behind the scenes'; a vision expressed succinctly in the final sentence of his essay 'One of the New Voters': 'The wheat is beautiful, but human life is labour.' It would be a mistake, however, to separate his political and moral concern from his nature mysticism. Jefferies came to reject the idea of design in nature: 'I look at the sunshine and feel that there is no contracted order: there is divine chaos, and, in it, limitless hope and possibilities.' Earlier, in *The Amateur Poacher* (1879), he had written,

> Let us get out of these indoor narrow modern days, whose twelve hours somehow have become shortened, into the sunlight and the pure wind. A something that the ancients called divine can be found and felt there still.

The divine, for Jefferies, represents possibilities of liberation that are both natural and human, spiritual and social – creative possibilities involving freedom from 'contracted order', enlargement of being, escape from 'narrow modern days' into the eternal moment. Aspects of Jefferies' thinking are anthropocentric, but, as his exploration of the ditch in 'The Pageant of Summer' amply demonstrates, his actual seeing corresponds to the modern ecological vision summed up as 'the first Law of Ecology' by William Rueckert, in Barry Commoner's words: 'Everything is connected to everything else'.[8]

In his ditch vision, Jefferies is one among several Victorian writers to develop an art of seeing which combines aestheticism with morality, natural observation with imagination (or 'magic'), science with mysticism. Other Victorian 'seers' to have significantly influenced English nature writing in the twentieth century include Gerard Manley Hopkins, Thomas Hardy, and John Ruskin, who, in *Modern Painters* (1856), famously said, 'the greatest thing a human soul ever does in this world is to *see* something'. Hardy's imagination owed a great deal to his Dorset childhood, as we see when he sets human figures against an immense landscape, as if against the universe, although in fact within the bounds of Wessex. This is especially noticeable in *The Return of the Native* (1878), in which Hardy evokes 'the vast tract of unenclosed wild known as Egdon Heath' and describes Clym Yeobright's microscopic vision of the Heath as he works as a furze-cutter, focusing with his failing eyesight upon the wildlife immediately around him. The effects of immensity and infinite natural abundance stem from Hardy's original perspective as a child, when the Heath, at the very door of his home, would have appeared immense. In his *Autobiography* (1934), John Cowper Powys described as 'sorcery' the child's 'power of finding the infinitely great in the materially small'.[9] This power, which Powys called 'the ecstasy of the unbounded', is perhaps the main source of the 'magical' effects we find in the ditch vision of Hardy, Jefferies, Powys himself, and other English nature writers. The troubling figure of Henry Williamson, at once a great novelist and an admirer of Hitler, cannot be dealt with in passing. But it must just be said that in his animal stories, such as *Tarka the Otter* (1927), he created an extraordinarily intimate sense of the life of the wild creature in its natural habitat.

For Edward Thomas as a boy, Jefferies' words about 'something that the ancients called divine' were 'a gospel, an incantation'.[10] In the years before the First World War, Thomas wrote numerous prose studies in which he explored both the English countryside (mainly in the southern counties) and the English tradition of nature writing. In his poetry, which he wrote in the last two years of his life,

Thomas continued – and renewed – the tradition of finding 'wild' life in domesticated landscapes. In *The South Country* (1909) Thomas spoke of 'social mysticism', which, no doubt with a memory of Jefferies, he ascribed to Thomas Traherne. Thomas referred to passages in which Traherne 'seems to advance to the position of Whitman, whom some have blamed for making the word "divine" of no value because he would apply it to all, whereas to do so is no more than to lay down that rule of veneration for men – and the other animals – which has produced and will produce the greatest revolutions'. What Thomas means by 'social mysticism' is further clarified by his observation that study of natural history 'should help to give the child a sense of oneness with all forms of life'.

From Edward Thomas's time until the present day, writers have continued to explore 'unknown' England, either by examining the familiar with new eyes or by following Gilbert White and Jefferies in finding the fullness of nature in a district or a ditch. The resulting visions are rarely innocent of politics and, broadly speaking, may be divided into the radical tradition, which emphasizes the value of the common life, and the conservative tradition, which uses the concept of 'organic community' to condemn popular culture and an urbanized society. Edward Thomas's principal counterpart between the wars and after the Second World War was Geoffrey Grigson, a poet and editor associated with W. H. Auden and the socialist poets of the 1930s, and an expert on English topography and wild flowers. Grigson was also instrumental in rediscovering writers and painters in the English visionary tradition, such as John Clare and Samuel Palmer.

According to Grigson, a 'lucky poet' retains 'a consciousness of his first territory, a consciousness with love'. He goes on to say, 'The territory may be – often has been – a garden which surrounded him and contained him, a miniature world or universe which seemed enormous and mysterious, and protective as well.'[11] By this definition Grigson himself was a lucky poet, since he was born and brought up in a vicarage at Pelynt in east Cornwall, and his 'first territory' was such a garden, with which he felt an original oneness. In his autobiographical writings, Grigson moves out from this centre into the surrounding parish, where, he says, 'I knew each tree, corner, footpath, rock and trickle, where I knew each of the fields by name.'[12] As he grew up, he added a localized sense of history to his love of natural objects and explored local antiquities and parish documents. In a word, he acquired knowledge of his parish similar to White's knowledge of his district, and the knowledge enabled him to write *The Freedom of the Parish* (1954), which is the book that perhaps comes closest to being a twentieth-century equivalent to *The Natural History and Antiquities of Selborne*.

In recent English nature writing that refuses 'an anthropocentric view of the world',[13] consciousness of territory involves rejection of human possessiveness and attention to the ways of other creatures. As we see in the poems and other writings of Colin Simms, this attention can require a linguistically innovative approach that avoids 'self-expression/that unacceptable indulgence'[14] and encounters the other. The word 'meeting' is of key importance in this approach, as in Simms's 'Meeting a riverine marten whilst waiting for otter, South Tynedale 1967', which begins, 'The "isness", the specific nature, of martens is an elusive matter, and will vary with any observer, even one who tries to avoid what is "said" already, what is "expected" opinion.' Aspects of Simms's writings recall the intense sympathy of John Clare's treatment of birds and animals, and his language is at times reminiscent of Gerard Manley Hopkins's inscapes, which depict the identity of unique beings. Simms's aim, however, is to shake off anthropocentric habits of language, in so far as that is possible. This is an aim that involves humour at the writer's own expense, as we see in the title of 'Marten deceives his pursuer (me ...)'. Marten 'won't have *our* own terms'; 'it is *his* way we only stumble at'. In this 'stumbling', this attempt to find 'terms' alive to the 'way' of other creatures, Simms's writing is excitingly inventive.

The political implications of Simms's work include, as Harriet Tarlo has shown, a location of places that resists their marginalization, and 'a sense of the land as workplace'. The same can be said of the writings of Jim Perrin. In his essay 'Caban', for example, Perrin, visiting a North Wales quarry, thinks first of 'the men whose brief, hard lives were spent wresting from the mountain the rock from which were carved rank upon rank of headstones in Deiniolen cemetery under which they now lie'.[15] Reading Perrin with his close attention to landscapes, individual human beings, and natural objects, and his wide range of literary references, underlines the fact that, as in the case of Edward Thomas and his 'social mysticism', radical politics, aesthetic values, and a sense of the spiritual can coexist in the English nature writing tradition. Perrin is a sophisticated writer, who brings what he calls 'my post-modernist perception' to bear on the language of the *conquest* of Everest, for example.[16] But he also records without irony how beauty affects him, as when he recalls a Wordsworthian experience of emerging from mist in the Derbyshire hills when he was twelve or thirteen:

> The valley-greens flared with fierce intensity, bracken seemed on fire, mist was gilded with the sun. What had been terror was now beauty. As I sat and watched it there was a stillness within me beyond anything I'd known. I was annihilated, had no existence, simply looked out at the inconceivable beauty of the world that had detached me from any concept of self in order that I might *see*.[17]

The escape from self is not dissimilar to Colin Simms's approach to the other, or Dorothy Wordsworth's acknowledgement of the hills 'all for themselves the sky and the clouds and a few wild creatures'. All such experiences accord with 'the fact' Edward Thomas recognized, 'that the earth does not belong to man, but man to the earth'.[18]

Richard Mabey, editor of a selection of Jefferies' writings and biographer of Gilbert White, has established a reputation as an explorer of England, or parts of England, as 'unknown' country which has continued the tradition of these writers into the twenty-first century. In the late 1960s he explored 'accidental corners' of Middlesex, 'wasteland', 'the edges of old tips', and generally derelict areas, an exploration that led to his book *The Unofficial Countryside* (1973) and a television film. Mabey's description of the latter gives a good idea of what his explorations revealed in the area of Greater London:

> We filmed kestrels nesting in tower-block window boxes and foxes hunting in cemeteries. We found giant hogweed, a vast

umbellifer from the damp regions of the Caucasus which had enjoyed a brief popularity in Victorian gardens, escaping to form feral colonies in the boggy surrounds of the Hoover factory. And in the derelict shell of Beckton gasworks in the East End we filmed black redstarts ... which normally haunt the low mountain slopes and stone villages of southern Europe.[19]

Work on the book gave Mabey 'a taste for wild corners that had slipped out of the system'. He discovered what appeared to be 'a parallel universe ... inhabiting the same space as us, living independently but learning to use our trade and our surplus energy and food for its own purposes'. *The Unofficial Countryside* reveals the abundance of wildlife inhabiting urban England.

A feature Mabey shares with all true naturalists is the ability to see anew when what he sees or is shown does not accord with his expectations. His visit to Dungeness in Kent, recorded in *Country Matters*, is a case in point. At first he sees the shingle promontory housing the nuclear power station as a 'wasteland': 'like one of those cryptic, unsettling landscapes in J. G. Ballard's novels, England's terminal beach'.[20] His view changes, however, when he sees Dungeness in the company of two ecologists, who take him to 'the top of the ridge, [where] a huge view suddenly opens out, not of a flat block of shingle but of long ridges, topped with vegetation and curving gently away towards the point of the Ness for nearly a mile'. The 'opening out' of confined spaces to reveal a larger and more varied natural world is a basic feature of writings in the tradition of White and Jefferies. The effect is rarely only aesthetic. In this instance Mabey comes to realize 'what makes Dungeness unique', and its ecosystem 'one of the most extensive and exquisitely formed in the world'.[21]

The most remarkable celebration of Dungeness is *Derek Jarman's Garden* (1995), a book consisting of Derek Jarman's record of the evolution of his garden, on the shingle facing the nuclear power station, from 1986 until the year of his death, 1994. Howard Sooley's photographs splendidly complement the prose record and poems. The book is very much more than the celebration of a place, as Jarman, with his diverse gifts, was a good deal more than a gardener. In the context of this essay, however, it is the garden, as a work of nature and a work of art, made out of 'wilderness', which is the focus of attention. 'My garden is ecologically sound,' Jarman writes, 'though work of any kind disrupts the existing terrain.'²² He introduces local flowers into the garden: 'so many weeds are spectacular flowers: the white campion, mallow, rest-harrow and scabious look wonderful'. With these, he 'makes a little wilderness at the heart of paradise'. He is aware from the beginning of the personal needs his garden serves – 'I saw it as a therapy and a pharmacopoeia' – and, as his illness progresses, he comes increasingly to mythologize 'my garden,/Gethsemane and Eden'. The personal importance of the garden, however, and the garden as a response to his illness and the deaths of friends ('Old age came quickly for my frosted generation,/cold, cold, cold, they died so silently') depend upon its actuality as a garden made in the local conditions:

> You see it is rather a wild garden; I really recommend this – out with those lawns and in with the stinging nettles and kerbside flowers: bluebells, pinks, purple orchids, drifts of buttercups – subtlety to the eye. (I don't see anything like this as I go about, just a desert of fuchsias, awful in July.) I would like anyone who reads my book to try this wildness in a corner. It will bring you much happiness.

I have argued in this essay that the tradition of English nature writing described here as 'ditch vision' has several strands – aesthetic, scientific, spiritual, moral, political – not all of which are present in every instance. One thing all the writers have in common is that they do not need Hawthorne's sense of wilderness, or 'naked Nature', to find natural depth and abundance in 'English earth'. Like Derek Jarman, all find 'wildness in a corner'.

From the Romantic period with the acceleration of industrialization, and increasingly in Victorian and modern England, nature was shrinking, being marginalized. Hence in part the focus on nature in little, on minute particulars. Hence the intensity with which Jefferies focused on the common rushes. In that essay it is, literally, a ditch that opens on to the unfathomable depths of nature. It is not 'naked

Nature' that English writers have had to fall back on. Jefferies represents a tradition that still continues, within a situation of ecological crisis, which he was aware of in an earlier phase. The nature to which he turned was humanized – a ditch is man-made. But he showed that it was full of natural life. It was not a last ditch in any metaphorical sense. According to the views of writers whom I have discussed here, from Gilbert White to Derek Jarman, it would make more sense to call their 'ditch' or 'wild corner' a source of life, and therefore a ground of values for humans in relation to the non-human world. Whether or not, in Bill McKibben's words, 'the comfort' they have found is 'inhuman', English writers have felt themselves to be 'part of something larger than themselves' in such places.

Notes

[1] Bill McKibben, *The End of Nature*, Penguin Books, 1990, pp. 201, 77.

[2] Quoted in Thomas Frick (ed.), *The Sacred Theory of the Earth*, North Atlantic Books, 1986, p. 37.

[3] Donald Worster, *Nature's Economy*, Cambridge University Press, 1994, p. 241.

[4] Oliver Rackham, *The History of the Countryside*, Dent, 1986, p. 64.

[5] William Cobbett, *Rural Rides*, Vol. 1, Dent, 1912, p. 64. This edition, with an introduction by Edward Thomas, reprints the edition of 1853.

[6] Edward Thomas, *A Language Not to Be Betrayed: Selected Prose of Edward Thomas*, ed. Edna Longley, Carcanet, 1981, p. 130.

[7] Quoted in E. D. H. Johnson (ed.), *The Poetry of Earth*, Gollancz, 1966, p. 63.

[8] William Rueckert, 'Literature and Ecology', *The Ecocriticism Reader: Landmarks in Literary Ecology*, ed. Cheryll Glotfelty and Harold Fromm, University of Georgia Press, 1996, p. 108.

[9] John Cowper Powys, *Autobiography*, Macdonald, 1967, p. 2.

[10] Edward Thomas, *The Childhood of Edward Thomas*, Faber & Faber, 1938, p. 134.

[11] Geoffrey Grigson, *The Private Art: A Poetry Note-Book*, Allison & Busby, 1982, p. 93.

[12] Geoffrey Grigson, *The Crest on the Silver*, Cresset Press, 1950, pp. 135–6.

[13] Harriet Tarlo, 'Radical Landscapes: Contemporary Poetry in the Bunting Tradition', *The Star You Steer by: Basil Bunting and British Modernism*, ed. James McGonigal and Richard Price, Rodopi, 2000, p. 173.

[14] Colin Simms, 'Mart out of the trees beneath the thistles', *Otters and Martens*, Shearsman Books, 2004, p. 117. Further quotations from Simms from this book.
[15] Jim Perrin, *Spirits of Place*, Gomer, 1997, p. 20.
[16] See 'Contumely of the Conquistadors', in *Spirits of Place*, pp. 139–43.
[17] Perrin, *Spirits of Place*, p. 133.
[18] Edward Thomas, *In Pursuit of Spring*, Nelson, 1914, p. 150.
[19] Richard Mabey, *Home Country*, Century, 1990, p. 82.
[20] Richard Mabey, *Country Matters*, Pimlico, 2000, p. 174.
[21] Ibid., pp. 174–5.
[22] Derek Jarman and Howard Sooley, *Derek Jarman's Garden*, Overlook Press, 1996, p. 30.

Richard Jefferies:
A Personal Discovery

> Never was such a worshipper of earth. The commonest pebble, dusty and marked with the stain of the ground, seems to me so wonderful; my mind works round it till it becomes the sun and centre of a system of thought and feeling. ('Hours of Spring')

About thirty years ago, I wrote a poem called 'At Coate Water'. It didn't work, but the poem contained one line I have never forgotten:

The man lived here who taught me how to see.

Later, I was glad I had abandoned the poem, especially on account of that one line. How could I attribute my 'God's gift of seeing', as my father (echoing John Constable) would have called it, to any one influence? I can't remember having taken much notice of my father's landscape paintings when I was a boy, but his perception of nature must have affected me from an early age. The same is probably true of my mother's love of nature, and from her I certainly acquired a strong feeling for lyric poetry, which in turn must have influenced my way of seeing.

But Richard Jefferies did open my eyes decisively at a particular moment. The problem I have in describing this is that I have continued to read Jefferies throughout my life, returning to a source but also developing a critical view of his work, so that I can't be sure of recalling my original reading without colouring it by later responses. Another problem is the question of influence itself: alighting upon common ground, we recognize ourselves in others and make *different* uses of what we receive from them.

All the same, I will begin with a sketch of the moment when I first discovered Jefferies. At about the age of twelve, I took down *Jefferies' England* from my parents' bookcase: a 1947 reprint of Samuel J. Looker's selection of the nature essays, first published in 1937. Reading in that book was a physical and emotional experience: it caused me to open my eyes, and to see things, as I had not done before. From before reading the essays, I remember a mainly active life in the Hampshire countryside where I was fortunate to live: playing, birds'-nesting, fishing, exploring on foot with a dog, cycling. But now I was seeing things – trees, leaves, grass, fields, landscape – as if for the first time; relishing their unique particularity, their beauty and the life in them, which are perhaps one and the same. The experience was very intense: ecstatic, and touched with a peculiar sadness.

Looking back on the experience, I realize that it probably had something to do with puberty. For at the same time as I was looking at nature with a new awareness, I was more self-conscious, more aware of myself as a separate person, capable of solitude and loneliness, sensitized to the difference between self and other which causes desire. This self-feeling, I later realized, was also implied in the Jefferies vision, in which an erotic element is integral to the idealization of natural beauty – as revealed, for instance, in 'Nature in the Louvre', in which Jefferies connects his response to the *Venus Accroupie* statue to his apprehension of nature as a boy. In his way of seeing, Jefferies gives us, with and in his apprehension of nature, himself, his isolation, his longing; in reading his later writings in particular, it is hard not to form a personal relationship with him. Later, I would see that this has its dangers. Part of the Jefferies appeal is to romantic individualism, to an exaggerated and potentially arrogant and self-pitying sense of separation.

When I first read Jefferies, the essay to which I returned again and again was 'Meadow Thoughts'. I still do, and this is the essay I shall look at most closely now. The opening has continued to have a magnetic attraction for me:

> The old house stood by the silent country road, secluded by many a long, long mile, and yet again secluded within the great walls of the garden. Often and often I rambled up to the milestone which stood under an oak, to look at the chipped

inscription low down – 'To London 79 miles'. So far away, you see, that the very inscription was cut at the foot of the stone, since no one would be likely to want that information. It was half-hidden by docks and nettles, despised and unnoticed. A broad land this seventy-nine miles – and how many meadows and cornfields, hedges and woods, in that distance? – wide enough to seclude any house, to hide it, like an acorn in the grass. Those who have lived all their lives in remote places do not feel the remoteness. No one else seemed to be conscious of the breadth that separated the place from the great centre, but it was, perhaps, that consciousness which deepened the solitude to me.

The word 'old' had an emotional appeal for me as a boy. The buildings I was most drawn to were old: weathered, with moss and lichen on walls and roofs, they were like parts of the landscape. Here, Jefferies immediately establishes a tone, and he does so, I would now say, with a poet's art. Others, including H. S. Salt, Looker, and W. J. Keith, who have responded to Jefferies' prose poetry have noticed this. Indeed, Salt, in his *Richard Jefferies: His Life & His Ideals* (1905), following Ellery Channing's application of the name 'poet-naturalist' to Henry David Thoreau, places Jefferies in the 'class of literature' thus designated and relates him to 'the idealistic tendency of modern poetry'. If we take prose poetry seriously as a form, as we should do, a case could be made for seeing Jefferies as one of the great Victorian poets, and as one who anticipates aspects of modern poetry. In this passage, alliteration and repetition are obvious poetic strategies, by means of which silence and seclusion are not words only, but feelings. Other poetic devices are indirection and implication. The milestone is 'despised and unnoticed', but Jefferies notices it, and quietly shows it to us. This sharing of vision harmonizes with the intimacy of his 'you see'. But there is also a counter-movement to communion in the prose poetry, in the sense of aloneness Jefferies conveys.

Jefferies shows us the 'broad land'; he suggests depth, natural abundance, space. He defines distance by 'this seventy-nine miles' from 'the great centre'. This, we know, is London, but the whole essay bears out the implication that the old house, or 'any house', hidden 'like an acorn in the grass', is also a centre.

Any house. To my mind, this is one of the most important truths to which Jefferies draws our attention. It spoke to my instincts as a boy, and it has become one of my settled beliefs. Any place is capable of being experienced as a centre of inexhaustible significance and manifold local and universal connections, especially to the people who live there. Of course, Jefferies was lucky in his place, as I was in the area in which I grew up almost a hundred years later, so that, even after the Second World War, I could still recognize 'Jefferies' England' in the places I knew. Coate gave Jefferies the sense of home on which much of his work was founded. Coate is no longer Coate as Jefferies knew it, of course. But his idea of place as a centre does not depend on any pastoral ideal; he was acutely conscious of social change, as well as of the fact that nature never stands still. Another Jefferies book I read early on was *Wild Life in a Southern County* (1879), the form of which corresponds to the place that is its subject. Starting on the Downs, the writer works down stream and brook and fields to the farm 'as a centre'. This kind of movement is characteristic of Jefferies. In his more pedestrian books it is practical – the subject is an area that can be encompassed by walking – but the movement round about a centre had deep emotional roots for him, and, as I shall later discuss, it had planetary and cosmic significance. By centring on place we make the Earth our home; if we haven't learnt this from Jefferies, the environmental crisis will prove its necessity to us.

Returning to 'Meadow Thoughts', we can see that Jefferies risks sentimentality. The danger is inherent in his subject, 'the old house'. He compounds it with his tone and his repetitions: 'many a long, long mile', 'Often and often I rambled up to the milestone'. It is also a hazard of his quality of tenderness, to which I shall return. In the same opening paragraph from which I have just quoted, he writes, 'The oaks stand – quiet, still – so still that the lichen loves them. At their feet the grass grows, and heeds nothing. Among it the squirrels leap, and their little hearts are as far away from you or me as the very wood of the oaks.' The ascription of human emotion to plants and animals might be described as animism, as W. H. Hudson defined it in *Far Away and Long Ago*.¹ Like so much in Jefferies, it is at once highly personal and part of the Romantic heritage. Whether or not he read Wordsworth and Coleridge, Jefferies shared his perception of joy in nature with them. In 'Meadow Thoughts' he writes of the happiness of the birds. Speaking of hares in *Wild Life in a Southern County*, he says, 'The joy in life of these animals – indeed, of almost all animals and birds in freedom – is very great.' Jefferies' perception of intense emotion in nature, including the love felt by lichen, is close to Wordsworth's 'faith that every flower/Enjoys the air it breathes'.

It also has to be said that another aspect of Jefferies' Romanticism is a certain vagueness. In 'Meadow Thoughts' he speaks of the 'presence' of 'an inexpressible thought … in the azure overhead'. 'There was something here that was not in the books.' A little later, 'There is something beyond the philosophies in the light, in the grassblades, the leaf, the grasshopper, the sparrow on the wall.' The word 'something' had a great, possibly at times a fatal, attraction for Jefferies. It manifests itself as the 'something that the ancients called divine' at the conclusion of *The Amateur Poacher*. It recurs throughout Jefferies' writings. In *The Story of My Heart*, for example: 'there lives on in me an unquenchable belief, thought burning like the sun, that there is yet something to be found, something real, something to give each separate personality sunshine and flowers in its own existence now', and 'The mind goes on and requires … something higher than prayer, something higher than a god.' One may wonder whether Jefferies found the magic formula in Tennyson's 'The Two Voices', in 'something is or seems,/That touches me with mystic gleams,/Like glimpses of forgotten dreams –//Of something felt, like something here;/Of something done, I know not where;/Such as no language may declare' … ''Tis life …/More life, and fuller, that I want.' Or whether Jefferies came upon it where Tennyson himself perhaps first encountered it, in Wordsworth's 'sense sublime/Of something far more deeply interfused,/Whose dwelling is the light of setting suns,/And the round ocean, and the living air, and in the mind of man.' But, in any event, though at times Jefferies derives a genuine lyrical afflatus from use of the word, his habitual recourse to it invites the scepticism of T. E. Hulme with his description of Romanticism as 'spilt religion' and of Romantic verse as flying 'away into the circumambient gas'.²

If Jefferies' perception of joy in nature has affinities with Wordsworth's, it is also distinct from the Romantic poet's. In his thinking, Jefferies came to reject a 'fit' between nature and the human mind. As he writes in *The Story of My Heart*: 'By no course of reasoning, however tortuous, can nature and the universe be fitted to the mind. Nor can the mind be fitted to the cosmos. My mind cannot be twisted to it; I am separate altogether from these designless things.' When he describes the grass as heeding nothing and the squirrels' hearts as being 'far away from you and me', Jefferies sees nature as concentrated upon itself, and utterly separated from the human observer. It is a question, though, whether Jefferies' apprehension of nature entirely supports his idea of nature, or contradicts it, the apprehension conflicting with the idea in a way that feeds his prose poetry. Certainly, with his mixture of animism and detached natural observation, in 'Meadow Thoughts' for example, Jefferies shows that nature is both like and unlike us.

'Meadow Thoughts' develops what Jefferies shows or implies in the opening paragraph: the concentration of nature. 'It is mesmerised upon itself.' By placing plants and creatures in their 'space' Jefferies gives great depth and breadth to the country. As he shows in, for example, a grasshopper that 'calls on the sward by the strawberries, and immediately fillips himself over seven leagues of grassblades', nature is not only the human province that can be measured in miles, but the domain of countless habitats, each with its own sense of space. To know the country '[it] is necessary to stay in it like the oaks'. What, though, does he mean by 'knowledge'?

Jefferies both shows and speaks of his sensitivity:

> So sensitive to it as I was, in its turn it held me firmly, like the fabled spells of old time. The mere touch of a leaf was a talisman to bring me under the enchantment, so that I seemed to feel and know all that was proceeding among the grassblades and in the bushes.

'Fabled spells', 'talisman to bring me under the enchantment'; clearly, Jefferies' knowledge is not of natural history alone. Rather, his perception is magical. One consequence of this is his consciousness of the inadequacy of words – indeed, of all art – to capture the magic. As he says later in this essay: 'Never yet have I been able to write what I felt about the sunlight only. Colour and form and light are as magic to me. It is a trance. It requires a language of ideas to convey it.' This may give us pause, however. Does 'a language of ideas' convey 'magic'? And is that what we read Jefferies for? Or do we read him for his perception of 'colour and form and light', his apprehension of 'magic'? And how would we define that? This is central to my concern here.

Immediately after speaking of 'magic', Jefferies risks breaking the spell he has cast by revealing that the experience occurred in the past. 'It is ten years since I last reclined on that grass plot, and yet I have been writing of it as if it was yesterday.' That this doesn't break the spell owes to the fact that Jefferies' immediacy is dependent upon retrospection, and his sense of Coate as a 'centre' upon his realization of its distance from 'the great centre', London.

At this point in 'Meadow Thoughts' one registers more acutely the nostalgic tone, the peculiar note of Jefferies' pathos, which is so moving in his late essays – unless it overbalances into sentimentality, as it does in 'Hours of Spring', for example, when he says, 'All the grasses of the meadow were my pets.' Even when I was a boy, I sometimes found Jefferies embarrassing. But what caused embarrassment was a misjudgement in the personal note, which was otherwise so moving. Now, I would ascribe the emotional Jefferies tone not only to his illness, the physical weakness and frustration and agony of mind of 'a worshipper of earth' whose object was slipping away from him, but also to the distance (in time and space) that separated him from Coate and heightened his perception of the place. In 'Meadow Thoughts' and other late writings, he is recording home thoughts and feelings, but as a man who no longer belongs. This, I think, is why Jefferies had such a strong appeal for me at the age of twelve, as he has had for others on the brink of adolescence. The appeal is to the newly realized sense of self of the growing person: growing *away* from the security of home and childhood, and growing *into* the position – the distance – from which one can see the home ground and love it consciously, with a love inseparable from a sense of loss. In my view, this is the peculiar Jefferies position in relation to Coate, and in relation to nature, in his late essays. It is the position of a person who belongs and does not belong; more specifically, of a person who becomes fully conscious of the meaning of belonging in the process of realizing his separation.

'There seems always a depth, somewhere, unexplored,' Jefferies says in 'The Pageant of Summer'. There, he writes of the 'endless grass, the endless leaves'. Jefferies owed to Coate his sense of the endlessness of nature, and the depth of the country, and, as I have described elsewhere,[3] he attempted in his later writings to recreate this endlessness and depth; in effect, to restore a sense of 'wild England' to the age of Victoria. In 'Meadow Thoughts', he depicts nature's abundance, and says, ironically, 'A blameable profusion this; a fifth as many [grass-blades] would be enough; altogether a wilful waste here.' He then says, 'The extravagance is sublime ... Nothing utilitarian – everything on a scale of splendid waste.' Here he is of course implicitly celebrating nature's challenge to Victorian values, especially utilitarianism. 'From the littleness, and meanness, and niggardliness forced upon us by circumstances, what a relief to turn aside to the exceeding plenty of Nature!' Jefferies' view of 'divine waste' is a riposte to both natural theology and the idea of evolution as 'blind' and purposeless. This is the view, coloured by a 'Greek' religious sense, that he develops most fully in *The Old House at Coate* (1948), in which he expresses his feeling that, in the sunshine, 'there is no contracted order: there is divine chaos, and, in it, limitless hope and possibilities'.

'Meadow Thoughts' concludes with Jefferies' visit to the spring on the Down, which involves an ascent in which he is characteristically both explorer and pilgrim. The spring is a place within the place, a centre within the centre, yet more deeply secluded: 'A rocky cell in concentrated silence of green things'. Here too is abundance – like an epitome of nature's 'open-handed generosity': 'the basin is always full and always running over'.

> Stooping, I lifted the water in the hollow of my hand – carefully, lest the sand might be disturbed – and the sunlight

gleamed on it as it slipped through my fingers. Alone in the green-roofed cave, alone with the sunlight and the pure water, there was a sense of something more than these. The water was more to me than water, and the sun than sun. The gleaming rays on the water in my palm held me for a moment, the touch of the water gave me something from itself. A moment, and the gleam was gone, the water flowing away, but I had had them. Beside the physical water and physical light I had received from them their beauty; they had communicated to me this silent mystery. The pure and beautiful water, the pure, clear, and beautiful light, each had given me something of their truth.

The spring is both epitome and symbol of nature's plenty, which the essay as a whole has shown. More, it is the source of Jefferies' imagination. Here is his ideal of pure beauty: an ideal springing not from Platonic vision alone, but from physical touch. And the 'green-roofed cave', the womb-like opening, gives access – and egress – to an element that is both sunlight and water, and natural and more than natural.

What I first responded to in Jefferies was his depiction of the life of nature, and this is what I periodically return to. Not nature as a history of separate objects, but the life in things, shining in individual entities and connecting them as a fluid force. It is a perception that might be described in both ancient and modern terms. One might fruitfully relate it to the Tao, 'the course, the flow, the drift, or the process of nature', which Alan Watts calls 'the Watercourse Way'.[4] James Krasner, discussing Jefferies' 'visual perception', has made connections between his way of seeing and modern physics and gestalt psychology, emphasizing that all three 'portray a world composed of dynamic fields of force that ebb and flow round one another'.[5]

As a boy, I would not have understood Jefferies in either of these terms. Rather, his essays opened my eyes to the colours and movements of nature, as I would later learn to see them in my father's paintings. In Jefferies' description of the River Barle, in 'Summer in Somerset', for instance:

Here is a pool by the bank under an ash – a deep green pool inclosed by massive rocks, which the stream has to brim over. The water is green – or is it the ferns, and the moss, and the oaks, and the pale ash reflected? This rock has a purple tint, dotted with moss spots almost black; the green water laps at the purple stone, and there is one place where a thin line of scarlet is visible, though I do not know what causes it. Another stone the spray does not touch has been dried to a bright white by the sun. Inclosed, the green water slowly swirls round till it finds crevices, and slips through. A few paces farther up there is a red rapid – reddened stones, and reddened growths beneath the water, a light that lets the red hues overcome the others – a wild rush of crowded waters rotating as they go, shrill voices calling. The next bend upwards dazzles the eyes, for every inclined surface and striving parallel, every swirl, and bubble, and eddy, and rush around a rock chances to reflect the sunlight. Not one long pathway of quiet sheen, such as stretches across a rippled lake, each wavelet throwing back its ray in just proportion, but a hundred separate mirrors vibrating, each inclined at a different angle, each casting a tremulous flash into the face. The eyelids involuntarily droop to shield the gaze from a hundred arrows; they are too strong – nothing can be distinguished but a woven surface of brilliance, a mesh of light, under which the water runs, itself invisible. I will go back to the deep green pool, and walking now with the sun behind, how the river has changed!

The colours are at once vivid and unstable, not appearances only, but integral to the moving, changing body of water. The truth of Jefferies' vision is in both its acuteness and its uncertainty: 'The water is green – or is it the ferns, and the moss, and the oaks, and the pale ash reflected?' '[T]here is one place where a thin line of scarlet is visible, though I do not know what causes it.' Jefferies' 'painting' of the river, one might say, is simultaneously a portrayal of his mind. Or one might rather say, as I prefer to, that he depicts a meeting, a relationship, between mind and matter. The meeting extends the power of his visual imagination to the limit, and overcomes it with the actuality of nature. 'The eyelids involuntarily droop to shield the gaze from a hundred arrows; they are too strong.' It is almost as if he has tried to wrest the heart from a mystery, and the sacred power has rebuffed him. He loses the visible in the invisible. It is a defeat; but the defeat is also the poet's victory.

The poetry in Jefferies is partly in his pictures. As he wrote in 'Wild Flowers':

> In the mind all things are written in pictures – there is no alphabetical combination of letters and words; all things are pictures and symbols. The bird's foot-lotus is the picture to me of sunshine and summer, and of that summer in the heart which is known only in youth, and then not alone. No words could write that feeling: the bird's foot-lotus writes it.

Writing in pictures is a poetic technique. It is prevalent in Victorian poetry, for example; and it was renewed, in a more complex form, in Imagism, which is a root of modernist poetry. It occurs widely also in nineteenth-century prose – in Dorothy Wordsworth, for instance, and John Ruskin, Gerard Manley Hopkins, and Thomas Hardy. It is not my case that all writing in pictures constitutes prose poetry; but when, as in Jefferies' late essays, it is combined with a distinctive personal rhythm, and reveals more than it shows or says, I would claim that it is.

At his best, Jefferies' verbal picturing is integral to his thinking. In fact, his most original thinking is primarily perceptual, with ideas emerging from what he apprehends – not only sees, but also touches, hears, smells, tastes. As in his description of the Barle, it is vision gained, and lost, and regained more vividly, from his immersion in the life of nature. Sometimes meaning emerges suddenly from sensuous apprehension and strikes Jefferies (and the reader) as a revelation; sometimes it remains implicit, charging the natural scene with a sense of mysterious presence. In both instances, Jefferies' poetic originality springs from his humility in face of nature. Paradoxically, he is most a poet when he sees that he cannot see and knows that he does not know. There is a kind of poetry that assumes mastery over language and subject, and there is another kind that arises from awe and love in face of a reality that the poet knows language is inadequate to convey. Jefferies' was the latter kind.

In this mode, Jefferies wrote in response to the power nature held over him, not as the exponent of his own intellectual power. I have at this point to admit that when I first read Jefferies, and progressed from essays such as 'Hours of Spring', 'The Pageant of Summer', 'Meadow Thoughts', 'Wild Flowers', and 'Nature and Books' to *The Story of My Heart*, I was disappointed. There were parts of the latter that impressed me, such as the first chapter and the description of the morning on London Bridge, but the book did not move or excite me as the essays had. Moreover, although I have read the spiritual autobiography on numerous occasions since, always in the hope of finding what I had missed, it has always been with disappointment. The reasons, I think, are its relative lack of particularity and immediacy, compared with the essays, and Jefferies' obsession with power – even spiritual power: his desire 'That my soul might be more than the cosmos of life' – which takes the place of his submission to nature's power in the essays. While expressing Jefferies' desire for 'soul-life' and for life in the body, *The Story of My Heart* contains a larger admixture of Victorian and imperialist ideology than has been generally recognized. It is especially significant that, with few exceptions, *The Story of My Heart* lacks Jefferies' vivid colour sense. This follows from the fact that in moving from perceptual to conceptual thinking he has abandoned his magic.

Colour was integral to Jefferies' sense of the sacred:

> To the heaven thought can reach lifted by the strong arms of the oak, carried up by the assent of the flame-shaped fir. Round the spruce top the blue was deepened, concentrated by the fixed point; the memory of that spot, as it were, of the sky is still fresh – I can see it distinctly – still beautiful and full of meaning. It is painted in bright colour in my mind, colour thrice laid, and indelible; as one passes a shrine and bows the head to the Madonna, so I recall the picture and stoop in spirit to the aspiration it yet arouses. For there is no saint like the sky, sunlight shining from its face. ('Wild Flowers')

The explicit Christian imagery is uncharacteristic (in similar contexts Jefferies usually cites Homer), but not the physical embodiment of thought in relation to animate nature. This is a memory of Jefferies' perceptual imagination, which inhered in the relationship between his mind and nature. It was to this that he owed his sense of magic.

> From tree, and earth, and soft air moving, there comes an invisible touch which arranges the senses to its waves as the ripples of the lake set the sand in parallel lines. The grass sways and fans the reposing mind; the leaves sway and stroke it, till it can feel beyond itself and with them, using each grass blade, each leaf, to abstract life from earth and ether. These then become new organs, fresh nerves and veins running afar into the field, along the winding brook, up through the leaves, bringing a larger existence. The arms of the mind open wide to the broad sky. ('The Sun and the Brook')

In both passages the imagery is that of touch, physical embrace: 'lifted by the strong arms of the oak', 'carried up', 'invisible touch which arranges the senses', 'the leaves sway and stroke' the mind, grass blade and leaf 'become new organs, fresh nerves and veins', 'the arms of the mind'. This is original Jefferies; at the same time, it is in the Romantic tradition, which opposed poetic thinking to abstract philosophy. It shares the Romantic fascination with the relationship between mind and nature, and the connection between human creativity and the dynamic, organic world.

It is also in line with the Romantic tradition that Jefferies' language of touch and physical embrace recalls the relationship with nature that he experienced as a boy, and ascribed to Bevis, and explored in *The Old House at Coate*. We are told of Bevis that, lying on the path at home in the summer evening, 'the touch of his mind felt' to the stars. Bevis's home feeling, which was Jefferies', can be described as an experience of planetary and cosmic 'centring':

> The heavens were as much a part of life as the elms, the oak, the house, the garden and orchard, the meadow and the brook. They were no more separated than the furniture of the

parlour, than the old oak chair where he sat, and saw the new moon shine over the mulberry tree. They were neither above nor beneath, they were in the same place with him.

There was no separation, 'no severance', Jefferies says.

> There was magic in everything, blades of grass and stars, the sun and the stones upon the ground.
> The green path by the strawberries was the centre of the world, and round about it by day *and* night the sun circled in a magical golden ring.

Even in *Bevis*, however, the 'magical golden ring' has an obverse side, which is exhaustion of all adventure, closure, the journey to which 'there was always an end'. In the context of Jefferies' thought as a whole, the 'end' represents the taming of 'wild England', in which nothing remained to be explored, and the death of mystery – an exhaustion, that is, which was both terrestrial and metaphysical. As I have argued in *Writers in a Landscape*, this was Jefferies' personal apprehension of the crisis of an urbanized and industrialized society, in which nature had been reduced to a margin and a sense of the sacred lost.

In this respect, Bevis's fable of the traveller who finds in 'Thibet' a bronze door covered with 'magic' inscriptions is profoundly significant. Through the door the traveller 'could see the country which had no other side to it'. He is able to reach through the door with his hand and pick up one of the leaves that 'had a secret written on it – a magic secret about the trees, and the plants, and the birds, and the stars, and the opal sun'. The traveller is dragged back from the door, but his mind and soul succeeded in entering:

> and he saw a white shoulder, like alabaster, pure, white, and transparent among the grass by the golden dome flower, and a white arm stretched out towards him, so white it gleamed polished, and a white hand, soft, warm-looking, delicious, transparent white, beckoning to him. So he struggled and struggled until it seemed as if he would get through to his

soul, which had gone on down the footpath.

The traveller knows that, beyond the door, 'from secret to secret you might wander ... still you could never, never, never get to the other side'.

Bevis's fable links Jefferies' boyhood experience with his mode of poetic perception as a writer. Colour and movement are integral to the vision in which he shows us that every leaf does have a secret. The secret is that '[t]he whole office of Matter is to feed life' ('The Pageant of Summer'). Matter is not dead, but alchemic, source and substance of transformative magic. Another crucial essay for understanding the connection between colour and magic in Jefferies' perceptual thinking is 'Out of Doors in February'. There, he says, 'Pure colour almost always gives the idea of fire, or rather, it is perhaps as if a light shone through as well as colour itself. The fresh green blade of corn is like this, so pellucid, so clear and pure in its green as to seem to shine with colour.' He goes on to say, 'it is out from that under-world, from the dead and the unknown, from the cold moist ground, that these green blades have sprung'. Here, we may recall that it was also from underground that the spring emerged to mingle sun and water and communicate to Jefferies 'this silent mystery'. In 'Out of Doors in February', he writes, 'It is this mystery of growth and life, of beauty and sweetness, and colour, starting forth from the clods that gives the corn its power over me.' For Jefferies, qualities such as 'beauty and sweetness, and colour', which philosophy generally designates as secondary, were primary, integral to 'growth and life'. Thus, colour, as he perceives it, discloses the magic of being, instead of painting appearances only. The secret of every leaf is this mystery.

There is an ambiguity in the passage from *Bevis* quoted above: is the traveller beckoned on by a female embodiment of nature, or is his own soul the female spirit that reaches out to him? The ambiguity has a special significance, since the female image recalls Andrew Rossabi's crucial insight, when he wrote, in his introduction to an edition of *The Story of My Heart*, 'in his next book, *The Dewy Morn*, Jefferies' soul becomes what she always was – a woman, the beautiful Felise, perfect child of nature, pure and fresh as the dawn, the embodiment of love'.[6] The great virtue of this formulation is that it effects a virtual identification between Jefferies' soul and the spirit of nature to which he was most sensitive.

In Bevis's fable of the traveller Jefferies projects an image of this soul. It is, of course, quite different from the conventionally male side of Bevis, the bossy, masterful boy, and from the same side of Jefferies, with his fantasies of military leadership and power in worldly affairs. Without indulging in generalizations about male and female 'principles', we can surely see the imbalance in Victorian ideas of the sexes, which opposed the dominant, rational male to the passive, sensitive, imaginative female. With this in mind, it is easy to understand the tension in Jefferies between will to power and sensitivity and tenderness. The latter were both qualities he showed in his writing and qualities he ascribed to his fictional heroines. The pressure was upon him from boyhood to conform to 'manly' ideals, instead of 'dreaming', which, in a working environment, would have been regarded as both effeminate and unproductive. It is evident from his writing that he internalized the conflict.

Some time after abandoning 'At Coate Water', I wrote the following poem:

Nobbut Dick Jefferies

('See'd ye owt on the downs?'
'Nobbut Dick Jefferies moonin' about.')

No one but him
Mooning in a backwater
Of the nineteenth century
We've walked apart from the houses
And here, on the edge
Of a common under pines
Light in every facet
Dances round his words.
Such tenderness
Is unbearable:
The point of a grassblade

> On the eyeball
> Even from the flowerhead
> Of a slender foxtail, a branch
> Grows over the earth's side
> And he has stopped where it bends
> Trying the body's weight
> Against the bough's strength
> The knowledge
> Will not disclose itself
> Nor the world make something
> Of him, though the extremity
> Starts from its roots.

Here, I pay tribute to Jefferies' vision of light, and record my early experience of it, on 'a common under pines'. The poem makes play with the contrast between 'common' and imagery of apartness and being 'on the edge'. At the core, it identifies Jefferies as a man who was at once marginal and central, and associates his tenderness with pain. Jefferies himself acknowledged the pain of his seeing. In 'Wild Flowers', for instance, he wrote, 'Today, and day after day, fresh pictures are coloured instantaneously in the retina as bright and perfect in detail and hue. This very power is often, I think, the cause of pain to me. To see so clearly is to value so highly, and to feel too deeply.' The pain, as well as being due to ill health, was inherent in his tender perception of a nature that did not return his love. It was also due to what I call 'extremity', and image as a branch growing 'over the earth's side'. The reference is partly to his isolation. A hostile view of Jefferies is that he was provincial in the narrow sense, belonging to 'a backwater/Of the nineteenth century'. Aspects of his writing lend support to this view. But it was not in his concentration on locality that he was provincial, but in his pedagogy, and his preaching, which, even at times in *The Story of My Heart*, sounds a note of soapbox oratory. As I have shown, his localism, in a positive sense, discloses the connection between place as 'centre' and the universe.

One thing I wanted to show in the poem was that Jefferies was a peculiarly exposed figure and that his extremity was deeply significant – it started from the world's 'roots'. I meant by this to portray him as a figure of the modern spiritual crisis, a man who broke through the nineteenth-century conventional framework of thought, and who saw and thought differently, and in consequence suffered from isolation and neglect. Later, in a paper that I incorporated in *Writers in a Landscape*, I drew a parallel between Jefferies and Vincent Van Gogh, with reference to the shared dynamism of their vision, the centrality of the sun to their consuming sense of the sacred, and their isolation. Now, I want to quote from Maurice Merleau-Ponty's great essay, 'Cézanne's Doubt':

> Cézanne's or Balzac's artist is not satisfied to be a cultured animal but takes up culture from its inception and founds it anew: he speaks as the first man spoke and paints as if no one had ever painted before. What he expresses cannot, therefore, be the translation of a clearly defined thought, since such clear thoughts are those which have already been said within ourselves or by others, 'Conception' cannot precede 'execution'.[7]

I may at times here, especially in my comments on *The Story of My Heart*, have seemed to be denigrating Jefferies the thinker. This has not been my intention. What I have tried to show is Jefferies' extraordinary poetic intelligence, which was based upon his gift for seeing nature as if no one had ever seen it before. His thinking was a product of his seeing, or, more accurately, his sensing. Jefferies' genius was perceptual; he did not see as people generally did, as a 'cultured animal', but as a great artist. Here, I deliberately choose the term that can cover both writer and painter. There is a good deal of evidence in Jefferies' work of his deep dissatisfaction with Victorian landscape art, and he provides in words, with his perception of colour and movement, a kind of verbal painting that corresponds to a new kind of painterly vision. My point is not that Jefferies substitutes words for paint, as a sort of imitation of Turneresque, Impressionist, Post-Impressionist effects, but that he shared the need to render nature anew to which the great painters also responded.

My argument is that Jefferies' finest expression of his new apprehension of nature occurs in his later essays, and that is where we encounter him at his most convincing as a thinker. In Maurice Merleau-Ponty's terms, that is where Jefferies 'executed' his vision. To follow it with 'conception', as he attempted in *The Story of My Heart*, was not only extremely difficult, but also perhaps not as necessary as he thought. We do not expect Van Gogh or Cézanne to explain to us in clear, abstract terms what their paintings are about. From a genuinely new painting or poem we do not require 'the translation of a clearly defined thought'. What we receive is embodied vision; in Jefferies' case, a magical perception of nature. It is this that changes our way of looking at the world and enables us to see it as if for the first time. Although I could not have explained it, this was what Jefferies gave me when I first took down his book of essays from my parents' bookcase.

Notes

[1] W. H. Hudson, *Far Away and Long Ago* (1918), Chapter 17.
[2] T. E. Hulme, *Speculations*, Routledge, 1960, pp. 118, 120.
[3] Jeremy Hooker, *Writers in a Landscape*, University of Wales Press, 1996, pp. 16–55.
[4] Alan Watts, *Tao: The Watercourse Way*, Penguin Books, 1979, p. 41.
[5] James Krasner, *The Entangled Eye*, Oxford University Press, Oxford, 1992, p. 146.
[6] Andrew Rossabi, 'Introduction', in Richard Jefferies, *The Story of My Heart*, Quartet Books, 1979, p. 19.
[7] Maurice Merleau-Ponty, 'Cézanne's Doubt', in *The Merleau-Ponty Aesthetics Reader*, ed. Galen A. Johnson, Northwestern University Press, 1993, p. 69.

Versions of Freedom:

NICOLAS BERDYAEV AND
JOHN COWPER POWYS

Towards the middle years of the twentieth century a major novelist, John Cowper Powys, encountered the thinking of an influential Russian religious thinker, Nicolas Berdyaev. For Powys it was a meeting of minds; he responded keenly to Berdyaev's ideas of spirit and creativity and, above all, Berdyaev's treatment of the link between personality and freedom. His response, however, was fundamentally oppositional and helped, usefully, to define his different approach to common themes. In this essay, I shall first give an account of Berdyaev's thinking about personality and freedom before proceeding to describe Powys's reaction to it, which I believe influenced some of his later work, including his masterpiece, *Porius* (1951). Powys was a great imaginative writer who encountered Berdyaev's thinking as a challenge. Berdyaev was one of the great religious thinkers of the twentieth century, and his work remains significant today.

Nicolai Alexandrovitch Berdyaev was born in Kiev in 1874. He was descended on his father's side from the military élite, and his mother belonged to the Polish and French aristocracy. He tells us in his autobiography that he lived as a boy, through his mother's Polish family connections, 'in the sphere of a semi-feudal aristocratic society'.[1] His family and social origins left a strong mark on him. 'I myself,' he writes, 'even while engaged in revolutionary activity and a convinced social democrat, never ceased to be fundamentally, though unconsciously, a nobleman.' In *Slavery and Freedom* (1943), he notes the juxtaposition in himself of two elements that produce the fundamental contradiction in his thinking about social life: 'an aristocratic interpretation of personality, freedom and creativeness, and a socialistic demand for the assertion of the dignity of every man, of even the most insignificant of men, and for a guarantee of his rights in life'. And, he says,

> When a levelling tyranny offends against my understanding of the dignity of personality, my love of freedom and creativeness, I rebel against it and I am ready to express my revolt in the extremest form. But when the defenders of social equality shamelessly defend their own privileges, when capitalism oppresses the labouring masses, and turns a man into a thing, then also I rebel. In both cases I reject the foundations of the contemporary world.[2]

Berdyaev was educated at a military academy, but reacted strongly against the military spirit and milieu. 'I have always broken with every group to which I belonged,' he tells us; 'I could never conform to any collective.' He seems even from boyhood to have had a sense of apartness, of belonging to another world, and to have been a philosopher. He was, however, a member of the Russian intelligentsia, and he involved himself intellectually in the revolutionary issues of his time. Initially, he was a Marxist, although he was always more of an idealist than a materialist, and by 1908 he had become a believing Christian. He became a lifelong, though extremely independent, member of the Orthodox Church. He was exiled once for his political activities by the old regime and, in 1913, arrested for blasphemy. He was also arrested twice under the communists, and in 1922 they banished him into exile.

Berdyaev left the Soviet Union 'overcome with grief and bitterness'. He had never wanted to leave, 'for I had faith in the possibility of spiritual regeneration and liberation of communist Russia from within'. From the beginning, he had seen communism as 'a challenge and a reminder of an unfulfilled Christian duty. Christians ought to have embodied the truth of communism: had they done so its falsehood would never have won the day.' In matters of economics and social justice he acknowledged the truth of Marxism. But Berdyaev the mature philosopher – and he had formed most of his ideas in embryo by 1916 – was an anti-materialist, opposed to bourgeois values that he saw as products of an enslaved life closed to the spirit under capitalism as well as communism. Politically, he described himself as 'a mystical anarchist' and a personalistic socialist.

In exile, Berdyaev lived first in Berlin, and, from 1923 until his death in 1948, in Paris, where he edited a journal concerned with Russian religious philosophical thought. During this period, he became one of the most influential modern religious thinkers.

Berdyaev, who described his thinking as 'intuitive and aphoristic rather than discursive and systematic', appears to be – indeed, is – full of contradictions, because he sees 'the life of man and of the world torn by contraries, which must be faced and maintained in their tension'. He believes in 'the priority of the subject over the object'; he is an existentialist, but, as he indicates, as St Augustine, Pascal, Kierkegaard, and Nietzsche are existentialists, rather than as Heidegger or Sartre or Jaspers. He is closest to Dostoievsky among modern thinkers; indeed, he says that he 'received Christianity' from the heroes of Tolstoy's and Dostoievsky's novels. As Berdyaev says, his thinking 'springs from a single, all-embracing vision'.

The keywords of Berdyaev's religious philosophy are personality, freedom, and creativeness. He always starts from the spiritual experience of the subject, the person, that is 'the image and likeness of God'. This is an extreme position, and the following passage from *Slavery and Freedom* is a characteristically extreme statement of it:

> In the existential system the sun is to be found not in the centre of the cosmos but in the centre of human personality and it is exteriorized only in the fallen state of man. The realization of personality, the concentration and actualization of its strength, takes the sun into itself, it inwardly receives the whole cosmos, the whole of history, all mankind.[3]

Personalism, however, is not egoism.

> Egoism destroys personality. Egocentric self-containment and concentration upon the self, and the inability to issue forth from the self is original sin, which prevents the realization of the full life of personality and hinders its strength from becoming effective.

Berdyaev sees personality's reflection of the divine image and likeness as 'its sole claim to existence'. If therefore God does not exist, neither does man.

> The image of human personality is not only a human image, it is also the image of God. In that fact lie hidden all the enigmas and mysteries of man. It is a mystery of divine-humanity, which is a paradox that cannot be expressed in rational terms. Personality is only human personality when it is divine-human personality.

Freedom of personality is not man's right; it is his duty. It is, Berdyaev argues in *Slavery and Freedom*, 'the realization of the divine idea of man, an answer to the divine call. Man ought to be free, he dare not be a slave, because he ought to be a man. Such is the will of God.' Man, therefore, is a divided being, and, as John Cowper Powys says in *Mortal Strife*, 'Life in its depth is war'.

> Man may know himself from above or from below, from his own light, from the divine element in him, and he may know himself from his darkness, from his elemental-subconscious, from the demonic element within himself. And he may do this because he is a dual and a contradictory being, a being polarized to the highest degree, god-like and beast-like, high and low, free and slave, capable of rising to the heights or of falling, capable of great love and sacrifice or of great cruelty and limitless egotism.[4]

God, for Berdyaev, 'is freedom: he is my liberator from the captivity in and enslavement to the world, and his kingdom is my kingdom of freedom and anarchy'. Berdyaev *experienced* freedom as divine. God 'is not Lord, but Liberator; he is the Saviour and Liberator from the slavery of the world'. Berdyaev says that he loves freedom above all else. 'Man came forth out of freedom and issues into freedom. Freedom is a primordial source and condition of existence.' Thus, the basis of Berdyaev's philosophy is not being, but freedom, and the only conception of freedom that he found satisfactory was Jacob Boehme's teaching concerning Ungrund ('groundlessness'), which Berdyaev identified with primordial freedom preceding all ontological determination. God is freedom; man made in God's image is freedom – 'The freedom of the spirit consists in the fact that man is not determined by anything but himself.'

God is freedom, not power. 'God has no power: he has less power than a policeman. Power is a social and not a religious phenomenon ... God can reconcile man to the sufferings of creation because he himself suffers, not because he reigns.' Berdyaev does not admit 'the conception of an almighty, omniscient, punitive deity beholding this stricken world of ours', any more than John Cowper Powys does. He 'can consent to and understand only the image of a loving, suffering, crucified God; I can, that is to say, only accept God through his Son'. Berdyaev rarely sounds like other modern theologians expounding the science of faith – but over this crucial issue, in accepting, in Christ, a powerless God who shares man's suffering, he partakes of the emphasis on the weakness of God which is peculiar to modern theology – not unique, but peculiar to the needs of the twentieth century.

If man does not affirm the image of God within himself he ceases to be man, disintegrating into the animal constituents of his nature, or becoming a slave to the machine. The relationship between man and God, however, is reciprocal; and Berdyaev states, 'Spiritual experience shows us that man longs for God, and that God longs for man and yearns for the birth of man who shall reveal his image.'[5] Indeed, he likes to quote Angelus Silesius: 'I know that without me God cannot exist for a single second. If I cease to be, He too must necessarily cease to be.'

It is by creativeness that man reveals his image to God. 'God awaits man's creative act, which is the response to the creative act of God.' Berdyaev sees divine wisdom in even the silence of the Gospels about creativeness. The first seven days of Creation were God's; the eighth day belongs to man.

> By an act of His Almighty and omniscient power the Creator willed to limit His own foresight of what the creative freedom of man would reveal, since such foreknowledge would have

done violence to and limited man's freedom in creation.⁶

But in what does human creativeness consist? Is Berdyaev indicating man's essential nature as a poet or maker, in the concrete terms that David Jones found in Jacques Maritain's neo-Thomist philosophy, or Eric Gill in Coomaraswamy's 'An artist is not a special kind of man, but every man is a special kind of artist'? This is not what Berdyaev thought; and it is precisely the lack of concreteness in his philosophy of the creative act – which, I believe, connects closely to the devaluation of sensation in his spiritual apprehension of life – that is the weakest aspect of Berdyaev's thought.

For Berdyaev, the goal of creativeness is 'real transfiguration'; the initial creative impulse is 'to bring forth new life, to transfigure the world and usher in a new heaven and a new earth'. This, however, is unattainable; and man's creative act is 'doomed to fail within the conditions of this world'. His attempt at transfiguration, at bringing forth a new heaven and a new earth, 'gives place to the production of aesthetic and cultural objects', which are 'symbols of reality rather than reality itself'. For Berdyaev, the world and everything in it are unreal: products of objectification, exteriorization, and alienation; only personality with its roots in abysmal freedom is real. The tragedy of human creativeness is that it objectifies itself in the finite and reveals a 'painful disparity between the creative idea and its embodiment in the world'. Thus the reality of the spirit is compromised in all its worldly manifestations, except in the communion between persons. With respect to their apprehension of life and experience of freedom, this is a point of fundamental difference between Berdyaev and John Cowper Powys. Differences of background played an important part, but the main difference sprang from the fact that Powys was primarily a poet and novelist who drew inspiration from the Romantic tradition with its roots in landscape and myth. Like Berdyaev, he was an original thinker, but fundamentally literary, and a sensationalist with a passion for nature.

Powys, who was born in 1872, had, like Berdyaev, aristocratic antecedents. His father, the Reverend C. F. Powys, claimed descent from a Welsh lord of the seventeenth century, and his mother counted the poets Cowper and Donne among her ancestors.

Brought up in Derbyshire, Dorset, and Somerset, Powys was educated at Sherborne School and Corpus Christi College, Cambridge. He initially worked in Britain as an itinerant lecturer for the University Extension Movement. From 1905 until his retirement in 1932, he lectured mainly in America, where he became known as an inspiring dramatic orator. Having returned to Dorset in 1934, he subsequently moved to Corwen in North Wales. From 1935 until his death in 1962, he lived in Blaenau Ffestiniog, Merionethshire.

In the preface to his first published novel, *Wood and Stone* (1915), Powys speaks of the concern of art to 'keep the horizons open' and to create in 'a certain spirit of liberation'; in *The Menace of German Culture* (1915) he opposes the 'great and divine idea of liberty' to the will to power; and in his philosophical work *The Complex Vision* (1920) he says that 'Personality is the only permanent thing in life'. From the beginning, then, in his fiction, politics, and philosophy, Powys is concerned with freedom and personality. In *A Glastonbury Romance* (1933) he writes,

> There is no *ultimate* mystery! Such a phrase is meaningless, because the reality of Being is forever changing under the primal and arbitrary will of the First Cause. The mystery of mysteries is Personality, a living person; and there is *that* in Personality which is indetermined, unaccountable, changing at every second!
> ...
> Apart from Personality, apart from Personal Will, there is no such 'ultimate' as Matter, there is no such 'ultimate' as Spirit. Beyond Life and beyond Death there is Personality, dominating both Life and Death to its own arbitrary and wilful purposes.[7]

Especially in *The Complex Vision*, Powys uses the words 'personality' and 'soul' interchangeably, and this book lays down the philosophical groundwork of *A Glastonbury Romance*: the soul is subject to the 'unfathomable duality, the emotion of love and the emotion of malice', and its life in the depths is war. To be sure, this is something quite different from belief in personality as a reflection of the image and likeness of God. It is, however, a philosophy that links the soul to the Absolute and ascribes to it immense creative and destructive power.

One of Powys's most important statements occurs in *Mortal Strife*:

> It is easy to sum up what has happened in our time. Individual men and women in great numbers all over Europe have ceased to believe in the soul. This means the substitution of *behaviouristic*, mechanistic, obedient Bully-Boys for men who stand on their own feet. An ordinary human soul not only contains God and Jesus and the Holy Ghost; it contains the Eternal Rebel 'called', as William Blake says of this great spirit, in its absolute and unconquerable loneliness ... 'by all the names divine, of Jesus or Jehovah'.[8]

Earlier, he linked Blake's reminder that the '"jealous Father of men" was born in the heart of man' with St Paul's 'Christ in us'. Powys's use of the quotations exemplifies his transference of powers traditionally ascribed to the Christian God to the human soul.

The process of transference begins early in Powys's writings – it may be seen in *The Complex Vision*, for example, where he describes Christ as having 'been created by the creative power of all souls'. He says, however, that 'while in one sense the figure of Christ is the supreme work of art of the world, the culminating achievement of the anonymous creative energy of all souls ... in another sense the figure of Christ is a real and living personality'.[9] *A Glastonbury Romance* treats Christ as a projection of human minds but also grants him an independent existence, and in his essay on St Paul, in *The Pleasures of Literature* (1938), Powys describes 'Christ in us' as both 'a natural presence' existing in every human soul, and 'a supernatural presence' bearing with it, 'as a universal feeling, the sense of there being *something more of the same kind* behind the whole astronomical world'.[10] However, the overall tendency of Powys's treatment of Christ is to assimilate his virtues to the human conscience, and to oppose him as the epitome and personification of love and mercy and pity to his evil, tyrannical Father. For Powys, St Paul's 'Christ in us' adapts to his doctrine of the magical power of the soul as, for example, St John's mystical theology does not.

In his philosophical writings Powys put a good deal of intellectual energy into producing a substitute for the Christian religion, a substitute that includes a selective translation of Christianity into his own terms. Thus, in *The Meaning of Culture* (1930) he undertakes to appropriate 'the good of religion' while casting away 'those props and crutches of infallible assurance upon which hitherto religion has depended'. One of the truths culture must take from religion is 'the earth-bound solidarity, in misery and in happiness, of all the poor creatures of earth'. Powys says that we owe to Christ 'the profoundest of all great Christian dogmas', the 'doctrine of the immeasurable and equal value of every living human soul'.[11] He thought of himself, following St Paul's words about *the whole of creation* groaning and travailing, as carrying the doctrine further. Thus, in *Mortal Strife*:

> Taught by Jesus to respect weakness and helplessness more than Power and Terror, our conscience, going further than the conscience of Jesus, feels that a worm is more deserving of worship just because it is so pitiful, than any Omnipotent Almighty.

In *A Philosophy of Solitude* (1933) Powys preaches a 'new life-cult'. This is 'a religion of the mind', and it is ' possessed of a sort of secular "Mass" …a green Mass, the culminating gesture of which is a deliberate, intentional, premeditated ecstasy'.[12] He substitutes the 'Non-human' for 'an all-too-human God':

> The Inanimate partakes of every one of those qualities that we have so long attributed to God. In the Inanimate we can lose ourselves and find ourselves as nowhere else. It is a great mystery, this austere remoteness of primordial Matter; but the feelings that are stirred up by it have the power of carrying us into a level of Being where we can satisfy our life-craving without the frenzy of Eros.

The Inanimate of Powys's Elementalism makes no demands on humankind, offers no obstruction to the magical power of the human mind, but feeds the life of sensations. By contrast, Powys's words about God the Father portray a monster. He is cruel, causing and permitting suffering. He stands for possessive love, which entails violent hatred. He is the despot who rules a closed universal system, which separates the elect from the damned and casts the latter into the outer darkness. He is Blake's Nobodaddy and Thomas Hardy's First Cause, united and grown more brutal on twentieth-century crimes. He is the God of all puritans, anti-sensationalist, and the enemy of sexual pleasure in particular. He is the ultimate terrorist of the human mind, the God who drove Powys's ancestor the poet William Cowper mad. He is not Freedom, but Tyranny; the great slave-master over personality and the nullifier of its magical power. He determines life, ruling out the possibilities that are open to a multiverse of auto-creative minds. Powys's Aquarian New Age opens upon possibility, upon a future different from the past. God is the Lord of all its adversaries.

There is, I think, a fiercer spirit of opposition to the Christian God, which coincides with a more passionate defence of freedom, in those of Powys's writings affected by his response to the rise of totalitarianism and the Second World War. The new spirit appears in *Mortal Strife* and culminates in *Porius* (1951). In the former it is summed up by a phrase like 'a Totalitarian God', or a sentence like 'Our superstitious cringing before the All-powerful – which makes of the whole cosmos a concentration camp'.[13] The new spirit may be sensed if we think of the priests in Powys's novels before *Porius* – men who are either relatively harmless (sometimes, as in the case of T. E. Valley, in *Wolf Solent* (1929) with a certain saintly power born of their wretchedness and humility), or dangerous mainly to themselves; some of them lovable; most of them more or less deranged, mixing sex and religion – and compare them with Minnawc Gorsant and the young Priest in *Porius*. The latter really mean business, and their business is to destroy or suppress freedom in the name of Christ. Minnawc Gorsant has even been instrumental in having a freethinker, Brochvael's son Morvant, murdered. The priests are deadly enemies of Pelagius, opposing the doctrine of Original Sin to his doctrine of the human being's free imagination, and of Myrddin, 'defender of lost souls', liberator of 'all the under-layers of earth-life'.

If the character of Matt Dekker in *A Glastonbury Romance* reflects Powys's affection for his own clergyman father, we owe Minnawc Gorsant partly to his observation of Hitler.

There are striking affinities between Powys's and Berdyaev's thinking, and especially between their versions of freedom, which both not only held as a sacred principle, but lived personally, in the face of a century of mass enslavement. I believe, however, that Powys's encounter with Berdyaev's thought, which occurred in the later 1930s, against the background of totalitarianism and the march towards war, influenced the hardening of his antagonism towards the Christian religion, despite (or perhaps because of) the affinities between his thought and Berdyaev's in certain respects.

Powys's most interesting published references to Berdyaev occur in *Mortal Strife*, *Dostoievsky* (1946), and *Rabelais* (1948). Berdyaev also wrote a book on Dostoievsky, but I doubt that it would be fair to Powys to compare his treatment of the Russian thinker and writer with Berdyaev's. While Powys, in one of his most self-indulgent books, depicts a Dostoievsky in harmony with Powys's thinking, and while Berdyaev interprets a Dostoievsky in tune with Berdyaev's religion, the latter seems to me much the more authentic, not least because Berdyaev did owe his philosophy in large measure to Dostoievsky. In this place, I shall confine my references to *Mortal Strife* and *Rabelais*.

Powys praises Berdyaev warmly, but qualifies his praise with criticism, and his praise is frequently double-edged. He finds *Slavery and Freedom* 'very noble and very moving'; but though he invariably refers to Berdyaev with respect, his frequent descriptions of him as 'clever', and as 'a subtle apologist', indicate distrust of his fundamental motives.

Powys's basic view of Berdyaev is that he reinvents God for the modern age. 'What the clever Russian Apologist Berdyaev is always doing', Powys says in *Mortal Strife*, 'is to soften and obscure the less just, the less merciful, the less sympathetic, the less poetic, the less credible outlines of Christianity, till the residue can in some measure arouse gratitude, fear, inspiration, love' – which Powys identifies as 'the urges that drive the exceptional person and the intellectual person to Religion'.[14] He is deeply suspicious of Berdyaev's use of the word 'spirit'. Powys is passionately anti-Hegelian, fiercely opposed to the idea of a closed universe, and he finds 'a distinct Hegelian tendency in the combination of logical vagueness with cosmic comprehensiveness of [Berdyaev's] use of the concept, *spirit*'. To Powys, 'The wholesome element of anarchy in our western world' is 'that *Freedom of the Spirit*, which Berdyaev praises only to betray'.[15] How, in his view, does Berdyaev betray it?

Speaking of Berdyaev's *Solitude and Society* (1938), Powys agrees with him about a number of things. Berdyaev is correct to regard modern communications as 'totally worthless in the growth of the soul'. He is correct to condemn Stalin's substitution of 'bureaucratic tyranny' for the Revolution. He is correct to curse 'mass-production, mass-hero-worship, mass-capitalism'. He is correct to reject totalitarianism. 'But,' Powys continues, 'having given the individual soul its liberty from Church and State and Race and Government, what must the disciple of the Fourth Gospel do but impose upon us, in place of these, the soul's *communion with* God.'[16]

We know what Powys thinks of the Fourth Gospel from his essay on St Paul. He thinks its author basks in the light of 'hermetically-sealed lovingness – the love of the Father for the Son and the love of Them both for Their Predestined Elect' – and has neither thought nor pity to spare 'for the cold, dark, unregenerate cosmos left outside this warm and privileged fold'. 'The appalling All-Powerful of the Fourth Gospel' is a Hegelian, a prison-keeper of a block universe, and his 'circle of "everlasting love" is so much smaller than his corresponding Inferno'.[17] Not for the first or last time in Powys's writings, the Christian God is condemned by pity and mercy, and 'Christ in us' is celebrated for affirming the power of the individual mind to *evolve* the Christian spirit.

Powys differs fundamentally from Berdyaev over the needs of the self. He rejects the idea of Original Sin and denies that the egocentric self is necessarily 'sinful, wicked, mad, *unhappy*', and in need of escaping from itself into the love of God. 'The soul of an ordinary democratic man', he claims, 'is not by any means the unhappy mad creature that it is Berdyaev's cue to make it.' 'Men and women have gone mad ere now, but it has not been from loneliness; it has not been from that super-sensuous embrace of the elements which is the reward of loneliness. It has been from Philosophy. It has been from Religion. *It has been from Love.*'[18]

This, of course, is Powys's dogma: that the self alone embracing the elements, and confronting the non-self, has all it needs. It is a dogma that recurs in his philosophical writings, but is qualified and even disproved in his fiction, where his heroes love, after their fashion, and have to recognize realities outside their minds.

Berdyaev was non-judgemental; the Gospel words that most profoundly impressed him were 'Judge not that ye be not judged' and 'He that is without sin among you, let him cast a stone at her'. So was Powys, and he claimed to be greatly relieved at Berdyaev's despatch of the 'last spectral emanation of the Jealous Father of Men'. For Powys, however, Berdyaev is the antithesis of Rabelais, and Berdyaev's 'process of the purging of providence' increasingly makes 'the world in which we live ... thin, unreal, and insubstantial; for it is hard to enjoy a life of unbounded possibilities in time and space while a god of Love and Woe yearns desperately and helplessly for our frail souls out of an eternity of sacrificial love'.[19]

To this it is fair to add that to Berdyaev the world was 'thin, unreal, and insubstantial'. He described himself in his autobiography as 'most akin to the element of fire': 'I am a stranger to the elements of earth and water. I have, therefore, seldom felt life to be well-grounded and secure, or relished it in the living.' He tells us that he feels distaste for the exaltation of emotion and for sensation, and that he is fastidious. 'I have therefore gone through life, as it were, with half-closed eyes and holding my nose.'[20] He is, in certain respects, like Nietzsche, a poetic philosopher; but Berdyaev is no poet. The idea of incarnating his ideas in images of nature and the things of the world would have been abhorrent to him; artistic embodiment through sensation would have meant objectification, materialization, and compromise of the spiritual experience of freedom. Powys, not unfairly, sees him reducing the body of the world to spirit. Berdyaev would probably have seen Powys as denying the spiritual source of freedom and disintegrating himself into the constituents of natural life.

Powys opposes the art of forgetting to the Christian emphasis upon 'pain and pity'. Significantly, he is aware of the theological opposition. In *Rabelais* he links Berdyaev with Jacques Maritain, Reinhold Niebuhr, and C. S. Lewis, describing them as apologists for 'the new orthodoxy'. They stress the power of evil; he believes in 'natural human goodness'. They round off the system of things in a 'Divine Circle'; he stands for pluralism and counters them with 'the poetic-humorous way of natural earth-born common sense'. This he ascribes to the tradition of Homer, Shakespeare, Rabelais, Cervantes, and Walt Whitman, who 'recognize in life and in nature hints and suggestions of an element of accident, of chaos, of anarchy, of a mysterious and unfathomable number of vast expanses, regions, dimensions, levels, planes, modes of being, possibilities of existence completely outside any conceivable "divine circle"'.[21] He says that it is as if the 'Christ in us' is at work in Rabelais' use of 'humour as his magic, in redeeming the unredeemable'. When Powys expounds his ideas and beliefs in opposition to Berdyaev and the other theologians, we may sense the figure of Myrddin Wyllt, which he would create in *Porius*, stirring to life in his imagination.

Porius shows a deepening of Powys's imagination; it also, I believe, manifests a hardening and a narrowing of his thinking. As in *A Glastonbury Romance*, much of the intellectual and imaginative energy in the novel springs from Powys's engagement with Christianity. In *A Glastonbury Romance*, Sam Dekker says, 'Our Glastonbury Christ is like Osiris. They've cut him into fragments; and out of each fragment they've made a different person.'[22] That, in part, is also what Powys has done in the novel: he has put fragments of Christianity into the creation of Sam, Matt Dekker, Mr Evans, Bloody Johnny, and other characters, and quickened the interaction of their religious ideas by his thinking and feeling about the subject. In *Porius*, dogmatic opposition replaces interaction. Myrddin represents, not so much an evocation of primeval powers, but more an evolution of the Christian spirit beyond Christianity, into the worship of all life. Against him stand the totalitarian fanatics represented in this speech by the young Priest:

> I want you to realize that until every living knee on this planet bows before Christ, and every thought, fancy, hope, imagination, desire, purpose, interest, in every individual soul, is com-

pletely bound and chained to Christ your victory will not have come! ... you must fight, we must all fight, with no other purpose in our minds save to compel every living creature in this whole world to fall down and worship Christ!

That, of course, is anything but the tone and language Berdyaev uses. It is, however, in the name of freedom that Powys rejects Berdyaev's God. Unlike most modernists, neither Powys nor Berdyaev invoked an idea of tradition that implied civilization must be secured by some kind of return to the past. Berdyaev is a prophet of the eighth day, the day of human creativeness. It is an idea that assumes that the world is incomplete. As he wrote in *The Divine and the Human* (1949):

> The greatest error of which historical Christianity is guilty is due to the circumscribing and deadening notion that revelation is finished and that there is nothing more to be expected, that the structure of the Church has been completely built and that the roof has been put on it.[23]

His eschatology is not aimed at frightening souls back into the orthodox fold; his thought at its most alive takes the roof off the Church, revealing that now is the time for the creative act that transfigures reality. For Powys too, as he wrote in *A Philosophy of Solitude*, 'the world is not a finished product; it is a creative flux; and what is known as evolution is the multifarious creation of myriads of self-creating wills'.[24] That is not Berdyaev's sense of possibility. However, in view of the dignity that both Powys and Berdyaev restored to personality as a free, creative agent, perhaps it is legitimate to invoke the tricky word and say that, despite their differences, they spoke about some important things in the same spirit.

Notes

[1] Nicolas Berdyaev, *Dream and Reality: An Essay in Autobiography*, Geoffrey Bles, 1950, p. 9. Except where otherwise indicated, subsequent quotations from Berdyaev are from this book.

² Quoted in *Christian Existentialism: A Berdyaev Anthology*, ed. Donald A. Lowrie, Allen & Unwin, 1965.
³ Nicolas Berdyaev, *Slavery and Freedom*, Geoffrey Bles, 1943, p. 42.
⁴ *Christian Existentialism*, p. 68.
⁵ Quoted in Evgueny Lampert, *Nicolas Berdyaev and the New Middle Ages*, James Clarke, 1945.
⁶ *Christian Existentialism*, p. 149.
⁷ John Cowper Powys, *A Glastonbury Romance*, Bodley Head, 1933, p. 693.
⁸ John Cowper Powys, *Mortal Strife*, Village Press, 1974, p. 156.
⁹ John Cowper Powys, *The Complex Vision*, Village Press, 1975, p. 221.
¹⁰ John Cowper Powys, *The Pleasures of Literature*, Cassell, 1938, p. 247, emphasis Powys's.
¹¹ John Cowper Powys, *The Meaning of Culture*, Jonathan Cape, 1930, p. 122.
¹² John Cowper Powys, *A Philosophy of Solitude*, Jonathan Cape, 1933, p. 95.
¹³ Powys, *Mortal Strife*, p. 48.
¹⁴ Ibid., pp. 37–8.
¹⁵ Ibid., p. 185.
¹⁶ Ibid., p. 159, emphasis Powys's.
¹⁷ Powys, *The Pleasures of Literature*, p. 175.
¹⁸ Powys, *Mortal Strife*, pp. 206–7, emphasis Powys's.
¹⁹ John Cowper Powys, *Rabelais*, Bodley Head, 1948, p. 337.
²⁰ From *Dream and Reality*.
²¹ Powys, *Rabelais*, pp. 376–7.
²² Powys, *A Glastonbury Romance*, p. 851.
²³ Nicolai Berdyaev, *The Divine and the Human*, Geoffrey Bles, 1949, p. 183.
²⁴ Powys, *A Philosophy of Solitude*, p. 56.

Alone in Life:

THE FRIENDSHIP OF ROBERT FROST AND EDWARD THOMAS

'It speaks, and it is poetry.' Edward Thomas's review of *North of Boston* (1914) accorded with Robert Frost's intention: 'I was after poetry that talked.'[1] It is well known that a preoccupation with what Frost called 'the sound of sense', with colloquial language and the living human voice as the medium of poetry, was crucial to both poets. But there is, I believe, more to say about what their own actual talks, their talks with each other, meant to them as men and poets. That is what I shall explore here.

Edward Thomas's essay 'This England', set in August 1914, reflects his walks with Robert Frost in Herefordshire, walks in which 'we talked – of flowers, childhood, Shakespeare, women, England, the war'.[2] The range of subjects suggests something of the depth and intimacy of their talks. Thomas's poem 'The sun used to shine', written in May 1916, recalls the same experience of walking and talking with Frost:

> The sun used to shine while we two walked
> Slowly together, paused and started
> Again, and sometimes mused, sometimes talked
> As either pleased, and cheerfully parted
>
> Each night. We never disagreed
> Which gate to rest on. The to be
> And the late past we gave small heed.
> We turned from men or poetry
>
> To rumours of the war remote ...

Alone in Life

Whereas the poem deals with memory, the essay is more immediate. Both essay and poem show the importance to Thomas of Frost's companionship. But the essay shows more: it reveals the friendship, implicitly, as a significant influence upon a new decisiveness in Thomas's life – a decisiveness that led both to his self-discovery as a poet and, eventually, to his enlistment.

Initially, the full implications of what has been revealed to him are obscure to Thomas:

> Then one evening the new moon made a difference ... At one stroke, I thought, like many other people, what things that same new moon sees eastward about the Meuse in France. Of those who could see it there, not blinded by smoke, pain, or excitement, how many saw it and heeded? I was deluged, in a second stroke, by another thought, or something that overpowered thought. All I can tell is, it seemed to me that either I had never loved England, or I had loved it foolishly, aesthetically, like a slave, not having realized that it was not mine unless I were willing and prepared to die rather than leave it as Belgian women and old men and children had left their country. Something I had omitted. Something, I felt, had to be done before I could look again composedly at English landscape.

Ultimately, Edward Thomas would find that what he had to do was fight for England. It was a decision he arrived at after turning over in his mind whether to join Robert Frost in America. In retrospect, however, we can see that the new decisiveness released in him by his friendship with Frost did more than help him to realize himself as a poet. It helped to bring him down to earth, to the recognition expressed in lines from 'Wind and Mist':

> I did not know it was the earth I loved
> Until I tried to live there in the clouds
> And the earth turned to cloud.

The speaker in the poem has been tormented by 'mist – mist/Like chaos surging back'. He describes himself as a detached 'eye' watching from the windows of the house, an eye that 'felt itself/Alone in all the world, marooned alone'. However actual it may have been, the mist is also a metaphor for a mental state, for the 'chaos' Edward Thomas himself had experienced as an 'isolated selfconsidering brain', as he described to Eleanor Farjeon.[3] The friendship with Robert Frost helped to rescue him from this condition and was therefore a decisive factor in his becoming the man who gave a handful of earth as his reason for fighting and a war poet focused on his love of the homeland.

Thomas understood the importance of speech to Frost's poetry. Frost, in turn, helped Thomas to see and hear the poetic speech contained in his written prose. The friends' talk was thus a vital part of their relationship as poets. It was talk that signified understanding, and not only with regard to what they talked about; it conveyed to each man that inwardness which the living voice alone can communicate. After Edward Thomas's death, Robert Frost described him as 'the only brother I ever had'. In 'To E. T.', included in *New Hampshire* (1923), he wrote, 'I meant, you meant, that nothing should remain/Unsaid between us, brother.' It was a friendship based on common intention and shared meaning. Jay Parini says of the friends' 'vital connection': Frost 'felt that for the first time in his life he had been fully understood'.[4]

Mutual understanding resulted in a profoundly creative relationship for both poets. The delight they shared, in each other, in nature and books, in walking and talking, shines in their reminiscences. An important aspect of their understanding was evidently that they could also share what deeply troubled them. Although we cannot know exactly what they said to each other about depression and fear of mental instability, we know from their letters[5] that Thomas was 'good at black talk', and both 'found pleasure in grovelling ... in such self-abasement'. Madness is a subject Robert Frost deals with in his poetry; as Jay Parini says, it 'had touched his family closely and would continue to haunt him'.[6] Edward Thomas had contemplated suicide, and was tormented by self-consciousness, which he described to Eleanor Farjeon as 'the central evil' and 'a disease'. In his book on Richard Jefferies[7] he called it 'the most tragic condition of man's greatness' and wrote, memorably, 'If the sea-waves were to be self-conscious, they would cease to wash the shore; a self-conscious world would fester and stink in a month. Many men survive the terror.'

Thomas's self-division appears in his poetry, in 'The Other', for example, and in a number of figures representing partial self-portraits in his prose, such as the man in *The South Country* (1909) who talks of 'we of the suburbs' and says, 'I am world-conscious, and hence suffer unutterable loneliness.' Such self-consciousness tormented Edward Thomas; he knew its 'terror', but survived it, and it was ultimately an aspect of his 'greatness' as a poet. The same can be said of the fears that haunted Robert Frost. In both cases, the suffering related to a profound loneliness. Paradoxically, it was a sense of this – the irreducible core of self that cannot be fully communicated – that Frost and Thomas shared.

In an early poem, 'Bereft', Robert Frost wrote,

Word I was in the house alone
Somehow must have gotten abroad,
Word I was in my life alone,
Word I had no one left but God.

Aloneness is the condition both of Frost's personal lyrics and of figures in his dialogue poems. One of its most memorable expressions occurs in 'Home Burial':

> The nearest friends can go
> With anyone to death, comes so far short
> They might as well not try to go at all.
> No, from the time when one is sick to death,
> One is alone, and he dies more alone.

It may be thought death makes this an extreme instance. It would be truer, I think, to see Frost's treatment of aloneness as always containing a sense of mortality. The same is true of Thomas's, as we see in 'Lights Out', for instance, where the poet, alone in his life, faces death. The situation is liminal: 'the borders of sleep,/The unfathomable deep/Forest'. It is 'the unknown' Thomas 'must enter, and leave, alone'.

The aloneness is a modern condition, which Marlow expresses powerfully in Conrad's *Heart of Darkness* (1899): 'We live as we dream – alone.' Within a broad historical context, it can be seen as the end of the Romantic tradition, with the poet both isolated from any social group and having only the glimmerings of a transcendental sense of nature to sustain him or her. Hence the pressure upon the poet as a separate individual, who experiences 'chaos'. The results can be seen in Frost's sense of poetry as 'a momentary stay against confusion' and in Thomas's adoption of the idea of the 'superfluous man'. It can be seen too in the feeling Thomas expressed in *The Country* (1913): *There is nothing left for us to rest upon*, nothing great, venerable, or mysterious, which can take us out of ourselves.'[8] This is the condition that leads Thomas to read the history of English poetry as the history of separation from 'a corporate view of life', with the poet standing apart 'in a kind of inevitable exile'. 'As for lyric poets,' he says, 'they appear but sudden sharp voices of birds flying over in a dark night.' The idea of 'home' that is central to the poetry of both Robert Frost and Edward Thomas is shadowed by the existential aloneness of 'exile'. Frost drew a parallel between birds' songs and human voices: 'Just so many sentence sounds belong to man as just so many vocal runs belong to one kind of bird.'[9] It was Thomas, though, for whom the contrast between human voices and birdsong, and the superior 'knowledge' of the latter, became an obsession.

Aloneness implies the difficulty of communication, perhaps even its impossibility. Edward Thomas felt this acutely. As he wrote in *Walter Pater: A Critical Study* (1913):

> men understand now the impossibility of speaking aloud all that is within them, and if they do not speak it, they cannot write as they speak. The most they can do is to write as they would speak in a less solitary world. A man cannot say all that is in his heart to a woman or another man. The waters are too deep between us.

It is tempting to contrast this with what Thomas was to write only a year or so later, when reviewing Frost's *North of Boston*:

> With a confidence like genius, he has trusted his conviction that a man will not easily write better than he speaks when some matter has touched him deeply, and he has turned it over until he has no doubt what it means to him, when he has no purpose to serve beyond expressing it, when he has no audience to be bullied or flattered, when he is free, and speech takes one form and no other.[10]

The temptation is to assume that Thomas found a freedom in his poetry because he learned to 'say all that is in his heart' to his friend. But it would be a fairy story, I think, to suggest that in meeting Robert Frost, in walking and talking with him, Edward Thomas discovered an exception to 'the impossibility of speaking all that is within'. Recognizing another person's aloneness is not the same as sharing it to such a point that in either or both it ceases to exist. However close the intimacy, an essential distance remains. In Frost's dialogue poems, for example, it is distance, more than closeness, that speech expresses: distance between speakers, and tension, and proneness to misunderstanding. The saying is also, of course, a seeing. A fine example of this occurs in Frost's great poem 'Home Burial', when the woman describes seeing her husband digging their child's grave:

> I saw you from that very window there,
> Making the gravel leap and leap in air,
> Leap up, like that, like that, and land so lightly
> And roll back down the mound beside the hole.
> I thought, Who is that man? I didn't know you.

She has said the man can't speak of his dead child, 'because you don't know how to speak'. It is clear from this description, however, that she is unable to *see* his feelings.

It is in considering the failures of figures in Frost's dialogue poems to know one another that one realizes Thomas exaggerates – even misrepresents – an important aspect of *North of Boston* when he says, 'Extraordinary things have not been sought for.' On the contrary, the stories in the dialogue poems, with their odd happenings and dramatic tensions between speakers, are closer than all but a few of Wordsworth's to Gothic pastoral.

In a word, Frost deals with not the ordinary, but the *strange*. Indeed, this is a word that recurs in *North of Boston*, where its presence in the personal lyric 'After Apple-Picking' establishes the vision that characterizes the book as a whole:

> I cannot rub the strangeness from my sight
> I got from looking through a pane of glass
> I skimmed this morning from the drinking trough
> And held against the world of hoary grass.

The strangeness that the poet gets from looking at the world in a certain way – or through a medium (here, ice, 'a pane of glass') – becomes part of the world he looks at. And strangeness, in the poems in *North of Boston*, ranges between the poles of the visionary and the disturbed. In 'The Mountain', for example, the dialogue makes a mystery of the mountain, which is compounded by the presence of contraries, in the brook that is 'always cold in summer, warm in winter'. I spoke earlier of 'glimmerings of a transcendental sense of nature' in Frost. The word 'glimmerings' suggests fitfulness, an uncertain light coming and going, illuminating the landscape strangely, that I believe accurately describes his poetry. This has a mystical element; it shows the influence of Ralph Waldo Emerson and his ideas of correspondence between inner and outer, and mind and nature; but it has too an uncertainty – at times, a desolation – that is foreign to Transcendentalism. There is, nevertheless, a suggestion of both Metaphysical and Romantic influences on Frost's recourse to the language of contraries. As he wrote in his notebooks: 'All a man's art is a bursting unity of opposites.'[11]

The presence of contraries, in nature and in the differences between man and woman, for example, is one of the things that makes the Derry landscape of *A Boy's Will* (1913), *North of Boston*, and *Mountain Interval* (1916) – the three books by Frost which Thomas knew – a haunted landscape. This is true both of its wildness, which intensifies the loneliness of its human inhabitants, and of life in the isolated houses. In 'The Fear', the woman says to the man as they return home at night,

> I always have felt strange when we came home
> To the dark house after so long an absence,
> And the key rattled loudly into place
> Seemed to warn someone to be getting out
> At one door as we entered at another.

The house is a refuge to Frost, but it is also, like the woods, a place of mystery and fear that evokes 'strange' feelings, as it does for the woman here. The same is true of Thomas's 'South Country' landscapes, which he often describes as 'hollow' and 'dark', and where isolated houses are haunted by a strange emptiness or presence. 'Two Houses' is characteristic of Thomas's treatment of the house as abode of time and death:

> But another house stood there long before:
> And as if above graves
> Still the turf heaves
> Above its stones:
> Dark hangs the sycamore,
> Shadowing kennel and bones
> And the black dog that shakes his chain and moans.
>
> And when he barks, over the river
> Flashing fast,
> Dark echoes reply,
> And the hollow past
> Half yields the dead that never
> More than half hidden lie:
> And out they creep and back again for ever.

This focus upon the 'haunted' house and 'hollow past' is a common theme in poetry of the period and can be found in, for example, Thomas Hardy, Walter de la Mare, and Rudyard Kipling. In some respects it provides a sense of the numinous to replace a lost transcendence. This is a large subject, which I can only touch on here. My aim at present is to pursue the sense of the 'strange' – not identical, but with affinities – in the poetry of Frost and Thomas.

Emerson influenced Robert Frost's mysticism. The principal influence on Edward Thomas's mysticism was Richard Jefferies with his sense of 'something that the ancients called divine' in the outdoor world. The fact that the actual Wiltshire and Hampshire landscapes of Jefferies and Thomas, with their numerous tumuli and other burial sites, are landscapes of the dead, with mysterious temporal depths, makes it natural to see them as 'spirit' worlds. There is, however, a morbid element in Thomas's 'dark echoes' and 'hollow past' that is more pronounced than anything in Jefferies. In my view, two things account for this. One is the fact that Thomas did not possess the 'belonging' he ascribed to Jefferies; he was, rather, an 'exile', never wholly at home in his English places. The other is the war.

Robert Frost was the first to see what Edward Thomas's poetry was: 'He didn't think of it for a moment as war poetry, though that is what it is. It ought to be called Roads to France.'[12] Though this may have been a novel insight at the time of Thomas's death, in retrospect it is hard to see how he could be regarded as other than a war poet. Wilfred Owen, crossing Winchester Downs in November 1917, 'could almost see the dead lying about in the hollows of the downs'.[13] Many other people must have had similar experiences during the war years, perhaps especially in landscapes such as the Winchester Downs that were ancient burial sites, though the whole country was death haunted. Thomas's South Country was strongly marked by the absence or ghostly presence of men who had tended the land – labourers killed in battle, such as the ploughman of 'A Private' and the ploughman's mate of 'As the team's head brass'. It was where

> Now all roads lead to France
> And heavy is the tread
> Of the living; but the dead
> Returning lightly dance:
>
> Whatever the road bring
> To me or take from me,
> They keep me company
> With their pattering,

Alone in Life

Crowding the solitude
Of the loops over the downs,
Hushing the roar of towns
And their brief multitude.

We can surely understand why, with such 'company' about him, Edward Thomas should often feel himself to be ghostly in wartime England or perceive a strange otherworldliness in natural effects. Words themselves are made of contraries; they are, as he wrote in his poem 'Words', 'light as dreams,/Tough as oak'; 'Strange and sweet/Equally,/and familiar'. Like Frost's Derry landscapes, Thomas's South Country is liminal, a border between life and death, and dream and reality. Poem after poem reveals it as a country composed of interacting contraries: light and dark, silence and sound, movement and stillness, the living and the dead, the dead and the unborn.

Edward Thomas's new decisiveness evident in 'This England' and carried through his self-realization as a poet meant that he survived self-consciousness, not that he transcended it. Talking with Robert Frost, and learning to 'speak' in his poetry, provided an acknowledgment of the core of experience that cannot be fully communicated. This is the paradox that the friendship of Thomas and Frost brings home to us: that a sense of the incommunicable can be shared. The strangeness that pervades *North of Boston* has an equivalent in some of Thomas's finest poems, such as 'The Unknown Bird' and 'Aspens', in which the poet finds metaphors for the core of subjective being. In 'Aspens' the trees 'at the cross-roads talk together'. They 'whisper' a potent word recalling 'Mowing', in *A Boy's Will*, in which the poet asks what 'my long scythe [was] whispering to the ground'. It is a word suggesting an intimacy that reaches beyond human speech. In 'Aspens' the whisper 'calls ... ghosts from their abode':

A silent smithy, a silent inn, nor fails
In the bare moonlight or the thick-furred gloom,
In tempest or the night of nightingales,
To turn the cross-roads to a ghostly room.

As in 'Two Houses', the past haunts the present, indeed, virtually replaces it. At this 'cross-roads', in this liminal situation, Edward Thomas has created a metaphor that comes as close as possible to expressing his own sense of inward being:

> Over all sorts of weather, men, and times,
> Aspens must shake their leaves and men may hear
> But need not listen, more than to my rhymes.
>
> Whatever wind blows, while they and I have leaves
> We cannot other than an aspen be
> That ceaselessly, unreasonably grieves,
> Or so men think who like a different tree.

The 'whisper' of 'Aspens' recalls an equally famous passage in which Thomas speaks meditatively of his poetic voice. In 'I never saw that land before', he reflects, 'if I could sing/What would not even whisper my soul/As I went on my journeying,//I should use, as the trees and birds did,/A language not to be betrayed.' The implication seems to be that all human language is 'betrayed' and the 'soul' cannot be whispered. Edward Thomas's poems, like Robert Frost's, use human speech to define its bounds. But is there another 'language' that transcends our limitations? In 'March' Thomas asks, 'What did the thrushes know?' 'The Word' concludes with 'a pure thrush word'. In 'March the Third', 'the birds' songs have/The holiness gone from the bells'. 'Health', in the sense of wholeness, evaded Edward Thomas, but existed for him beyond self-consciousness, in a 'holiness' still to be heard in nature. While Robert Frost's poems are marked by failures of communication between his speakers, Edward Thomas's are haunted by natural voices, voices of wind and water and, especially, birds, that convey something more than the human voice is capable of saying. This may seem a negative conclusion to an essay that has emphasized the importance to two poets and their work of their mutual understanding. Yet it is to acknowledge that the two men who, walking and talking together, achieved such intimacy were fine lyrical poets. For the lyrical poem springs from the aloneness at the heart of human subjectivity, and speaks eloquently of the unsayable.

Notes

[1] Quoted in Jay Parini, *Robert Frost: A Life*, Pimlico, 2001, p. 88.
[2] Edward Thomas, *The Last Sheaf*, Jonathan Cape, 1928, p. 218.
[3] Eleanor Farjeon, *Edward Thomas: The Last Four Years*, Oxford University Press, 1958, p. 13.
[4] Parini, *Robert Frost*, p. 150.
[5] Matthew Spencer (ed.), *Elected Friends: Robert Frost & Edward Thomas to One Another*, Handsel Books, 2003.
[6] Parini, *Robert Frost*, p. 100.
[7] Edward Thomas, *Richard Jefferies: His Life and Work*, Hutchinson, 1909.
[8] Emphasis Thomas's.
[9] Robert Frost, *Selected Letters of Robert Frost*, ed. Lawrence Thompson, Holt, Rhinehart & Winston, 1964, p. 140.
[10] Thomas, *A Language Not to Be Betrayed*, p. 128.
[11] Robert Frost, *The Notebooks of Robert Frost*, ed. Robert Faggen, Belknap Press of Harvard University Press, 2006, p. 128.
[12] Frost, *Selected Letters*, p. 217.
[13] Wilfred Owen, *Selected Letters*, ed. John Bell, Oxford University Press, 1998, p. 291.

The Bounded and the Wild

The American poet Robinson Jeffers wrote 'Subjected Earth' during a vacation in the British Isles in 1929. In the poem Jeffers records walking in 'flat Oxfordshire fields' and remembering 'impatiently' his Pacific coast, 'Where colour is no account and pathos ridiculous, the sculpture is all,/Breaks the arrows of the setting sun/Over the enormous rounded eye-ball of ocean'. In 'the soft alien twilight/Worn and weak with too much humanity', the English landscape shows him earth as 'meek-smiling slave', which he addresses:

> If sometime the swamps return and the heavy forest, black beech and oak-roots
> Break up the paving of London streets;
> And only, as long before, on the lifted ridge-ways
> Few people shivering by little fires
> Watch the night of the forest cover the land
> And shiver to hear the wild dogs howling where the cities were,
> Would you be glad to be free? I think you will never
> Be glad again, so kneaded with human flesh, so humbled and changed.

The Oxfordshire fields are 'flat' in this poem, the flints 'little', the pheasants 'half tame'. Jeffers asks whether earth would 'be glad to be free' if primeval conditions returned. He thinks it would never be glad again, because too subjected: 'kneaded with human flesh … humbled and changed'. Significantly, the American poet identifies freedom with the wild. He measures the tame English landscape by his own mountainous Pacific coast and ocean.

Jeffers's American reaction to England in 1929 had precedents. Ralph Waldo Emerson visited England in 1833 and again in 1847.

He met the elderly Coleridge and Wordsworth, and in *English Traits* (1856) conveyed his sense of their limitations. Although too polite to say so, he clearly found them representative of what he calls England, 'an old and exhausted island'. 'England', he says, 'is a garden. Under an ash-coloured sky, the fields have been combed and rolled till they appear to have been finished with a pencil instead of a plough.' Emerson calls America, by contrast, 'that great sloven continent', where 'sleeps and murmurs and hides the great mother, long since driven away from the trim hedge-rows and over-cultivated gardens of England'.

Emerson's friend, Henry David Thoreau, found in 'Wildness ... the preservation of the World'. In 'Walking' he wrote, 'I wish to speak a word for Nature, for absolute freedom and wildness, as contrasted with a freedom and culture merely civil.' The Puritan settlers had feared and disliked the American wilderness and seen it as Satanic, abode of devilish heathens, the Red Indians. But by the eighteenth and nineteenth centuries wilderness had become associated with freedom and perceived as the opposite of corrupt civilization. For Emerson and his fellow Transcendentalists, nature and humankind are in harmony. Nature, Emerson says, is where 'the currents of the Universal Being circulate through me; I am part and parcel of God'. This is a profoundly optimistic philosophy, which not all writers of the nineteenth-century American renaissance shared. Writers as different from one another as Thoreau and Hawthorne, however, speak positively of 'naked Nature'. The huge democratic optimism of Walt Whitman embraces the American continent.

Love of the primitive is not itself a primitive emotion. One of its most moving expressions occurs in the work of one of the most urbane of writers, at the conclusion of F. Scott Fitzgerald's *The Great Gatsby* (1925), when Nick Carraway looks across the Sound:

> And as the moon rose higher the inessential houses began to melt away until gradually I became aware of the old island here that flowered once for Dutch sailors' eyes – a fresh, green breast of the new world. Its vanished trees ... had once pandered in whispers to the last and greatest of all human dreams; for a transitory enchanted moment man must have

held his breath in the presence of this continent, compelled into an aesthetic contemplation he neither understood nor desired, face to face for the last time in history with something commensurate to his capacity for wonder.

From this we might conclude that wilderness is an aspect of the American Dream. Not entirely. Charles Olson said, 'I take SPACE to be the central fact to man born in America ... I spell it large because it comes large here. Large, and without mercy.'[1] We should be aware, however, that the American cult of wilderness flourished as the need to preserve wilderness arose, from the 1860s. The nature philosophies of Emerson and Thoreau preceded it. American naturalists and ecologists such as John Muir, Aldo Leopold, Rachel Carson, and Gary Snyder are mainly men and women of the later nineteenth and twentieth centuries.

American and British ecologists, moreover, share a common father-figure in Gilbert White, whose *The Natural History and Antiquities of Selborne* (1789) records the wildlife of a parish. 'All nature', White wrote, 'is so full that the district produces the greatest variety which is most examined.' The American ecologist Aldo Leopold, whose *A Sand County Almanac* was first published in 1949, taught a similar lesson: 'The weeds in a city lot convey the same lesson as the redwoods; the farmer may see in his cow-pasture what may not be vouchsafed to the scientist adventuring in the South Seas.'[2]

It is a matter of perspective. 'Ditch vision' is the expression I use to describe the way of seeing nature's fullness by looking closely at a small area: parish or cow-pasture, ditch or hedge or city lot. It describes a tradition of British nature writing. In Britain the bounded is necessarily the way into the unbounded, the wild. But the way is not exclusive to Britain, or absent from America.

I first became conscious of ditch vision in a specific passage in Richard Jefferies' writings. At the beginning of his essay 'The Pageant of Summer', he provides a wonderful sense of the depth and abundance and life of nature – and one suddenly realizes he is describing a ditch. But I might as easily have found the idea in the poetry of John Clare, for instance, in 'Emmonsails Heath in Winter':

The Bounded and the Wild

I love to see the old heaths withered brake
Mingle its crimped leaves with furze and ling
While the old Heron from the lonely lake
Starts slow and flaps his melancholly wing
And oddling crow in idle motions swing
On the half rotten ash trees topmost twig
Beside whose trunk the gipsey makes his bed
Up flies the bouncing wood cock from the brig
Where a black quagmire quakes beneath the tread
The field fare chatters in the whistling thorn
And for the awe round fields and closen rove
And coy bumbarrels twenty in a drove
Flit down the hedgerows in the frozen plain
And hang on little twigs and start again.

Emmonsails Heath was ancient grazing land near Clare's home at Helpstone in Northamptonshire. It was not the heath of unaccommodated man in *King Lear*, or the heath Thomas Hardy describes at the beginning of *The Return of the Native*. This is Clare's home ground, which he has known and loved since a child. It is his, but it is also the place of a community, as the vernacular music shows: *crimped, oddling, brig, awe, bumbarrels*. It is both humanized and wild, not 'subjected' like Jeffers's Oxfordshire. Here 'the gypsy makes his bed'; the archetypal wanderer, who lives outside or on the margins of society, is at home.

I have said the place is not 'subjected', and it is not domesticated. Nature is vital here: 'Up flies the bouncing wood cock'; the bumbarrels (long-tailed tits) 'start again', ending the poem without closure, continuous with life's movement. Yet in another sense the place is subjected. Clare's parish was subjected to Enclosures, which to him were 'like a Bonaparte'. The words 'strange', 'stranger', and 'hermit' recur in his poetry. He experienced isolation, and removal from his original home. His poetry is often poetry of memory, intensely poignant from remembered happiness and present pain. His many poems about birds and their nests express his longing for home.

English nature poetry is historical and psychological in its very fibre. It could not possibly be about 'naked' nature, because there is scarcely any earth in England unmarked by human beings or outside the pressures of history. Gary Snyder says, 'For Americans, "nature" means wilderness, the untamed realm of total freedom.' He adds, 'Something is always eating at the American heart like acid: it is the knowledge of what we have done to our continent, and to the American Indian.'[3] American eco-writers tend to idealize what they call 'the Palaeolithic mind',[4] the world of hunters and gatherers. But if something is eating at the heart of the English nature poet like acid it is the life and death of the agricultural labourer – the poverty, the toil, the dispossession. John Clare is the ghost in the fields.

Robinson Jeffers saw in his wife, Una, what Thomas De Quincey saw in Dorothy Wordsworth: 'She was the very wildest (in the sense of the most natural) person I have ever known.' William Wordsworth said of his sister, 'she gave me eyes, she gave me ears'. Her description of daffodils bears this out:

> When we were in the woods beyond Gowbarrow park we saw a few daffodils close to the water side. We fancied that the lake had floated the seeds ashore and that the little colony had so sprung up. But as we went along there were more and yet more and at last under the boughs of the trees, we saw that there was a long belt of them along the shore, about the breadth of a country turnpike road. I never saw daffodils so beautiful they grew among the mossy stones about and about them, some rested their heads upon these stones as on a pillow for weariness and the rest tossed and reeled and danced and seemed as if they verily laughed with the wind that blew upon them over the lake, they looked so gay ever glancing ever changing. This wind blew directly over the lake to them. There was here and there a little knot and a few stragglers a few yards higher up but they were so few as not to disturb the simplicity and unity and life of that one busy highway.

Dorothy delights in the common flowers, in their beauty, in their vital life – they 'tossed and reeled and danced'. She almost humanizes them: some rested their heads ... *as* on a pillow', 'and *seemed* as if they verily laughed', 'they *looked* so gay'. But she respects their non-human being; the emotion is hers, not theirs.

Dorothy's response to the daffodils is well known to be a source of her brother's 'I wandered lonely as a cloud', a poem in which the dancing flowers are vital. But it is noteworthy that Wordsworth appropriates the daffodils, as Dorothy does not, setting himself apart from company by emphasizing his loneliness, and retaining the flowers for his 'inward eye'.

Regard for the common or humble object, or person, is an aspect of Wordsworthian Romanticism. A contrary feature is egoism. William Hazlitt, reviewing *The Excursion*, said, 'The power of his mind preys upon itself. It is as if there were nothing but himself and the universe.' This relation to the universe can look in either one of two opposing directions: the transcendental or the lonely. Loneliness is a condition of the Romantic tradition, equally present in British and American nature poetry. It was surely one of the main things that attracted Edward Thomas and Robert Frost to one another when they first met in England in October 1913. Both Thomas and Frost are sensitive observers of the natural world. Their landscapes of Hampshire and New Hampshire are different, but not radically dissimilar, as, say, Jeffers's California is from both. One thing linking the poets is their loneliness, the subjectivity they could reveal to each other as, perhaps, to no one else. Thomas called his experience melancholy. He and Frost had what the latter called, in the title of the famous poem of that name, 'desert places':

> They cannot scare me with their empty spaces
> Between stars – on stars where no human race is.
> I have it in me so much nearer home
> To scare myself with my own desert places.

This poem depicts wilderness in a negative sense, as snow-covered land around home. It is an internal condition, something in the poet himself, an inner emptiness, to which the snow corresponds.

As Frost uses nature to express inner states, so does Thomas too, as in 'Aspens':

Ditch Vision

All day and night, save winter, every weather,
Above the inn, the smithy and the shop,
The aspens at the cross-roads talk together
Of rain, until their last leaves fall from the top.

Out of the blacksmith's cavern comes the ringing
Of hammer, shoe, and anvil; out of the inn
The clink, the hum, the roar, the random singing –
The sounds that for these fifty years have been.

The whisper of the aspens is not drowned,
And over lightless pane and footless road,
Empty as sky, with every other sound
Not ceasing, calls their ghosts from their abode,

A silent smithy, a silent inn, nor fails
In the bare moonlight or the thick-furred gloom,
In tempest or the night of nightingales,
To turn the cross-roads to a ghostly room.

And it would be the same were no house near.
Over all sorts of weather, men, and times,
Aspens must shake their leaves and men may hear
But need not listen, more than to my rhymes.

Whatever wind blows, while I and they have leaves
We cannot other than an aspen be
That ceaselessly, unreasonably grieves,
Or so men think who like a different tree.

As Thomas said to Eleanor Farjeon: 'I was the aspen. "We" meant the trees and I with my dejected shyness.' 'The whisper of the aspens' corresponds to Thomas's poetic voice. His grieving constitutes a lonely inner world, for which he finds partial expression in nature. For Thomas, poetry itself is the voice of loneliness. 'As for lyric poets,' he wrote, 'they appear but sudden sharp voices as of birds flying over in a dark night.'

War shadows Thomas's English landscape, an implicit presence when it is not mentioned explicitly. His landscape is liminal, threshold to the land of the dead. Here, the lively community of smithy and inn has its ghostly mirror-image, silent and empty. Thomas is a poet of his own desert places: an elusive subjectivity, but corresponding also to the ghost world of England in 1915.

It is important not to simplify the differences between British and American nature poetry. The connections are too many and too intimate. As in the case of Thomas and Frost, so also in that of D. H. Lawrence, one of the most vital of English nature poets, who was powerfully influenced by Walt Whitman. Lawrence's animal vitalism was, in turn, a strong influence upon Ted Hughes. Hughes also inherited Edward Thomas's wartime landscapes, as we see in 'Thistles' with its imagery of Viking violence. Every thistle is 'a revengeful burst/Of resurrection, a grasped fistful/Of splintered weapons'.[5]

For Hughes war is a condition of the one nature, human and non-human. At times, as in this poem, he celebrates this. It is a continuity in his northern landscape, an energy in both land and language, 'the gutturals of dialects'. 'Thistles' celebrates a distinctively male energy and persistence: fighting fathers and sons. The poem draws on history and turns towards myth and an idea of the sacred, indicating the direction of Hughes's later poetry. 'A revengeful burst/Of resurrection' unsettles the central idea of the Christian universe. Hughes's world is post-Christian, post-war, a world of the nuclear age. As he wrote: 'Any form of violence – any form of vehement activity – invokes the bigger energy, the elemental power circuit of the Universe.'[6]

This idea of power is very different from Emerson's idea of the circulation through him of 'the currents of the Universal Being'. One may feel that in Hughes the power of male will is close to Robinson Jeffers. Jeffers framed his philosophy of 'Inhumanism' at the end of the First World War. It involved 'a shifting of emphasis and significance from man to not-man; the rejection of human solipsism and recognition of the transhuman magnificence'.[7] Jeffers preached 'turning outward from man to what is boundlessly greater'. In the years following the First World War he built Tor House and Hawk

Tower on the coast of California. His principal symbols were hawk and rock, and, with a view overlooking the Pacific Ocean, he commanded a cosmic perspective. It has been said that Jeffers 'thought of California as the place where Western civilization reaches its geographical, intellectual, and spiritual end'.[8] His primitivism – if that is the right word – identifies God with the physical universe, with rock and ocean. His setting, in 'Birds and Fishes' for instance, is 'the granite edge of the continent'. But, as this poem reveals, his primitivism is sophisticated and draws upon his civilized learning. He alludes in 'Birds and Fishes' to Job and *The Merchant of Venice*, and there is humour in his irony when he says 'the mob-hysteria' of the birds 'is nearly human', and concludes with a reference to Portia's famous speech about mercy:

> The wings and the wild hungers, the wave-worn skerries, the
>   bright quick minnows
> Living in terror to die in torment – man's fate and theirs –
>   and the island rocks and immense ocean beyond,
>   and Lobos
> Darkening above the bay: they are beautiful?
> That is their quality: not mercy, not mind, not goodness, but
>   the beauty of
>   God.

Primitivism, as others have observed, is, like wilderness philosophy, a fruit of civilization. Jeffers's cosmic perspective is American, Californian; it partakes of the immensity of the Pacific Ocean. In passing, we may observe what Jeffers sees, and what he does not see. He sees birds and fish and rocks and ocean; his vision encompasses humankind and 'the beauty of God'. He looks from a height, in more than one sense. His pulpit is 'the granite edge of the continent'. He does not notice things intimately in the manner of John Clare. Jeffers's concern is not the particular sensitive life of nature.

Another poet of the American Pacific coastal region, Gary Snyder, has what is initially a more relaxed vision, deriving from the Beat generation and his Zen Buddhism, as we see in 'Burning the Small Dead',[9] in which burning dead branches from 'whitebark pine' is seen in relation to the cosmos:

> a hundred summers
> snowmelt   rock   and air
>
> hiss in a twisted bough.
>
>   sierra granite;
>   Mt. Ritter –
>   black rock twice as old.
>
> Deneb, Altair
>
> windy fire

The poem springs from Snyder's experience in 'the Back Country' in the 1950s, from his work as a lookout in the mountains and from his experience of logging. He spaces word and image to reveal connections between trees, mountains, and stars, and between time and natural processes and the moment. He does not invoke any abstract concept, such as 'the elemental power circuit of the Universe', but he depicts universal energy as 'windy fire', 'the same in small dead branches burning', in 'hiss in a twisted bough', and in the stars.

There is no contemporary British nature poetry that is an exact equivalent of Snyder's, and it is doubtful that any British poet could say, like Snyder,

> As a poet I hold the most archaic values on earth. They go back to the late Palaeolithic; the fertility of the soil, the magic of animals, the power-vision in solitude, the terrifying initiation and rebirth; the love and ecstasy of the dance, the common work of the tribe.

Snyder's traditions and landscapes make this more than an empty boast: Thoreau and John Muir and American wilderness philosophy, Native American cultures, and West Coast elemental spaces. Added to these, the ecological movement in the United States, of which

Snyder is one of the leading thinkers and activists.

In the eponymous book published in the 1970s Snyder renamed the United States 'Turtle Island':

> A name: that we may see ourselves more accurately on this continent of watersheds and life-communities – plant zones, physiographic provinces, culture areas: following natural boundaries. The 'U. S. A.' and its states and counties are arbitrary and inaccurate impositions on what is really here.

Snyder, like all authentic contemporary nature poets, has absorbed the lessons of Rachel Carson, whose *Silent Spring* (1962) simultaneously exposed the chemical destruction of wildlife and emphasized 'the intricate web of life whose interwoven strands lead from microbes to man'.[10] His poem 'Front Lines' begins, 'The edge of the cancer/Swells against the hill.'[11] The focus is logging, the destruction of a forest, but the disease is a whole way of life: 'the rot at the heart /In the sick fat veins of Amerika'. It involves machines (chainsaw, jets) and ways of looking described as analogous to rape: 'Landseekers, lookers, they say/To the land/Spread your legs.' In Snyder's ecological vision wild things and creatures are people, their destruction equivalent to murder: 'skinned-up bodies of still-live bushes'. Wilderness still exists here: 'Behind is a forest that goes to the Arctic/And a desert that still belongs to the Piute.' But wilderness is now the front line of the war to save nature from human greed.

The ecological crisis in its modern phase has produced a new nature poetry, in which women poets have played a prominent part. The subject requires special care, to avoid identifying women with nature in the fashion of patriarchal ideology for which the identification is a form of subjection. The new nature poetry involves empathy, fellow-feeling, but this is not exclusive to women. John Clare is one of the most empathetic of poets. John Keats is another: 'if a sparrow comes before my Window I take part in its existence and pick about the Gravel'. There is, however, a kind of 'taking part' that only women can know. Thus, Gillian Clarke, in her poem 'Birth', describes the birth of a calf: 'Hot and slippery, the scalding/Baby came.'

We waited while the calf struggled
To stand, moved as though this
Were the first time. I could feel the soft sucking
Of the new-born, the tugging pleasure
Of bruised reordering, the signal
Of milk's incoming tide, and satisfaction
Fall like a clean sheet around us.[12]

As 'Birth' shows, with her early poems in the 1970s, Gillian Clarke introduced something new into Welsh poetry, which for centuries had been the domain of male poets. Nature poets are great observers, but observation, as the word implies, places the poet apart from what he sees. This seemingly simple poem is revolutionary through the woman poet's identification with the animal's process of giving birth. The word 'baby' links calf and child. Physically and emotionally, the woman relives the process of giving birth. She shares the animal's natural experience from within, instead of observing it as an onlooker.

Participation in natural processes makes women poets especially sensitive to ecological crisis. Clarke's poem-sequence 'Making the Beds for the Dead'[13] is about 'the plague year' of 2001, the year of the foot-and-mouth virus. 'Fox', subtitled 'September 2001', describes a fox that has been 'feasting with crows/on the carcass of a sheep':

What she can't eat she stashes
in her dozen larders
against hard times.

On the farm track she laps rain
from a cloven pool,
leaving cells to multiply
in the soup of a hoof print.

Calling the fox 'she' induces a sense of intimacy. Other words in the poem connect the animal and the human. But here life process and web of connection have taken a diabolic turn, as the imagery intimates: 'cloven', 'hoof print'. The cattle sip from a 'chalice' that is poisoned, and the wild fox inadvertently brings death on to the farm. Religious images have recurred in Clarke's poetry from the beginning, establishing for the woman poet a priestly function. Nature poetry is rarely 'only' nature poetry, since it connects to both the sacred and religious, and the social and historical, and cannot do otherwise, for nature is ground of all life. Ted Hughes and Gary Snyder are poets who assume functions of the shaman. Clarke's imagery of 'cloven pool' and poisoned 'chalice' is more shocking because of her sense that nature is sacred and the poet is nature's priest.

Welsh and English nature poetry is rich in place names. Pant-y-Cetris in 'Calf' is an example of names that are themselves poetry of a long-settled country. Like Clare's Emmonsails Heath they bespeak homeliness, where the human and the natural coexist. Poetry of place, in this sense, resists the encroachment of modernity, whether as Enclosures or mechanical uniformity. Snyder changes the name of the USA in his war against ecological destruction; in Britain, poets invoke local names as part of the resistance.

Recalling Jeffers's description of Oxfordshire, and by extension England, as 'subjected earth', it is instructive to look at a cycle of poems set in Oxfordshire by an English poet. Kim Taplin's 'This year, next year', published in her book *The Harbour Wall*,[14] records a year from March to February. It is a poem-cycle written with feeling in awareness of the state of the world in the 1980s, as well as in response to grievous events in the poet's personal life. This makes it nonetheless poetry in the tradition of Clare and Jefferies. Its cumulative force needs to be seen in a lengthy quotation, as in these lines from 'July':

> The Cherwell is alive with damsel-flies.
> This is the month of little field-edge flowers,
> hop-trefoil, creeping buttercup, heart's ease and clover,
> when marshy Peter's Spout smells warm and minty
> and meadowsweet is heavy in the air.
> Phoebe keeps finding tiny thumbnail frogs.
> There are sweet peas for picking every day,
> lifting the lassitude of the sultry Dog-star.

Swallows and swifts possess the evening sky.
Across the river Mr Hunter
in a brown overall is stacking bales;
the setting sun is glowing on his face.
We walk the fieldpath to the fair at Tackley,
Indian file through the popping barley.
On the way back our feet brush dew-damp grass.
Was that an early bat or a late swallow
skimming down the lane?
                       With dark comes rain at last
bringing relief as withheld tears do,
and someone quickly pulling windows shut
unwittingly caught a hawk-moth in the house
where it had followed strands of honeysuckle.
After squalls all night from the south and west
we found next day the bean-row had blown down
and the hawk-moth sitting still inside the glass,
a creature hardly ever seen by day,
with alien candy stripes of pink and green.
It sat all day beside the open window
and in the evening vanished silently.
On the last day of July Nat was born.

Notation and impression, as in Dorothy Wordsworth's journals and Richard Jefferies' essays, lie behind the style of the poem, giving it immediacy, a quickness of living detail. Impression crystallizes beautifully in image: for example, 'the lassitude of the sultry Dog-star'. Natural detail coexists with crucial events in the poet's life-experience, such as the birth of her son, Nat. The poem is alive with abundant particulars: damselflies, named field-edge flowers, named places and individual people, thumbnail frogs, a hawkmoth. Jeffers saw only 'flat Oxfordshire fields' and images of wildlife that emphasized its tameness. It is Kim Taplin's Oxfordshire that is truly wild, because she sees it with feeling and in minute detail. She is active and senses the life of the fields; she and her companions are *in* the fields, not just looking at them. Here, the bounded world opens on a depth of natural and human life. Enter the hawkmoth, 'caught', but bringing a strangeness into the house, something alien, other, and mysterious. Taplin does not need rock and hawk and the Pacific Ocean to obtain a sense of the wild; she finds it in 'the hawk-moth sitting still inside the glass'. If we were being hypercritical, we could even say that Jeffers's cosmic perspective is less wild, because he sees it as an *idea* of wildness.

An element of abstraction, more or less, characterizes the great tradition of English nature writing in the nineteenth century. Writers such as Gilbert White, Dorothy Wordsworth and the Romantic poets, John Ruskin, Jefferies, Gerard Manley Hopkins, and Thomas Hardy found the wild in the bounded by looking at landscape with little or no human presence. The tradition continues into the twentieth century, in which J. A. Baker's *The Peregrine*, first published in 1967, is perhaps its most remarkable product. Other English writers in the nineteenth century had discovered survivals of the wild on the Yorkshire Moors or Egdon Heath, and in recent times Ted Hughes found his savage country in Yorkshire and Devon. Baker's wild England, by contrast, was coastal Essex. How did he manage this?

In the following passage Baker describes the peregrine's perspective as it rises higher and higher:

> Looking down, the hawk saw the big orchard beneath him shrink into dark twiggy lines and green strips; saw the dark woods closing together and reaching out across the hills; saw the green and white fields turning to brown; saw the silver line of the brook, and the coiled river slowly uncoiling; saw the whole valley flattening and widening; saw the horizon staining with distant towns; saw the estuary lifting up its blue and silver mouth, tongued with green islands. And beyond, beyond all, he saw the straight-ruled shine of the sea floating like a rim of mercury on the surface of the brown and white land. The sea, rising as he rose, lifted its blazing storm of light, and thundered freedom to the land-locked hawk.[15]

Orchard shrinking, woods closing together, fields turning to brown, river uncoiling, valley widening: the hawk's perspective reconverts man-made landscape to original wild land. The human presence is reduced to 'the horizon staining with distant towns'. And what the wild represents, as it did to Jeffers, is freedom: 'The sea ... lifted its blazing storm of light, and thundered freedom to the land-locked hawk.'

Freedom for the peregrine means imaginative power for the writer. Baker identifies with the hawk and virtually becomes it:

> Standing in the fields near the north orchard, I shut my eyes and tried to crystallise my will into the light-drenched prism of the hawk's mind. Warm and firm-footed in long grass smelling of the sun, I sank into the skin and blood and bones of the hawk. The ground became a branch to my feet, the sun on my eyelids was heavy and warm. Like the hawk, I heard and hated the sound of man, that faceless horror of the stony places. I stifled in the same filthy sack of fear. I shared the same hunter's longing for the wild home none can know, alone with the sight and smell of the quarry, under the indifferent sky.[16]

This is powerful *writing*: an exhilarating dramatic narrative that uses images to sustain a high order of prose poetry, as Jefferies at his best does. Baker adopts a view identified with the hawk: 'I heard and hated the sound of man, that faceless horror of the stony places.' We may forget that misanthropy is a human trait. So is the 'hunter's longing for the wild home none can know'. It is of course the human imagination that Baker releases in identifying with the hawk, and the human need to restore a bounded landscape to the wild and mysterious.

Baker's need, as a man suffering from a disease that was progressively constricting him, was to identify with the wild and the free. One result was to reveal nature to us, to make us aware of wild England, as Henry Williamson had done in *Tarka the Otter*, another book written by a man who needed to escape the limitations of the agonizing human condition. This leads me to reflect, finally, on writers' – especially male writers' – need to identify with powerful animals, such as hawks. This has to do, surely, with power: animal power, which also signifies imaginative and spiritual power, as in the case of

Hopkins's windhover representing Christ in Majesty. The keyword from the second passage quoted from *The Peregrine* is, perhaps, 'will': 'I shut my eyes and tried to crystallise my will into the light-drenched prism of the hawk's mind.' Will power drives the imaginative identification. One may recall William Hazlitt: 'The language of poetry naturally falls in with the language of power.' Hazlitt was speaking of Shakespeare, to whom it is only partly applicable, for Shakespeare is the poet of unaccommodated man as well as kings and queens, and of field and forest as well as the Court. However, the connection between wildlife, language, and power would seem to hold in the case of some of the writers I have discussed. It applies to Robinson Jeffers, and to Ted Hughes's 'elemental power circuit of the Universe'. This is one reason why we cannot make an absolute distinction between modern American and British nature poetry.

There is a strong and growing body of contemporary nature poetry in Britain and America, with diverse poets sharing a common sense of ecological crisis. It is unlikely that for them the language of power will suffice, for this is the language that suits expressions of violent energy, of the world of the predator, and the view from above, the cosmic perspective. Hopkins's windhover represents Christ's mastery of the Creation. It could not represent God as William Blake perceives him, 'in the lowest effects as well as in the highest causes; for he is become a worm that he may nourish the weak'.

The language of power enables a vision of nature from one direction, and works in association with the will and force of human mastery. It prevents ways of seeing from other directions, which express needs that we are now especially aware of. There are alternative languages that enable different perspectives. One of these is the language of patient scientific observation, in the tradition of Gilbert White and Charles Darwin. Another is the language of personal vulnerability, of the lonely self, which is an aspect of Romanticism. Ditch vision may be especially valuable to the contemporary nature poet: language capable of getting down into the ditch, into the bird's nest, under bark, down among microbes in the soil. Such a poet may find a fitting model in Dorothy Wordsworth, or in John Keats as he takes part in the existence of the sparrow.

Notes

[1] Charles Olson, *Call Me Ishmael*, Jonathan Cape, 1967, p. 15.
[2] Aldo Leopold, *A Sand County Almanac*, Ballantine Books, 1970, p, 292.
[3] Gary Snyder, *Earth House Hold*, Jonathan Cape, 1970, p. 119.
[4] See, for instance, Max Oelschlaeger, *The Idea of Wilderness*, Yale University Press, 1991.
[5] Ted Hughes, *Selected Poems 1957–1981*, Faber & Faber, 1982, p. 63.
[6] Interview with Ted Hughes, in Ekbert Faas, *Ted Hughes: The Unaccommodated Universe*, Black Sparrow Press, 1980, p. 200.
[7] Robinson Jeffers, 'Preface', in *The Double Axe*, Liveright, 1977, p. xxi.
[8] James Karman, *Robinson Jeffers: Poet of California*, Story Line Press, 1995, p. 3.
[9] Gary Snyder, *No Nature: New and Selected Poems*, Pantheon Books, 1992, p. 95.
[10] Rachel Carson, *Silent Spring*, Penguin Books, 2000, p. 74.
[11] Gary Snyder, *Turtle Island*, New Directions, 1974, p. 18.
[12] Gillian Clarke, *The Sundial*, Gomer Press, 1978, p. 29.
[13] The sequence is included in Gillian Clarke, *Making the Beds for the Dead*, Carcanet Press, 2004.
[14] Kim Taplin, *The Harbour Wall*, Enitharmon Press, 1990, pp. 21–32.
[15] J. A. Baker, *The Peregrine*, New York Review of Books, 2005, p. 140.
[16] Ibid., pp. 144–5.

Alun Lewis:

'The Tragic Condition'

Nearly fifty years ago, after visiting Edward Thomas's memorial stone at Steep in Hampshire, I wrote a poem in memory of Edward Thomas and Alun Lewis.[1] It was a vulnerable piece, a young man's poem, but with a serious theme. In that rich countryside, not far from Gilbert White's Selborne, I was thinking of the tragic contrast between the two poets' gifts of natural observation and the uses to which the gifts were put when they became soldiers. Behind the tension within each man between poet and soldier, I was aware, too, of the tormenting self-consciousness they shared. This could be something demonic, self-destructive. Edward Thomas described self-consciousness as 'the terror' and wrote of himself that it amounted to 'a disease'. Alun Lewis also felt the severe depressions to which he was prone as a disease. He told his wife, Gweno, that 'When I was really sick to death ... and my mind was like a thing decomposing and putrefying in me ... I used to think everyday how simple it is to die'.[2]

Like Edward Thomas, Alun Lewis was a man of deeply troubled selfhood. This was partly what made him such a fine writer, in his poems, stories, and letters, but at a terrible cost. Garrisoned at Longmoor, in an area of Hampshire dear to Edward Thomas, between May 1940 and July 1941, Lewis followed Thomas's walks and visited his memorial stone and thought a good deal about the man who had been, in certain respects, so like himself. He wrote a poem addressed to Thomas, and concluded 'All Day It Has Rained' with the lines: 'where Edward Thomas brooded long/On death and beauty – till a bullet stopped his song'.[3] 'To Edward Thomas' strongly suggests that Thomas wished to escape from his 'weary/Circle of failure' in death; indeed, that death attracted him. The poem may be glossed by Lewis's later review of a selection of Thomas's poems, in which he speaks of 'a voice in him – Death, the ultimate response that he, despite himself, desired'.[4]

Both poets were haunted by death as an escape from the torments of self-consciousness. But preoccupation with death in wartime, and especially by soldiers, is common, so that this peculiarity of each man was also what enabled them to express what many felt. Thomas saw the war in 1914–15 as the presence of death and of the dead in England. Lewis internalized his war; it was 'the dark cancer in my vitals' of 'The Soldier'. In 'After Dunkirk' he wrote,

> But inwardly I have wept.
> The blood has flown inwardly into the spirit
> Through the gaping wound of the world.

Though this is acutely self-conscious, it also assumes what many were experiencing: 'the gaping wound' was the 'wound of the world', not Lewis's private wound. As a democrat and socialist, Lewis hated what militarism did to people. In India, he felt the guilt of a soldier of an army of occupation. At the same time, he was an efficient officer; and above all he cared for the welfare of his men, his 'Welsh boys'. An especially significant moment occurs in his story 'They Came', when the soldier whose wife has been killed in a bombing raid says to himself, 'My life belongs to the world, ... I will do what I can.'[5] The soldier's voice is that of Lewis, who wrote to his wife, 'I'm not going to funk the reality and cruelty of this phase of world history.'

Alun Lewis was not a man to protect himself. As poet and soldier, he was riven by inner conflict. In India, as Freda Aykroyd was to write in her memoir of their relationship, his 'divided love for me and Gweno' 'drove him to despair'.[6] Despair was Lewis's familiar, and as long as he lived he did not attempt to escape from it. To Gweno, he wrote, 'I cherish the power to think and feel above all; even when it's agony to think.' These are the words of a writer for whom experience of despair was an integral part of his subject matter. Nothing in this contradicts the fact that he loved Life, which he often capitalized, as he did Death also.

In my view, what is more valuable than playing amateur psychologist with Lewis is to enter into what he made of himself as a writer. Lewis made a distinction between his stories and poems. As he wrote to Freda: 'When I think of it, I think the poems are an act of daring, always daring, to plunge & tear & enter; & the stories are an act of recognition & steadiness, of *myself where I am.*' The truth of this may be borne out by a comparison of his finest story, 'The Orange Grove',[7] and his most powerful poem, 'The Jungle'.

'The Orange Grove' describes the nightmare drive of Staff-Captain Beale into what is to him the wilderness of Central India. He carries the corpse of his murdered driver in the back of the lorry, obsessed with the need to deliver it to a military post in accord with the proper formalities. It is implied that nationalist insurgents who want the British out of India have killed the driver. Beale, his mind turned by the nightmare, is loyal to his man. Eventually he links up with a tribe of gypsies, 'jungle wanderers', who are at home where he is completely lost. The theme of home and homelessness is reinforced by the image of an orange grove in Palestine as an ideal society. The story may be read as a metaphor for Lewis's sense of desperate lostness in India; but with remarkable objectivity, through the experience of one man, it embraces the theme of a rootless civilization attempting to impose itself upon a people with a profound sense of belonging, and in consequence having its groundlessness and emptiness exposed.

Lewis's approach to writing poetry was different. He thought of his poems as 'an act of daring, always daring, to plunge & tear & enter'. What this could mean finds expression in a letter to Gweno from India, in which he speaks of his vain wrestling 'in the long battle of thoughts and words'. He describes having been 'enticed, seduced and destroyed by the long octopus arms and hungry hard mouth of a shapeless poem'. He says that he knew that he 'couldn't live with the thoughts that encircled this particular poem'. He is describing what was evidently a not uncommon experience for him: writing in a state of chaos, when his mind was subject to subconscious forces, and attempting to win order from the struggle.

Chaos was what Alun Lewis as a poet risked. 'The Jungle' is the supreme example of what this man, who refused to protect himself from inner demons or seek safety from external enemies, could achieve. It is an intensely self-conscious poem, which speaks of a state of ultimate isolation:

> Only aloneness, swinging slowly
> Down the cold orbit of an older world
> Than any they predicted in the schools.
> Stirs the cold forest with a starry wind,
> And sudden as the flashing of a sword
> The dream exalts the bowed and golden head
> And time is swept with a great turbulence,
> The old temptation to remould the world.

The sense of extreme isolation, the defeated idealism, and the dreaming head recall the concluding lines of 'To Edward Thomas':

>   the dream
> Emerging from the fact that folds a dream,
> The endless rides of stormy-branchéd dark
> Whose fibres are a thread within the hand –
>
> Till suddenly, at Arras, you possessed that hinted land.

In each case, the poem ends with the inner world succumbing to its extinction. Both are intensely inward, and 'The Jungle' is suffused with a feeling of guilt and personal failure, shown, for example, in the astonishing image of 'the stagnant pool' holding 'Autumn rotting like an unfrocked priest'. But the remarkable thing about 'The Jungle' is that it uses the language of 'we', in contrast to the solitary wanderer in 'The Orange Grove': 'Wandering and fortuitous the paths/We followed to this rendezvous today'. The first verse paragraph of the third section of the poem enlarges 'the black spot in the focus' to include a distressing autobiographical passage, but concludes, 'we know/The greater enmity within ourselves'. The second section displays Lewis's versatility with a compacted pre-war social history that shows us the common ground he shared with Auden and Orwell, as distinct from his affinities with romantics such as Yeats and Rilke. Here, with special reference to South Wales, he summarizes 'the humming cultures of the West':

The weekly bribe we paid the man in black,
The day shift sinking from the sun,
The blinding arc of rivets blown through steel,
The patient queues, headlines and slogans flung
Across a frightened continent, the town
Sullen and out of work, the little home
Semi-detached, suburban, transient
As fever or the anger of the old,
The best ones on some specious pretext gone.

'The Jungle' demonstrates Lewis's daring, the risk he was taking in confronting despair and personal chaos. It is a self-conscious poem, with a 'darkness' that lacks the objectivity of 'The Orange Grove'. Yet it shows also how Lewis strove to the end for the democratic vision, the expression of common experience, however sharply he felt his personal predicament. Though he wrote to Gweno, 'I ... never lose you, thank God, in the jungle of my mind', he did not forget that for his men both the inner and outer jungles were a common experience. And to Gweno he said, also, of his fellow soldiers, 'we are all living through an identical experience in the same way'.

Alun Lewis's literary models included the great realists. In 'Last Pages of a Long Journal'[8] he criticized contemporary writers who sought loneliness and introspection: 'They have gone wrong. They must come back to Tolstoy, to the art which works through a vast human sympathy, through the community of human beings.' In a letter to Freda Aykroyd he said of Zola's *Germinal*, 'To write with such simple sincerity and to be at such pains to state the ugly truth of it all is an act of devotion to life.' Lewis's 'ugly truth' was the truth of two worlds, inner and outer: dark, despairing self-consciousness, and social evil – war, the forces opposed to democracy, a rotten civilization. He wrote sincerely of both. On Boxing Day 1943, not long before his death on 5 March 1944, he wrote to Freda, 'I'm not going to ask for leave because it's too much an escape & I should probe the void here instead because it's the void of the greater part of mankind.' This was the commitment that cost Alun Lewis his life, but it also made Lewis the writer. He tried to explain to Gweno:

> And if you ask why a man appears to prefer what is casual, rough, hazardous and incomplete to what is warm and personal and loving, I suggest you read Edward Thomas's poems again. It is, if you like, curious that the idealist should live casually with regard to himself and the preservation of himself, that he should find the haversack, the trench, the journeying, most suited to the pursuit of high ends.

It may be that Alun Lewis exaggerated his closeness to Edward Thomas, since their circumstances, and their wars, were different. But they both fought battles within themselves, against the inner darkness. Both, too, made themselves as writers in conflict with, but also out of, the self-consciousness that tormented them. Edward Thomas described 'the terror' of self-consciousness. But he also called it 'the most tragic condition of man's greatness'.[9] Alun Lewis's achievement bears out the truth of these words.

Notes

[1] 'At Steep' originally appeared in Jeremy Hooker, *Landscape of the Daylight Moon*, Enitharmon Press, 1978.

[2] Alun Lewis, *Letters to My Wife*, Seren, 1989, p. 92. Subsequent quotations from his letters to Gweno are from this edition.

[3] All quotations from Alun Lewis's poems are from Alun Lewis, *Collected Poems*, ed. Cary Archard, Seren, 1994.

[4] Alun Lewis, *A Miscellany of His Writings*, ed. John Pikoulis, Poetry Wales Press, 1982, p. 119.

[5] Alun Lewis, *Collected Stories*, ed. Cary Archard, 1990, p. 176.

[6] See Freda Aykroyd, 'Remembering Alun Lewis', in Alun Lewis, *A Cypress Walk*, Enitharmon Press, 2006. Subsequent quotations from Alun Lewis's letters to Freda Aykroyd are from this book.

[7] Lewis, *Collected Stories*, pp. 213–25.

[8] Lewis, *A Miscellany of His Writings*, pp. 119–23.

[9] Thomas, *Richard Jefferies*, p. 305.

Mary Butts and Her English Landscape

Admirers of Mary Butts place her among the great modernist writers of the first half of the twentieth century, yet many readers will still ask, 'Who was Mary Butts?' – as they would not ask about Virginia Woolf or T. S. Eliot, however little we *really* know about their lives. It is fair to assume, therefore, that little is known of Mary Butts in her native region, East Dorset, with which she closely identified. No one speaks familiarly of Butts's Dorset as we do of Hardy's Wessex. She was, however, conspicuous among her contemporaries, by whom she was seen in different ways.

An elderly Parkstone resident recalled, in a piece published in 1983, seeing Mary with her mother: 'Mrs. Colville-Hyde was a great and important lady in the district ... Her daughter, Mary, was often with her, and was the first lady I ever saw smoking. I remember being shocked and thinking it quite dreadful.'[1] Butts would shock people with less conventional expectations.

In London during and after the First World War, and on the continent, and especially in Paris, during the 1920s, Mary Butts was friendly or acquainted with practically every writer and many artists of note. She was a protégée of Ford Madox Ford. Ezra Pound and Jean Cocteau were her friends. In memoirs and letters of the period, Butts, with her red hair and bohemian behaviour, appears a striking figure, adored by some and disliked by others. In Wyndham Lewis's *The Apes of God* (1930) she is 'a big carroty anglish intellgentsia ... and buxom heiress'. (In her journal she remarks, astonishingly, of Lewis, 'A pleasure to be raped by him: yes, that's true.')[2] Aleister Crowley, self-styled Great Beast 666, whom she had helped with his occult studies, referred to her as 'a large white red-haired maggot'.[3]

Insult and eulogy alike testify to Butts's personal power. Her lover, the American composer Virgil Thomson, described her as 'an Englishwoman of noble birth, a roisterer, and a writer of intensely personal fiction ... I used to call her "the storm goddess" because she was at her best surrounded by cataclysms.'[4] On hearing of her death, her fellow great modernist writer, Dorothy Richardson, wrote, 'In ways, I feel no one could touch her. She had, don't you think, an innocent eye? Both in & out of her cups she was a seer. And the sophisticates by whom for so long she was surrounded, could not corrupt her. Her four-dimensionality was genuine, never whipped up, or bogeyish with desire to shock.'[5] Thinking of Butts five years later, Richardson wrote, 'Mary, for me, remains "Ashe of Rings" [her first novel], & a generous kindly creature ... She was only 23 when we used to see her, looking 40 in her voluminous black cloak & curtains of red curls, sybillising at the Dôme, evening after evening, elbows on table & head bent above magic circle, surrounded by a group of listening males.'[6]

These are glimpses only. Some facts may help us see a little more of Mary Butts. She was born in 1890 at Salterns, Parkstone, near Poole Harbour. Her father was a wealthy man from an ancient family, who, as a young man, had fought in the Crimean War. Her mother was younger and from a mercantile family. Mary's father, whom she adored, died in 1905, and her sense of displacement began when, the following year, she was sent away to a girls' school at St Andrews.

Butts's life in London began in 1909 when she became a 'general student' at Westfield College. In London she began to make her way in the literary world. Her first short-lived marriage was to John Rodker, whom she helped during the war as a conscientious objector on the run. Rodker's Ovid Press published early volumes by T. S. Eliot and Ezra Pound. Butts and Rodker had one daughter, whom she left mainly to the care of others.

In 1920 Mary Butts met the man who seems to have been the love of her life, Cecil Maitland, who had been wounded at Gallipoli. She shared studies in magic with Maitland and they spent the summer of 1921 at Aleister Crowley's 'Abbey' in Sicily. According to her biographer, Natalie Blondel, 'Mary Butts and Cecil Maitland began to undertake astral journeys, often while smoking hashish.' Her journal records out-of-body experiences; for instance, on 10 October 1916, 'On the pavement off the Fulham Rd waiting for a 31 bus I nearly came through.'[7]

It was probably through her friendship with Jean Cocteau that she became addicted to opium. Butts's love relationships, with men and women, all seem to have ended unhappily, possibly because of her attraction to the 'psychically sick'. Her writing is remarkable for its time in her non-judgemental treatment of transgressive sexual relationships. Hence in part its attraction to writers such as Robert Duncan in the San Francisco gay community. Robin Blaser's essay about her, 'Here Lies the Woodpecker Who Was Zeus', is one of the finest things written about Butts.[8] His afterword to her *Imaginary Letters* contains the following words:

> Of course, it is difficult to understand the passionate. They are seldom safe in their own hearts, let alone in their relations with others. On the evidence of the books, she adored men and, I think, frightened them. Somehow, her life threw her among homosexual and bisexual men. She understood their distance from women, the underworld of their thought, even to madness. She understood the unrequited, the youthfulness of sexuality and its terror.[9]

The bohemian life with its drug-taking and drinking took its toll and Mary Butts's life was saved when her mother brought her back to England in 1930. Mary moved with her second husband to Sennen Cove in Cornwall in 1932, and there ended her life, alone, in 1937, dying of perforated ulcers.

It is a sensational story, but if we think we know much about Butts from such a record we should heed the words of one of her most understanding friends, Wesson Bull: 'Mary had her secrets from us all, and to seek to lay bare her whole personality is to find she has a way of escaping us a little.'[10] Or a lot. She may have been a roisterer, a drug addict, a neglectful mother, an unhappy lover, but, first and foremost, she was a writer, and a woman making her way as a writer in a world dominated by men. Whatever her circumstances, she worked consistently, producing five novels, a considerable number of short stories, a childhood autobiography, a journal, poems, letters, two pamphlets, and many reviews.

Mary Butts's art was her lifeblood and a wound fed it. She was a person of extremes: a woman who sought passionately for meaning in relationships, and through the occult and, finally, religion, and always in her art. Adoring her father, she identified with his family and its values. She bitterly resented her mother, whom she blamed for her disinheritance – the loss of her original home and its treasures, which her mother sold after the death of Mary's father.

To understand Mary Butts at all we have to appreciate her childhood experience and her feelings for the home she lost. She wrote *The Crystal Cabinet: My Childhood at Salterns* towards the end of her life, and it was published posthumously in the year of her death. It begins with a wonderful description of the house 'which lay on the shore of Poole Harbour', which is part rhapsodic evocation of her home and its surroundings as they were and part bitter denunciation of change: 'the filth, the tram-lines and villas that pass for civilization'. She describes 'a mysterious belt of wood' towards the house, and continues,

> Several woods meeting on rising ground, ending in a dark half-moon to enclose the garden and the house. Inside this cusp, the orchard and kitchen garden, below these the ancient white stables. Then the belt of shrubbery. Then the House. But the House turned its back on the hill and the woods; its green lawn ran out softly between the points of the moon, between tall beeches, with a garden on each side, and a terrace garden behind it opposite the front door, built out of the foot of the hill. On the other side, between the beeches, the lawn flowed down to fields, studded with oaks and descending easily to the high road; and two hundred yards on the further side of the road, flooding in at the high tides of the equinox, the Harbour ran; across the Harbour, like a child in its womb, lay Brownsea Island with its high bank of woods; and behind Brownsea the green body of the Purbeck Hills, like a naked god laid down asleep.[11]

A number of crucial motifs appear in these opening passages, principally Butts's sense of the ideal rural beauty of her original home and its surroundings, and her bitterness and anger at its subsequent urbanization, a process she refers to as 'The Tide', which sums up everything she loathed about modernity, both material change and spiritual loss. Notable also are images of enclosure: woods 'ending in a dark half-moon to enclose the garden'; lawn 'between the points of the moon'; 'the Harbour, like a child in its womb'. This is an imagery born of myth, which conveys a sense of magical security. In this passage it culminates in 'the green body of the Purbeck Hills, like a naked god laid down asleep'. Mythical images sexualize the landscape, making it over as a feminine power in relation to a dormant male.

The idea of the land as a protective magical circle with a woman as its beleaguered guardian recurs in Mary Butts's fiction. Her first novel, *Ashe of Rings*, written during the war, begins,

> Rings lay in a cup of turf. A thin spring sun painted its stones white. Two rollers of chalk down hung over it; midway between their crest and the sea, the house crouched like a dragon on a saucer of jade.[12]

Rings is a house situated within chalk earthworks. It is a fictionalized Badbury Rings, which, like Salterns, was for Butts a temenos, a sacred enclosure. Imagery of dragon and saucer of jade identify the place as a centre of cosmic energy. Ashe is the family name; the title of the novel identifies the family – the father and, after him, daughter – with the place. In effect – to anticipate – Rings is an image of England.

Returning to Mary Butts's childhood at Salterns, we see how, from the outset, she acquired a mythical consciousness and a sense of the power that is magic. The source of this was partly classical – a Greek vision that, initially through her father's teaching and stories, became identified for her with English landscape. Her places were holy, like Eleusis, like Delphi. In her novels and stories her characters have a mythical figuration. Her fiction has a surface realism, but in and behind it there is another reality, and the visible discloses the invisible.

In her world the mythic is closely related to the poetic. It would not be untrue to say that her whole way of seeing was determined by poetry. From childhood she literally lived with William Blake's vision. Her father was the grandson of Thomas Butts, Blake's friend and patron, and among the many valuable antique treasures at Salterns was a collection of Blake's works – watercolours, engravings, portraits, and sketches. In *The Crystal Cabinet* she tells us that, brooding on certain of these, 'slowly, not the execution but the conception, the kind of seeing that there was in William Blake, in the end affected me both unconsciously and profoundly'.[13]

This 'kind of seeing' may be glossed as a perception of the divine in or through the visible world. It relates also to the marriage of opposites, which is central to occult research. Other strong poetic influences upon her seeing were Shelley, Wordsworth, and the Border ballads. In 'Thomas the Rhymer', for instance, she observed 'the transition', 'when a place becomes another place; and you know what you have suspected before – that all the time it has been two places at once'.[14]

Butts describes a quality of poetry as 'the evocation of the invisible'. Her sense that her childhood world was more than appeared on the surface – a sense she retained lifelong – informed her animism. This was at once a child's-eye view and a mature philosophy backed up by reading and scholarship, as we see in the following:

> Grown up people say that children like to pretend that the things they love are alive. This is nonsense – they *are* alive, and animism a natural possession of childhood. Alive, not with a copy of their own life, but with its life, the *mana*, proper to the thing itself. The virtue Chaucer knew about.[15]

Her use of the word 'mana' has behind it her extensive reading in the works of classicists and anthropologists, such as Sir James Frazer and Jane Ellen Harrison. It expressed her power of awareness:

> 'Mana', the word which science has taken from the Polynesians ... It is what Chaucer meant by 'the law of kind', that which makes a horse a horse and a sword a sword, a man a

man ... and so on with every object, animate and inanimate throughout nature.[16]

Mary Butts the writer is a sophisticated modernist. She spoke of her technique as 'the knight's move', which conveys 'both the necessary oblique manner of writing and the qualitative change conveyed by supernatural transformations'.[17] Again, in 'Ghosts and Ghoulies', she said, 'the first law ... of the interaction of other worlds with ours ... can be somehow described by a parallel with the knight's move in chess. The other moves are comparable with ordinary activities. Only the knights move two squares and a diagonal, on and sideways and can jump.' This points to a style that is elliptical, oblique, imagistic, with a highly conscious use of language. The pleasure of reading her is collaborative: the reader's intelligence is stretched by meeting her intelligence, as is the case in reading other modernists, such as James Joyce and Virginia Woolf. Butts's characters are psychologically complex, troubled, in some cases unstable (her second novel is entitled *Armed with Madness*), sophisticated moderns living a bohemian existence in London or Paris, or Dorset.

This, however, is only part of the truth. The Ashe father and daughter, and the Taverners, especially the women, Scylla and Felicity, in *Armed with Madness* and *Death of Felicity Taverner*, have a mystical sense of connection with the land. They are at once guardians and spirits of place. This connection with nature gives Butts's writing its extraordinary poetic vitality. It *animates* it and is indeed the expression of an animistic vision. As she wrote: 'Our forefathers thought "animistically", endowed everything that lives with life, like or unlike his own. (All artists still do.).'

In 'Our Native Land', a review in *The Bookman* in 1933, Mary Butts wrote of

> The enigmatic veil with which Nature has furnished the smallest weed in the hedge, a snail-shell, a pebble; as much as the most stupendous mountain ranges, the stateliest sunset.
>
> No use to peer & try to snatch at that veil. Yet the whole life of poet or painter, no less than scientist or common man, has been determined by its lifting – if only for an instant – if

only from a quite ordinary tree, a bend in a stream, a shoulder of a hill, a plant, a stone.

In such passages she is writing about herself. Salterns was her original holy place, and beyond it were Badbury Rings to the north and, across Poole Harbour, Purbeck, with Corfe Castle, and South Egliston and the coast below Tyneham Cap. This coastal area is the landscape of the Sacred Wood and the houses in the Taverner novels. From this part of England she abstracted what was for her the spirit of England.

In her journal Mary Butts included an 'eloge' on her friend Christopher Wood, the painter. This must be quoted at length:

> We both came from the same part of England, the short turf & chalk hills which are like nothing else on earth. They sprawl across counties, & our history & the history of man is written on them in flint & bronze & leaf & grey stone. Written on very short grass full of small black & white snail-shells. A dry country of immense earth-works & monstrous pictures done on the chalk stripped of its grass. From Avebury [Wiltshire] to Stone Cliff [Sussex] it is the same, sprawled across a kingdom, the history of England open. Also its secret history in letters too large to read. Secrets whose simplicity appals. People bred there go away & do different things, but at some time they have read the too large letters, & it becomes their business to re-write them legibly & in characters of whatever it is that they have to do. And, if they are conscious people, it is best for them at times to realize this, to remember what they are & what they are doing, to return to the place whose fruit & flesh & grass & salted air, whose sap has grown the bodies they have to take about.[18]

She perceives the South Country as a landscape where 'the history of man is written'. England's 'secret history' is written here 'in letters too large to read'. The business of the native-bred artist is to 're-write' the secrets 'legibly' – in words or paint for instance. A form of translation of landscape into art is their business, because they are born of this place, 'whose fruit & flesh & grass & salted air, whose sap has grown the bodies they have to take about'.

This myth of the organic oneness of person and place is a powerful one for a poet or painter: a myth that encourages works of animistic imagination. It is also a dangerous abstraction. And it springs from danger; from experience of crisis, which both affects the individual and is social. In Mary Butts's case, her vision was sharpened by loss. Immediately after the passage quoted earlier, which ends with an image of 'the green body of the Purbeck Hills, like a naked god laid down asleep', she says, 'Place I shall never see again, now they have violated it, now that body has been put to vile use, such as men from cities do to such places as these, such uses as its own people do not know how to prevent'.

The Crystal Cabinet records Butts's childhood at Salterns with a sharpness born of loss of the place and her inheritance, and of a general idea of violation. The war and what it represented were integral to her sense of disinheritance, and of belonging to a 'lost generation'. They were a determining influence upon her life and work, and she felt them as a wound from which she and her generation never recovered: 'I belong to the war-ruined generation; those years lie like a fog on my spirit, mud, slough of despair, cynicism, panic.'[19] *Ashe of Rings* was written during the war. In an afterword written in 1933, she described it as 'a war-fairy-tale, occasioned by the way life was presented to the imaginative children of my generation'. 'Some very curious things went on, in London and elsewhere, about that time; a tension of life and a sense of living in at least two worlds at once.' It is a death-haunted novel involving conflict between occult powers of good and evil. The central figure represents a beleaguered 'priesthood of life'.

This mythopoeic female function would remain central to Mary Butts's fiction. It represented a response to crisis, of which the war was not the only cause. As she wrote in 1933:

> As by now people have realized, between the years A. D. 1914 to 1917 something was done to the new generation of men that had never been done before. One can think of no parallel to that unique war and that peace that was no peace, coming

at a time when the rational spirit had evoked a science to break down faith, and let loose forces in nature only too capable of destroying our race. These facts go on staring us in the face, and as a result we are living in a spiritual chaos for which again there is no parallel.[20]

These words come from a review reprinted in a book devoted to Mary Butts's life and work called, significantly, *A Sacred Quest*. She speaks here of generational conflict arising from the war; such conflict between the young and the old recurs in her fiction. Crucially, she sees the war as an episode in an ongoing process of destruction, in a world in which 'the rational spirit had evoked a science to break down faith, and let loose forces in nature only too capable of destroying our race'. We are living, she says, in an unparalleled 'spiritual chaos'.

Butts's metaphor for this chaos was the same as T. S. Eliot's: the Waste Land. She both admired Eliot and saw him as a rival. Like Eliot in *The Waste Land* (1922), she drew on Frazer's *The Golden Bough* (1890) and Jessie L. Weston's *From Ritual to Romance* (1920), as well as the classical literature and the classical and Nordic mythology that were part of her imaginative lifeblood. The Grail Quest motif, which is integral to the Waste Land theme, recurs in her writing and is the notably ambiguous centre of *Armed with Madness*. The myth and its associated imagery serve to express the central experience of her writing: questing for meaning – the life-giving grail – in the spiritual chaos of the modern world.

As Scylla reflects in *Armed with Madness*:

What was she worried about? Money, of course, and love affairs; the important, unimportant things. Hitherto God had fed his sparrows, and as good fish had come out of the sea. But everywhere there was a sense of broken continuity, a disease. The end of an age, the beginning of another. Revaluation of values. Phrases that meant something if you could mean them. The meaning of meaning? Discovery of a new value, a different way of apprehending everything. She wished the earth would not suddenly look fragile, as if it was going to start shifting about ... There was something wrong with all of them, or with their world. A moment missed, a moment to come. Or not coming. Or either or both. Shove it off on the war; but that did not help.[21]

Whether or not one invokes Nietzsche, as Scylla does, this awareness of a fragile earth, and sense of 'something wrong with all of them, or with their world', is central to the modern experience; its expression, through psychological and emotional instability, is what makes Mary Butts a significant modern writer.

In her world, worry about money and love affairs rests on a more fundamental problem – 'a sense of broken continuity, a dis-ease' – that is religious. Her personal trajectory was from magic to religion, but to a religion that, in a sense, validates a magical view of life. Her last published novels, *The Macedonian* and *Scenes from the Life of Cleopatra*, combine scholarship and imaginative construction to show us – they are highly visual works – figures who stand in close relation to the divine. Two brief passages will illustrate the point. In *The Macedonian*, Alexander says,

> Since the first moments I can remember, I have had the gods for company, or a god. I called it my dâimon, as Socrates his, until I knew it was not. I and my dâimon are one. Do you not see? I may not be man. I have been shown what God is until it has changed my blood. I have gone into the forms that are shapes of God. That is torture ... And I have seen the other Alexander, who is dying as much as this one lives.[22]

In *Scenes from the Life of Cleopatra*, the Egyptian queen speaks 'like a divine woman':

> Then a time came when they put me into the Sacred Robes and I stood before the people ... and offered myself – or was offered – myself to myself. Then it is that I came out of myself and Something – call it the Goddess – becomes me and I That ... I do not want – I am – power.

We may see in this a fictional projection of the desire for power of a woman writer in a man's world and her dealings with magic. It reflects also 'the ancient priesthood of life'.

The ancient world held for Mary Butts what was threatened in her own: 'Egypt, because of its religion, particularly attached to the divine, every act of life being so many threads attaching men to the unseen'. Egypt was the Salterns of her childhood, 'every act of life … so many threads attaching [her] to the unseen'.

Her mental warfare, like Blake's, was in defence of the sacred, which, like Blake's green and pleasant land, was identified for her with the country, with rural England, whose quintessential embodiment was East Dorset. Consequently, in *Death of Felicity Taverner*, she dramatizes conflict between the Taverners as guardians of the land and a figure that is the mortal enemy of everything they – and she – love and believe in. Scylla's 'bit of England' means 'the flawless, clean and blessed, mana and tabu earth', conceived as in Butts's eloge for Christopher Wood: 'strictly of their flesh, whose birds and beasts and eggs and fish, and fruit and leaf and air and water had nourished their bodies, "composed their beauties", whose pattern was repeated in them, the stuff of a country made into man'. Their adversary, Nick Kralin, is effectively a devil-figure; anti-poetic, 'a man whose interests were all cerebral'. His 'terrible power' is the power of 'Not-Being, Un-Meaning, Un-doing. … Nodens, God of the Abyss'. His practical plan is to buy up the land and ultimately dispossess the Taverners.

Scylla's husband, Picus, listens to Kralin outlining his scheme to 'build a hotel and a row of bungalows along the low cliff, light the sea lane and drain it'. He would advertise 'one of the least-known places in England'.

> Picus listened to this, and all that he was sure that he felt was a pain somewhere deep in the middle of his inside. He heard Kralin telling him about a gold-course, and where the garages and the parking-ground could be. As he listened he could hear at the same time a long cry, a wail, a lamentation from outside that never stopped. A mourning somewhere in creation that the freshest earth there is should lose its maidenhood, be-

come handled and subservient to man, to the men who would follow Nick Kralin.

This is what Mary Butts saw being done to her original home ground, her 'bit of England'. In the novel it is prevented only because Kralin is murdered.

Violation of the sacred recurs as a theme in Butts's fiction. A notable instance features in the story 'From Altar to Chimney-Piece', which is a satirical portrait of Gertrude Stein and, through Stein, of the post-war intelligentsia. Miss Van Norden (the Stein figure) shows the Englishman objects in her Parisian flat. The objects used as ornaments are 'frames, supports, stands for the ciborium, the box … to hold the wafers of the Host', from a country church in Spain:

> 'These Greek letters are the only relic of piety about them', she added, 'and cleaning will soon wear them off. Interesting parochial baroque – and from the country of its origin too. For they are not old.' She picked up one and began to rub it on a filthy handkerchief of khaki cotton, on which she spat. The old paint was dry and cracked and the signature of Christ rubbed off at a touch.[23]

In this action, as 'the letter Chi' is rubbed off the 'ornament', the satire on the reversal of values – from sacred object of communal worship to aesthetic personal possession – is obvious. What makes it effective is the detail of the old woman's horrible unconscious sacrilege when 'She picked up one and began to rub it on a filthy handkerchief of khaki cotton on which she spat'. 'Khaki' is an almost subliminal touch, calling to mind the spiritual chaos represented by the war.

Mary Butts's personal trajectory was from her interest in the occult and astral journeys to her conversion, in 1935, two years before her death, to Anglo-Catholicism. Then, she wrote to Charles Williams, 'literally my spiritual recovery began to date from the day the first of your books came into my hands'. Although she lived to reject magic as a Crowley-like preoccupation with the occult, magic as the imaginative apprehension of mystery continued to inspire her.

She assented to the words of her friend, Richard Ellis Roberts, which she quoted in *The Crystal Cabinet*:

> Without God there can be no man; without supernature there can be no nature; without philosophy there can be no psychology; without theology there can be no science; without mysticism there can be no commonsense.

But what saved her from this reversal of values was, she says, Badbury Rings:

> without the Rings, I know what would have happened to me – whirled away on the merry-go-round of the complex and the wish-fulfillment and the conditioned reflex, with Jung and Pavlov, Julian Huxley and Bertrand Russell, in all the consciousness of my group. On those rocking-horses I might have pranced for ever, with the rest of us, in a ring we mounted with zest.

Her Christian faith was informed by the magical view of life. Long years of reading anthropologists and classicists lie behind her description of Christ as 'the young god-man on the holy earth-tree'. This image, which draws upon the Anglo-Saxon poem 'The Dream of the Rood', would have appealed to another writer, the Catholic David Jones, who knew how deeply the war had stirred up and mixed pagan and Christian sources.

Mary Butts's vision of her 'bit of England' is far from being immune to criticism. Patrick Wright, in particular, has made an incisive critique from a sociological point of view.[24] He has demonstrated the operation of 'exclusion and anathema' as 'principles active at the foundation of Mary Butts's sacred geography', showing the 'two primary forms' they take in her writings: 'one political, the other racial'.

The charge of racism focuses on the portrayal of Kralin, who is described as 'no more than half a Russian – more than half a Jew'. It is not suggested that he is diabolic *because* he is a Jew. However, there does seem to be more than a touch of anti-Semitism here. Butts pronounced anathema on what she called 'The Tide', an all-embracing term for what she hated about the modern urban world, which included population growth and development in East Dorset. This exclusive vision is anti-democratic and constitutes a kind of English racism, based ultimately on what she believed to be her ancient family inheritance and the hierarchical order that it represented. To my mind, her exclusiveness – her snobbery – is the poison in her Holy Grail.

As Natalie Blondel says, Mary Butts was 'an early ecologist and conservationist'. This is true, but it came at a price. Her poem 'Corfe' begins,

> Corfe, the hub of a wheel
> Where the green down-spokes turning
> Embrace an earth-cup of smoke and ghosts and stone.
> The sea orchestrates
> The still dance in the cup
> Danced for ever, the same intricate sobriety
> Equivocal, adored.
>
> But when I remember you, Corfe, I remember Delphi
> Because your history also is a mystery of God.

Her bit of England, centred on Corfe in this poem, is holy; a sacred enclosure, like Delphi. Here, again, her favourite imagery of rings recurs as a sacred symbolism: 'hub of a wheel', 'earth-cup', 'dance in the cup'. The cosmic dance, which is the source of original creative energy, is centred on the sacred place. That place was Mary Butts's spiritual protector, and she was its imaginative guardian. It is an elevated vision; unfortunately, it is also an exclusive one. 'Corfe' is also known as 'A Song to Keep People out of Dorset'. Mixing styles and registers, the poem concludes with a ballad measure. The last three verses read as follows:

> Turn back our folk from it, we hate the lot
> Turn the American and turn the Scot;
> Take unpropitious the turf, the dust
> If the sea doesn't get em then the cattle must.

> Make many slugs where the stranger goes
> Better than barbed wire the briar rose;
> Swarm on the down-tops the flint men's hosts
> Taboo the barrows, encourage ghosts.
>
> Arm the rabbits with tigers' teeth
> Serpents shoot from the soil beneath
> By pain in belly and foot and mouth
> Keep them out of our sacred south.

This is intentionally comic, but perhaps not so funny to readers who recognize themselves as the excluded, as most of us are.

Butts shared her dislike and fear of mass society and mass culture, and her idea of a beleaguered civilized minority, with most modernists. This has not prevented her fellow artists from being recognized for their significance, and it should not be allowed to obscure her achievement. But where exactly does Mary Butts the writer belong? Following her death, Hugh Ross Williamson placed her with D. H. Lawrence and T. S. Eliot:

> To say that Mary Butts was as 'difficult', as original, as individual an artist, and that her work might be termed a mediation between extremes, is perhaps the best way to introduce her writing to those ignorant of it. Her books combine Eliot's intellectual classicism with Lawrence's emotional romanticism; and it is that combination which makes them unique.[25]

Though this is high praise, any such 'placing' is liable to blur a writer's individuality. It misses important things in Mary Butts's case too, including the ground she shared with other major women writers, and her interest in the supernatural and the ghost story, which gives her affinities to writers as different as M. R. James, Arthur Machen, and Charles Williams, as well as Kipling and E. M. Forster. It also misses a sympathetic understanding of sexual transgression, very different from either Lawrence's aggressive heterosexuality or Eliot's puritanism. Mary Butts was her own woman.

Her landscape, however, was not hers alone. In *Armed with Mad-*

ness, the American Carston exclaims, 'This is the England we think of. Hardy's country, isn't it?' Of course, it is not. Hardy's Wessex is rich in folklore and myth. It is also the site of modernity, and not in urbanization and mechanization alone. As early as *The Return of the Native* (1878), Hardy's subject was 'the mind adrift on change, and harassed by the irrepressible New'. But Hardy the Victorian was a social novelist and a realist, and the modernist Butts was not. Her Dorset is more a place of myth, poetic, abstract, more a psychological realm. More like John Cowper Powys's Wessex, in fact.

Landscapes of south and southwest England feature as sacred presences in both Butts's and Powys's fiction. Similar images occur. For instance, Butts's 'the green body of the Purbeck Hills, like a naked god laid down asleep' calls to mind Wolf Solent's view of 'that ocean of greenness out of which rose, like the phallus of an unknown god, the mystical hill of Glastonbury!'[26] Both Butts and Powys were strongly influenced by Blake and the Romantic poets. Both were, perhaps, primarily poets working in forms of fictional prose; certainly, they were mythic storytellers, not realist novelists. The grail and the Waste Land theme, and the spiritual hunger in chaotic times which these symbolize, obsessed both writers.

In their work, compared with the world of Thomas Hardy, there is a social narrowing. At times, reading of the lives of Butts's country gentry, one may be reminded of a passage in J. A. Hobson's *Imperialism* (1902):

> Could the incomes expended in the Home Counties and other large districts of Southern Britain be traced to their sources, it would be found that they were in large measure wrung from the enforced toil of vast multitudes of black, brown, or yellow natives, by arts not differing essentially from those which supported in idleness and luxury imperial Rome.[27]

Although it would be unfair to apply this without qualification to Butts's small group of impoverished artists and intellectuals, it comes to mind because of their abstraction from the larger historical society. Butts's bit of England is withdrawn not only from England as a whole, but also from its own region and location – the reality of East Dorset.

For all her privileging of a minority, however, her primary landscape is not easily forgotten: 'the short turf & chalk hills which are like nothing else on earth'; the place of 'whose fruit & flesh & grass & salted air, whose sap' she felt herself to have been born. A similar feeling, springing from a sense of loss and dislocation during and after the war, was not uncommon in her generation. It resulted in a form of spiritual patriotism, which became a potent force among English writers and artists of the period. One thinks of Edward Thomas, of E. M. Forster and the 'condition of England' novel, of Woolf's *Between the Acts* and Eliot's *Four Quartets*. In these, and in the work of artists such as Christopher Wood, Paul Nash, and Henry Moore, the body of the land incarnates an essential English spirit. Mary Butts's landscape deserves to be known alongside theirs.

Notes

[1] Quoted in Nathalie Blondel, *Mary Butts: Scenes from the Life*, McPherson, 1998, p. 448, note 2.

[2] Mary Butts, *The Journals of Mary Butts*, ed. Nathalie Blondel, Yale University Press, 2002, p. 133.

[3] Quoted in Blondel, *Mary Butts*, p. 104.

[4] Ibid., p. 176.

[5] Dorothy Richardson, *Windows on Modernism: Selected Letters of Dorothy Richardson*, ed. Gloria G. Fromm, University of Georgia Press, 1995, pp. 328–9.

[6] Ibid., p. 484.

[7] Butts, *The Journals*, p. 60.

[8] Robin Blaser, 'Here Lies the Woodpecker Who Was Zeus', in *A Sacred Quest: The Life and Writings of Mary Butts*, ed. Christopher Wagstaff, McPherson, 1995, pp. 159–223.

[9] Robin Blaser, 'Afterword', in Mary Butts, *Imaginary Letters*, Talonbooks, 1979, pp. 74–5.

[10] Harcourt Wesson Bull, 'Truth is the Heart's Desire', in *A Sacred Quest: The Life and Writings of Mary Butts*, ed. Christopher Wagstaff, McPherson, 1995, p. 87.

[11] Mary Butts, *The Crystal Cabinet: My Childhood at Salterns*, Carcanet, 1988, p. 15.

[12] Mary Butts, *Ashe of Rings and Other Writings*, McPherson, 1998, p. 5.

[13] Butts, *The Crystal Cabinet*, p. 34.

14 Mary Butts, 'Ghosties and Ghoulies', in *Ashe of Rings and Other Writings*, p. 342.
15 Butts, *The Crystal Cabinet*, p. 81.
16 Mary Butts, 'Traps for Unbelievers', in *Ashe of Rings and Other Writings*. p. 323.
17 Quoted in Blondel, *Mary Butts*, p. 173.
18 Butts, *The Journals*, p. 360.
19 Ibid., p. 293.
20 Mary Butts, 'The Dark Tower', in *A Sacred Quest: The Life and Writings of Mary Butts*, ed. Christopher Wagstaff, McPherson, 1995, p. 137.
21 All quotations from *Armed with Madness* and *Death of Felicity Taverner* are taken from Mary Butts, *The Taverner Novels*, McPherson, 1992.
22 Quotations from *The Macedonian* and *Scenes from the Life of Cleopatra* come from Mary Butts, *The Classical Novels*, McPherson, 1994.
23 Mary Butts, *With and Without Buttons*, Carcanet, 1991, p. 183.
24 For his discussion of Mary Butts, see Patrick Wright, *On Living in an Old Country*, Verso, 1985.
25 Quoted in Blondel, *Mary Butts*, pp. 429–30.
26 John Cowper Powys, *Wolf Solent*, Penguin Books, 1964, p. 403.
27 J. A. Hobson, *Imperialism: A Study*, 3rd edn, Unwin Hyman, p. 151.

Frances Bellerby, Poet

In 1975, Alan Clodd sent me a copy of Frances Bellerby's *The First-Known and Other Poems*, which he had published at Enitharmon Press. The poems moved me deeply and my instinct was to write to their author and tell her so. I was unable to do this, because Bellerby had died shortly after the book was published. I had not heard of her before Alan Clodd sent me her book. I proceeded to acquire and read all her published work, to write an essay on her poetry, and eventually to make a selection of her short stories, which Alan Clodd published, alongside a selection of her poetry edited by Anne Stevenson. Frances Bellerby is not an unknown poet. Her friend Charles Causley made an earlier selection of her poetry, she was praised by discerning critics, such as Kathleen Raine and Alan Brownjohn, and her poems occasionally appear in anthologies of twentieth-century poetry. But there is, I believe, a message in the way in which I came to learn about her.

Put quite simply, without Alan Clodd's intervention, I might never have heard of Frances Bellerby. It is easy to miss significant poets in our culture. At any given time, a few powerful 'voices' influence a generation – at one time W. H. Auden, at another Ted Hughes and Sylvia Plath – and a few well-known publishing houses sustain the mainstream. In this situation, other good writers languish in the margins; some of them – Basil Bunting and Roy Fisher for instance – eventually being taken up by the big publishers, and others continuing to write in relative obscurity. This is a large subject, and with Frances Bellerby in mind, I want to make only one important point here. It has often been argued, with justice, that women poets have been unfairly marginalized compared with men. Less often, *subject* has been observed to be the marginalizing factor, and when subject and gender coincide the poet's voice is less likely to be heard. A case could be made that women poets who held religious convictions, and others whose sensibility was religious, wrote some of the most vital English poetry in the twentieth century. I am thinking of figures such as Kathleen Raine, Elizabeth Jennings, E. J. Scovell, Ann Ridler, Mary Casey, and Frances Bellerby – some of them with established reputations, others not as well known as they should be. If one thinks of a seriousness more political than religious other names come to mind, such as Sylvia Townsend Warner and Valentine Ackland. Of course, knowing a name isn't the same as understanding a poem or body of work. That is why I want to return to Frances Bellerby, because I hope to understand better what so moved me in the book of poems Alan Clodd sent me in 1975.

On first reading *The First-Known and Other Poems* I was drawn, like Charles Causley, to the poet's expression of 'the ambience, and the essence, of place'.[1] While still quite a young woman, Bellerby, after separation from her husband, seems to have lived alone, and from the early 1940s until her death she made her home in isolated cottages in Cornwall and Devon. Her poems convey an intense sense of isolation, in conditions in which she responds with exquisite sensitivity to landscape and the effects of weathers and seasons. Her West Country is a luminous realm in which darkness is shot through with blazing light. The following lines from 'On the Third Evening'[2] are typical of the situation of the poet and her sense of quest:

> On the third evening
> coming out of the hillside wood
> and for the first time hesitating,
> I saw that the hedgeless road
> on the one hand leapt up towards the west
> to vanish in streaming light,
> on the other plunged into a wooded cleft
> already deep with night.

Aspects of Frances Bellerby's poetry recall Thomas Hardy and Edward Thomas, but her vision of light is metaphysical and closer in spirit to Henry Vaughan.

Frances Bellerby's isolation was peopled with spirits, especially those of her dead brother, killed at the age of eighteen in 1915, and her mother, who committed suicide in 1932. As with Vaughan, deaths of her beloved inspired her vision of eternity. She was also especially close to the natural world and had an acute sense of the being of individual creatures, such as the lizard, spider, otter, heron, and other birds. The poems make clear her feelings for these, whose lives and deaths she shares. Julian, the young man in her novel *Hath the Rain a Father?*, speaking to the young girl, Elizabeth, expresses what was evidently Bellerby's own belief. Indeed, his speech is more like a sermon, as the following extract reveals:

> Man thinks he is made in the image of God. Who told him so? It is *Life* that is made in the image of God, in the thousand, million images of God. The whole of Life, not only animal life – and who can ever know what the whole of Life consists of, so who can ever know in what guise God is stepping near? It may be Man's guise, for the greater includes the lesser, but Man is no more and no less 'in the image' than are the other shapes of Life. Not only animal-shapes, not only plant-shapes. Stones and rocks, the sea, the clouds, the rain, the frost, sun, moon and stars, the leaping fire, the wind, the shadow of the apple tree upon the moonlit grass ... Images of God, these and all other manifestations of pure Life. The Old Testament poets knew more about this than we do, with their 'God my rock'. Hold a stone in your hand with reverence, with awareness, and it is God you hold. This is my body, this is my blood.[3]

This, surely, is Frances Bellerby speaking through her fictional character. The intensity is hers – the love for and sense of mission to all creatures. Born and brought up in an intensely religious household, Bellerby lived a life of service – to poor and disadvantaged people, before the accident that curtailed her professional work, and to non-human creatures lifelong. Here also we see a religious vision, which draws heavily upon the Christian Incarnation but is not confined to orthodoxy. Her life was very different from Mary Butts's, but both women retained the animistic vision of their childhood.

It is necessary to hear a whole poem to appreciate Frances Bellerby's lyrical gift. 'The First-Known' is characteristic of the emotional power that her words and rhythms embody:

> I am free to come and go –
> That is the bargain I have made.
> The door stands wide. Is never closed.
> The threshold's worn by me and the dead.
>
> When the wind rages, and the rain,
> hurled half-across the impassive room,
> streams down my lifted face like tears,
> I hear the calling of my name
>
> Tossed in the tempest, here and there,
> by that immortal first-known voice
> – my friend, my lover, my unseen
> gaoler in this hidden place.
>
> One day, one night, one dawn, one dusk,
> I will call back, not hesitate,
> nor search my memory, heart and mind,
> for that dear Name. But still not yet.
>
> Freedom's my chain. Take that and give
> truth. Uncloud my hindered eyes,
> unstop my ears, that once for all
> I see, and hear, and recognize.

The poem is meditative, the thinking and feeling of a real subject, with 'memory, heart and mind'. It is deeply personal, containing a life story that may not be fully comprehensible without reference to Robert Gittings's invaluable biographical essay that prefaces the *Selected Poems*.[4] But the feeling in the poem communicates itself strongly, through a voice that is now matter of fact, now hesitant, now rapt as it projects grief on to the tempest, and expresses powerful emotion through repetition: 'One day, one night, one dawn, one dusk'.

The paradox of freedom that is 'my chain', which places 'truth' beyond reach, reverses the normal 'order' of life and death and expresses the desire for an ultimate communion with 'that immortal first-known voice'.

'The First-Known', like many of Frances Bellerby's poems, is a poem about 'the dead', but, despite the grief, it is not cast in a traditional elegiac mode. It may be contrasted with Thomas Hardy's marvellous 'The Self-Unseeing' with its equivalent ecstasy as he recalls a childhood moment with his parents, 'here', in a specific room, 'Where the dead feet walked in'. Hardy's revisioning is a poem of memory, when 'Blessings emblazoned that day', but recalls what is inexorably past, not the eternal present. Hardy's 'former door/Where the dead feet walked in' differs completely from Bellerby's 'threshold worn by me and the dead', for in the latter case the living poet shares the boundary with the dead, calling in question the finality of death.

This is perhaps the most difficult aspect of Frances Bellerby's thinking to understand and it turns on her idea of 'perfection'. Robert Gittings quotes her words in response to the death of her brother, dearly loved and a hero to her, which she '"saw through tears, as absolute perfection" in the light of a triumphant fulfilment of his own wish'.[5] Such a view can only be understood in the context of a sacramental vision of life. She dedicated her *Selected Poems* 'To the brief and everlasting life of my brother'. *The First-Known and Other Poems* carries a dedication in the same spirit to her mother: 'Because of the beginning/and because of/an end/which was not after all/the end'. Charles Causley quotes what she said about the theme of love and death which is central to her work:

> I know that human love (one expression of the Principle of Love) is far stronger than death. I knew this from the start, and all my experience has proved it beyond least shadow of doubt. In fact, I do not think love and death are in opposition at all, though love and life may be. Death does not check love, nor halt its development and deepening in so far as the living are concerned.[6]

For Frances Bellerby, knowledge 'from the start' meant the completeness – the perfection – of love within her original family. 'Home' is a recurring word in her poetry, as it is in Edward Thomas's. In both instances the word carries a sense of ultimate belonging, but in Bellerby's poems it is metaphysical. Thus, in 'Strange Return', she wrote, 'My long journey's sole purposed end/was, at last, at last, a return home.' This is what I mean by speaking of her quest: a spiritual adventure that cannot be reduced to nostalgia for a long-lost familial unity. In theological terms, we may think of a passage from St Paul quoted in *Hath the Rain a Father?*: 'God has made known to us the mystery of His will – that in accordance with his eternal plan He should reunite all things in Christ, both things in Heaven and things in earth.'[7] The belief is usually implicit in her poems, and sought for, in hope, rather than triumphantly affirmed. The end of 'The Heron' is an exception:

> Then will the difference
> Vanish as the God of Love transfigures the everlasting
> Dead that they may shine with lively light in the flowing
> Time of forgiveness of all winters, when the Vixen
> Dances with her cubs and the Spider's care is great
> And order has burnt up chaos and the world is calm.

Frances Bellerby was the only daughter of an exceptionally close-knit family, her clergyman father was 'an ardent and "Socialist" Anglo-Catholic, with a mission to the poor',[8] and so her life from the start was set in a pattern of sacred relationships. This applied especially to her brother and mother (to a degree, she was later alienated from her father for a period, when his relationship with her mother failed); it also applied to her feelings for nature and the animal creation. We may speculate how the original intensity was racked up further by her later experience. As an athletic young woman Frances Bellerby suffered a terrible accident that eventually rendered her disabled. In later life she was a victim of breast cancer. She lived with bouts of almost unbearable pain; and in these circumstances she wrote her poems and stories. From the stories in particular, we can see the relationship between physical and mental and emotional anguish and vision – a kind of heightened seeing that was, as it were, switched on and off by her suffering. The opening words of her story 'Soft and Fair' provide an idea of what she experienced: 'Time is, perhaps, little more than a flimsy curtain, which under the least pressure of intensity gives way.'[9] Her story 'The Little Lamps' gives what is surely the most autobiographical expression of her vision. It concerns 'witnessing of a private and unique manifestation of the exquisite life beneath the surface of life', which the narrator, quoting Tchehov, relates to the death of a child, in which 'there was felt the presence of a mystery that promised a life peaceful, beautiful, eternal'. In the same story, the narrator says, 'There is pain of which one can make a fierce friend, and there is pain which is the destroying enemy.'[10] In her agony, Bellerby saw her 'body as a millstone round the neck of my spirit'.[11] 'I died then,' she said after an operation in 1951. Afterwards she thought of herself as a Lazarus. Being trapped in a disabled body, with the memory of her vital athleticism, profoundly affected her experience of existence in 'the valley of the shadow', where, in the words of her poem 'The Valley', she was able 'to see beyond sight'. It also enabled the spiritual intensity with which she identified with the lives and deaths of non-human fellow creatures. There is, as it were, a rhythm of seeing in her poetry, in which light and darkness form a living pulse, related to the intensity and diminution of pain, as day and night and weathers change in her landscapes.

Her sense of past and present, time and eternity, her idea of perfection, and the relation between these and her imagery of light and shadow and darkness are connected directly to her sacred relationships. 'Brother and Sister' shows how naturally at times she crossed the threshold between life and death:

> Would you say that field is the one?
> Look, my dear, there's the great
> pink chestnut, and the straight path
> from iron gate to iron gate –
> the old sort, that you wind yourself through.
> Yes, that field is the one.

> Then the tree's shadow must still make a tent.
> What are we so troubled about, the two of us?
> There's shelter, freedom, and the whole of time
> whilst that slow sun follows its long course,
> and in and out of the shadow-tent play,
> those deathless children, to our hearts' content.

It is difficult to say exactly what the feeling is in this poem – if there is anything exact about feeling that springs from a person's whole life. Frances Bellerby's poems often have a plangency that combines, as in this case, with a sense of triumph. The 'field' of this poem, like the door in 'The First-Known', is a threshold that the living and the dead cross. The setting is 'the valley of the shadow', which is here 'the shadow-tent' in which brother and sister play. The sister (we may assume the speaker is the poet) speaks to her brother as she did when he was alive. More than this, he is alive for her, and together they are 'those deathless children'.

In the words of her long poem 'The Heron', Bellerby's subject is that perfect moment when 'lower-case time's/Done, and capital Time that cannot be wasted,/Nor killed even humanely, becomes visible, tangible,/Closer than lover'. Grief is the disguise of 'the principle of Love'. This poem about a dead heron rises to an eloquent affirmation of non-human creatures' 'share of the riches of the God/Of Love':

> Who himself offers no protection,
> Guides to no sanctuary, but anneals tenderness
> To a passion, making each individual life a supreme
> Unique dedication, and each individual death
> A tragedy to purge with pity and terror the innocent
> Children of men with their bloodstained hands.

'The Heron' and the other poems I have quoted display the intensity that I heard in Frances Bellerby's poetry when Alan Clodd sent me a copy of *The First-Known and Other Poems*. It is quite possible that without his gift of the book, in our culture of factions of mainstream and experimental poetry, I might have never encountered her poetry. It is the uniqueness of the voice that one hears – a distinctive, plangent lyricism, but with a power that does not make it absurd when she quotes the Old Testament or, as in 'The Heron', invokes the 'pity and terror' of the Greek Tragedians.

Notes

[1] Charles Causley, 'Introduction', in Frances Bellerby, *Selected Poems*, Enitharmon Press, 1970, p. ii.
[2] All quotations from Bellerby's poetry in this essay from Frances Bellerby, *The First-Known and Other Poems*, Enitharmon Press, 1975.
[3] Frances Bellerby, *Hath the Rain a Father?*, Peter Davies, 1946, p. 25.
[4] Robert Gittings, 'Biographical Introduction', in *Selected Poems by Frances Bellerby*, ed. Anne Stevenson, Enitharmon Press, 1986. Subsequent quotations from Gittings are from this biographical essay.
[5] Quoted in Robert Gittings, 'Biographical Introduction', in Frances Bellerby, *Selected Poems*, Enitharmon Press, 1986, p. 13.
[6] Quoted in Charles Causley, 'Introduction', in Frances Bellerby, *Selected Poems*, Enitharmon Press, 1970, p. iv.
[7] Butts, *Hath the Rain a Father?*, p. 99.
[8] Gittings, 'Biographical Introduction', p. 9.
[9] Frances Bellerby, *Selected Stories*, ed. Jeremy Hooker, Enitharmon Press, 1986, p. 51.
[10] Ibid., pp. 110–11.
[11] Gittings, 'Biographical Introduction', p. 19.

Three 'Powys Poems' with a Commentary on Each

I first heard the name Powys when I was a student and my tutor, the poet F. T. Prince, leant me a copy of Llewelyn Powys's *Advice to a Young Poet*. It wasn't until some years later, however, that I came to know about the Powys brothers and to read and write about their books. From youth, I had been absorbed in the work of Thomas Hardy, which in some respects reflected the lives of my forebears, and which presented a physical world in the south of England which I knew and loved. But Hardy wrote of historical change, and he himself had become a historical figure. My initial interest in Powys writings was, therefore, in how they imagined Wessex in a period closer to my own time.

    I confess that at first I felt, rather superstitiously, a kind of 'fate' in my discovery of the Powyses, though its causes were rational enough. I met my first wife, Sue, in the tiny Dorset village of Plush, which was only a short walk from Mappowder, a village rich in Powys associations, of which I was then totally ignorant. Gerard Casey, who would later become a close friend, lived in Mappowder with his wife, the poet Mary Casey. Or rather the Caseys lived in the village during returns from farming in Kenya, in a cottage next to Mary's mother, Lucy, the youngest and then one of the few surviving members of the Powys family. It was through Lucy and Mary, but above all through Gerard, that I came to know about the Powys brothers. In some ways, the Powyses – the family as a whole, but especially John Cowper, Theodore, and Llewelyn – are figures of myth, and I felt that I had been drawn within their mythic orbit. The reasons for my fascination could be explained, nevertheless, through friendship, and love of Dorset, and – more complexly – a need to know Wessex as a place of imaginative possibility in the modern

Three 'Powys Poems'

world. At the same time, as I came to understand them as a critical reader, they spoke to me as a poet. I wrote two poems early on in my relationship with the Powys brothers and their writings, and one much later; all are as much autobiographical as they are addressed to the particular subject.

Song of the Ashes

For John Cowper Powys

His ashes sang on Chesil Bank,
'Old Cheat-the-worms you chose to go
In fire's sensation, body's final fling,

Not in green villages put cold to bed
With ploughmen in their huts of sward,
Not anchored by a stone.

Where all is strange the senses
Twisting whimper like a clueless hound
And terror whips its own heels raw:

You found a way in what you were.
You have amazed the hump-back bass
By striking, silver-black, at ambush

In the surf, and played the angler
With his trace of wire. The weaver's spine
Inflicts no pain, for your intelligence

Became the poison and the wound;
Nor can you suffer more the ocean's histories,
Returning sated like a shag to roost,

White Nose and Portland,
Chesil's tide-plucked bow of stones,
Are but one shell whose echo cannot sound

Down shelf on shelf the deep-sea crypt,
Adrift on mountain chains, mid-ocean rifts,
An image of the land they mock,

Where all lives tend back where they came –
What is so strange as to be born?
Fear fear and in the fire be fire.'

So sang calm ashes on the sea,
Dissolving on a tide which they made visible.

This (minus one revision) was the earliest of my three 'Powys poems'. I can't be certain when I wrote it, but it was sometime between 1970 and its appearance in my first independent publication, *The Elements*, a pamphlet in the Triskel Poets series, published in 1972. Owing to its somewhat rhetorical style, I have never republished it till now. Its importance for me, however, is twofold.

First, it was the occasion of the start of a friendship from which, over the following years, I gained immeasurably. I took some copies of the newly published pamphlet to the John Cowper Powys Centenary Conference at Cambridge in 1972 and proudly/shyly gave away several to people that I met there for the first time. One of these was Gerard Casey. I shall never forget how, on the second morning of the conference, as Gerard walked slowly and gravely beside me he stopped and said, in his deep, deliberate voice, 'Jeremy, I was moved by "Song of the Ashes". *I* scattered the ashes on Chesil Beach.' Of course I hadn't known. I wouldn't have given him a copy of the pamphlet if I had.

As I reread the poem now, I realize how important the discovery of John Cowper Powys was for me. At that time it meant, above all, a partial liberation from fearful self-consciousness, and a confidence in my own elementalism. *Autobiography* was the key book. In recounting his own phobias and manias J.C.P. made it possible – as Wilson Knight once remarked – for young readers to realize that they're not as peculiar as they think they are. So it was for me. The book pointed me towards the possibility of self-acceptance, and a use of the intelligence to combat anxiety and depression. Strangeness is the human condition; it shouldn't be policed by obsession with a dogmatic idea of 'maturity'. J.C.P.'s 'message' was his example, his way of being: 'Fear fear and in the fire be fire.'

Easter at White Nose

i.m. Llewelyn Powys

Over downland, where the field
Of wheat in an arc
Drops into space,
We find the clean-cut lettered stone:
THE LIVING THE LIVING HE SHALL PRAISE THEE

The chalk is a globe bitten
Through its axis, the white line
Of retreating cliffs
Jagged with marks of teeth.
Far up in the salt wind,

Hearing the sea crumple
Mouthing its stones, I could lie
Here like ash if death only
Meant contemplation
Under the gently reddening

Sunlight and salt.
Old atheist, the new corn
Has forced a green way
Through flints to the edge
Of your stone. Like St Francis

You have stretched naked
On the naked ground, thankful
At Easter for the unholy
Resurrections, and sure
There was no other.

> These flints teach the same
> Dogma and the brute wheat
> Supports you with its fine green
> Shoots; perhaps it is only
> A wish almost as old to sense
> That I speak to a mind
> In the smooth domed hill.

I read Llewelyn Powys before I read either of his brothers. In the late summer and early autumn of 1969 I was staying with my first wife, Sue, at Child Okeford, in a cottage we rented from Andrew Wordsworth and his wife. Andrew had known Llewelyn and had several of his books. I had read some Llewelyn before, but now became passionately interested in the man and his work. For me, it was a time of recovering physical and mental health. Climbing Hambledon Hill at all hours and reading Llewelyn Powys made the recovery possible In his letters and essays – to my mind, always the best of Llewelyn – and through contact with the Dorset earth, I found a kind of 'grounding' which placed me back in my body and in contact with the world.

The occasion of the poem was perhaps two years later, at Easter. I shall never forget the day when, beginning to climb White Nose, Sue and I walked into a wind off the sea and over the grass which was the very essence of health, bringing a quickening of all the senses. That wind was the spirit of life.

And this is what I identified with Llewelyn, so that, coming to his stone, and thinking of his dogmatic atheism, I was intensely aware of living in the face of death and the question his belief posed. I felt with him too a certain intimacy, as the end of the poem indicates. His importance to me and to Sue may be gauged from the fact that when our son was born, in July 1972, we named him Joseph Llewelyn.

That summer, after Joe was born, I wrote most of the poems published in *Soliloquies of a Chalk Giant* (1974). Here, in creating a 'voice' for the Cerne Abbas Giant, I felt that I moved some way towards finding my own. At the time, focused on the work itself, I wasn't aware of how much I owed to John Cowper and Llewelyn Powys. But clearly I owed a great deal to them. Their contact with the earth of the South Country was crucial, as was their celebratory enlargement of being. Through them I was able unconsciously to assume the land and its history as my heritage, and to find an imaginative grounding beyond the ironic mode that dominated post-war English poetry. And nothing could be more quickening, and more deepening, than the conversations over nearly thirty years with Gerard Casey, whose loving knowledge of the Powyses never lost a certain healthy sceptical distance. In thus retaining his independence, Gerard also helped me to value mine.

St Peter and St Paul, Mappowder

With thoughts of T. F. Powys

1

Muck on country lanes,
good dirt,
and fields of Blackmoor Vale
and distant Bulbarrow.

A place where a man
might hide himself from the world.

This, however, was a man
on no map known to us
though he chose to live here,
close to the churchyard wall
communing with the dead.

His tomb is a stone book,
the last enigmatic page
given over to the grass.

2

Obliteration
was his word for death,
a final consignment
of all he was to silence,
a gift to God's Acre.

There is, perhaps, a mystery of the self
that reaches beyond the self,
a silence that deepens
beyond the word.

3

I have sat where he sat
in a pew of the empty church
listening, wondering
about this man.

I have followed his steps
on the Dorset lane,
smelling the good smell
of sun-warmed dirt,
watching skylark and pewit
over fields towards Bulbarrow,
entranced by tiny things,
grass seed and celandine,
ditches humming with summer.

I have read his words
and thought at times
I glimpsed a mind I might know.

But each time he escaped
as perhaps he too, listening
for the dead beyond the wall,

escaped from himself, reaching
into depths he could not fathom.

Theodore Powys was the last of the brothers whose work I came to know. The style of his novels and stories calls upon traditional sources as diverse as John Bunyan and Jane Austen, yet bears his unique signature. His delightful humour is integral to his unsettling vision, with features that are at once Nietzschean and profoundly theological. Who was he? What did he really believe? These questions arise with T. F. Powys perhaps more than with any other writer. With Mr Weston and other characters, he makes fun, not of God, but of all our *ideas* of God. Yet he has too, more intensely than his brothers, that Powysean religious sense, which Mary Casey called 'the feeling of wonder and awe in the presence of life and of the unknown powers behind life'.[1] Once, when I was visiting Gerard, he took me into Mappowder Church and left me to sit in the pew at the back, where he had told me Theodore had sat, in solitude. I cannot say I communed with his spirit. What I felt was more like a sense of the very limits of language, in which Theodore may have found God, or nothing. It is his religious scepticism that I treasure most, the voice of *Soliloquies of a Hermit* that says, 'I am without a belief; – a belief is too easy a road to God.'[2] I think of him as one who reached 'into depths he could not fathom'. My poem about Theodore belongs to a sequence called 'God's Houses', published in *Scattered Light* in 2015. T. F. and John Cowper Powys have both strengthened in me a scepticism of scepticism, which may also be equated with Keats's negative capability. I too was brought up in the religion that fostered their imaginations and gave me an abiding sense of 'the unknown powers behind life'.

Notes

[1] Mary Casey, *A Net in Water: A Selection from the Journals of Mary Casey*, ed. Judith M. Lang and Louise de Bruin, Powys Press, 1994, p. 148.

[2] Theodore Francis Powys, *Soliloquies of a Hermit*, Andrew Melrose, 1918, p. 1.

Notes on 'Poetic Vision'

> How white the gulls
> in grey weather
>   Soon April
>   the little
> yellows[1]

I would suggest that this short poem by Lorine Niedecker is more resonant for our times than Wordsworth's 'host of golden daffodils', since the latter has long been a poetic commonplace and may therefore be a substitute for seeing anew. Niedecker's poem makes us see for ourselves; it activates the mind. White gulls, grey weather, *yellows*: here is a revelation of colour. Is 'yellows' a verb or a noun, or both? Does it refer to little April flowers, or to a process, 'the little/yellows'? To both, surely. We see little yellow flowers, *and* yellow rising, growing, becoming present, against white and grey. Here are nature as product and nature as process: plant and force. And nature is present in *little*, in things that are small, common, easily overlooked. This twentieth-century instance of Blake's world in a grain of sand is not a descriptive poem, but a poem that makes us see.

Mary Casey's 'After Reading Basho' is another short poem, richer in traditional poetic means than Niedecker's:

> a long gray evening
> falling rain and grieving
> at nightfall the dearest star
> a most frail shining[2]

Responding to the seventeenth-century Japanese haiku poet, whose work has a revelatory quality allied to Zen Buddhism, Mary Casey produces an instant of intuition. The poem has a sonorous Tennysonian quality, with long vowel sounds reinforcing the melancholy of 'gray evening', 'falling rain', 'grieving', 'nightfall', 'most frail'. Alliteration connects 'frail' to 'falling' and 'nightfall'. The diction is emotive (for example, 'the dearest'). The poem expresses an emotional state but is also visionary, pointing beyond the melancholy. As often in visionary poetry, it uses imagery of light: 'star/a most frail shining'.

Both short poems draw on techniques of Imagism, the early twentieth-century movement that marked a decisive break with Victorian descriptive and didactic poetry and emphasized the need for verbal precision, economy, concreteness, 'hard light, clear edges' (Ezra Pound). Imagist techniques contained potential for expressing a sense of mystery – in the Zen element, for example, the instant of revelation or intuition, and in the art of intimation or suggestion. Richard Aldington described 'the sense of mystery' as 'the experience of certain places and times when one's whole nature seems to be in touch with a presence, a genius loci, a potency'.[3]

From this we may infer that the Imagist *presents* images, and the *presentation* evokes a sense of *presence*. In this way the element of mystery enters into modern poetry. It isn't vastly different from Wordsworth's 'spots of time' and one can trace connections between Romantic and modern poetry. One also has to recognize differences arising from the decay of orthodox religious belief and the use of different poetic techniques.

The following short poem is by John Riley:

at the boundary of mind's reach
at the edge of heart's sensing
violence of colour
and the wind rising[4]

This was perhaps the last poem written by John Riley, who was killed in 1978. He was a poet at the cutting edge of English modernism. Influenced by Americans such as Charles Olson and Robert Creeley and Russian writers and thinkers such as Osip Mandelstam, Riley had been received into the Russian Orthodox Church. In his visionary poetry the ultra-traditional and the ultra-modern combine. Vision occurs 'at the boundary of mind's reach/at the edge of heart's sensing'. Thus, it is a human and a personal experience requiring mind and heart; but it intimates something that transcends them, something that *breaks in*. This is imaged in elemental terms: 'violence of colour', 'the wind rising'.

Riley in this poem is using his art to see, in a religious sense. He approaches as near as language can to a moment of transfiguration when words no longer serve.

I have written about poetry in more mundane terms in 'At the Edge', the afterword to *Their Silence a Language* (1993):

> The imagination is not only a mental faculty, but is rooted in the whole body with its connections to the world ... I think of poetry as an art of seeing, an art by which, in my blindness, I learn to see. As a poet I work at the edge of sight, which is the edge of meaning and of language. It is the edge between the little I know and what may be chaos or could be a greater order. Here I waste effort, stumbling in the dark; here, sometimes, I find an opening.[5]

I think there is an affinity between my sense of an 'opening', the idea of presence, and John Riley's sense of imminent transfiguration, since all indicate faith in a reality that exists beyond language, though we need language to point to it.

'Vision' is a word with several meanings in the dictionary:

an appearance of a prophetic or mystical character

seeing ... something not actually present to the eye

seeing with the bodily eye[6]

The word comprehends revelation, and dream or trance, as well as 'exercise of the ordinary faculty of sight'. Poetry comprehends the whole range of meanings, at times uniting them and at other times concentrating on one.

Seventeenth-century Metaphysical poetry, especially the poetry of Henry Vaughan and Thomas Traherne, unites bodily and mystical vision. A passage from Traherne's *Centuries* provides a well-known instance:

> The corn was orient and immortal wheat, which never should be reaped, nor was ever sown. I thought it had stood from everlasting to everlasting. The dust and stones of the street were as precious as gold: the gates were at first the end of the world. The green trees when I saw them first through one of the gates transported and ravished me, their sweetness and unusual beauty made my heart to leap, and almost mad with ecstasy, they were such strange and wonderful things. The men! O what venerable and reverent creatures did the aged seem! Immortal Cherubims! And young men glittering and sparkling Angels, and maids strange seraphic pieces of life and beauty! Boys and girls tumbling in the street, and playing, were moving jewels. I knew not that they were born or should die; But all things abided eternally as they were in their proper places.

Traherne's recollection of his vision of the world as a child has a religious optimism and is expressed with an ecstasy that one would be surprised to find in modern visionary poetry. There are, however, modern poems resembling his sense of 'all things' abiding eternally 'in their proper places'. Frances Bellerby's 'In Place' is a notable instance:

> In clear gilt sunlight
> At one-seventeen p.m.
> On this twenty-fifth day of April
> Rests this lizard
>
> On this primrose leaf.
> Elect for the poised and almost weightless weight
> This particular lolled tongue of a leaf in the hedge
>
> Enables perfection.[7]

Bellerby emphasizes the concrete and particular. This is what 'enables perfection'. The difference from Traherne inheres mainly in two things: Bellerby's self-conscious insistence on her theme, and her perception of the design as natural:

> Here, then, is executed the perfection of a design
> Brought from and through all Time
> Into this moment – into this timed moment
> Out of all Time past and all to come –
> Into this accurate timed moment which being perfect
> Could not be out of place
> In Eternity.

Eternity, the poem says, depends upon a perfect timed moment, not Time upon Eternity.

Frances Bellerby's vision in 'In Place' is, perhaps, more at home with our contemporary ecological awareness than with Traherne's divine vision. This is also sometimes true of overtly religious poetry, as in R. S. Thomas's 'The Bright Field', in which, in spite of the biblical images, one is more aware of the 'small field', which 'the sun break[s] through/to illuminate', than of the light of eternity outside nature. Nature rather than the supernatural is, usually, the locus of our new religious poetry, which resacralizes the natural world that nineteenth-century materialism divested of religious mystery and significance. We are living in a poetic revolution as we learn to apprehend the human place in nature anew.

Prophecy as a form of poetic vision occurs in the Hebrew prophets. Later, it occurs in Walt Whitman's celebrating the making of American democracy, and in W. B. Yeats's 'The Second Coming' and other poems imaging the fate of Western civilization. William Blake is a great visionary poet in his political and social prophecies and his affirmation of the power of the imagination. He teaches the importance of seeing not merely with but through the eye: in the words of *The Marriage of Heaven and Hell*, 'If the doors of perception were cleansed everything would appear to man as it is, infinite.' In this form, religious vision is revelatory: a perception of the eternal in the temporal.

In contrast to great positive visionaries of past times, sceptical vision is a mode understandably common in the modern world. Geoffrey Hill is a classic example of a religious poet with a sceptical intelligence. 'Of Commerce and Society, IV' provides an early example: 'Statesmen have known visions.'[8] In the context of modern history, these words remind us how dangerous visions can be, and how jaded the word 'vision' has become. By the visions of a Stalin or a Hitler the people perish; at any level self-proclaimed visionaries are best avoided, and uncritical use of traditional visionary language results in vacuous verse. Hill is aware, as Yeats discovered, that the poet has dangerous responsibilities. W. H. Auden famously wrote that poetry makes nothing happen. Poets such as Yeats and Hill, however, know that poems can inspire people to go out and kill or be killed. In consequence some of the most challenging modern poetry is profoundly sceptical of the truth claims of vision and aware of the power of language to deceive.

Seeing, in a humbler sense than the word 'vision' implies, is an art of great value. It may be characterized by Roy Fisher's words about Birmingham (which he does not name) in 'City': 'Most of it has never been seen.'[9] In his poetry Fisher shows us what has gone unnoticed in the urban world, not appearances alone, but deep social structures, historical processes, and things in people's minds, imagined things. His challenge is to remind us that we need constantly to see things anew.

John Ruskin provided the classic statement of this need when he wrote in *Modern Painters*, 'the greatest thing a human soul ever does in this world is to *see* something, and tell what it *saw* in a plain way. Hundreds of people can talk for one who can think, but thousands can think for one who can see. To see clearly is poetry, prophecy, and religion, – all in one.'

Ruskin is heir to the Romantics in his emphasis upon seeing 'something', as distinct from the sublime or conventionally valuable object or scene, and on telling what is seen 'in a plain way'. Coleridge's great statement in *Biographia Literaria* (1817) of Wordsworth's object in his poems in *Lyrical Ballads* stands behind Ruskin:

> To give the charm of novelty to things of every day, and to excite a feeling analogous to the supernatural, by awakening

the mind's attention to the lethargy of custom, and directing it to the loveliness and the wonders of the world before us; an inexhaustible treasure, but for which, in consequence of the film of familiarity and selfish solicitude, we have eyes yet see not, ears that hear not, and hearts that neither feel nor understand.

Following Ruskin and his Romantic predecessors, Edward Thomas and Ivor Gurney carry this way of seeing into twentieth-century English poetry. The influence of Richard Jefferies upon Edward Thomas is evident in Thomas's description of Jefferies' imagination:

> The clearness of the physical is allied to the penetration of the spiritual vision. For both are nourished to their perfect flowering by the habit of concentration. To see a thing as clearly as he saw the sun-painted yellowhammer … is part of the office of imagination.[10]

To make images, Thomas says in *Richard Jefferies*, 'clear concentrated sight and patient mind are the most necessary things after love, and these two are the children of love'.

'But These Things Also' is a fine example of Thomas's loving observation of the humble object:

> The shell of a little snail bleached
> In the grass; chip of flint, and mite
> Of chalk; and the small bird's dung
> In splashes of purest white.

As he uses his eyes to see and value common things anew, so Thomas also transcends the limits of his physical vision:

> Over the land freckled with snow half-thawed
> The speculating rooks at their nests cawed
> And saw from elm-tops, delicate as flower of grass,
> What we below could not see. Winter pass.

His seeing and hearing produce details of remarkable accuracy: 'land freckled with snow', 'elm-tops, delicate as flower of grass', 'speculating rooks'. But he goes further, using his senses to intimate the limits of human vision and reveal what lies beyond it, in the rooks' perspective, with their senses attuned more sensitively than ours to the passing of winter.

In 'The Escape' Ivor Gurney provides a complete restatement of the Romantic doctrine of poetic vision:

> I believe in the increasing of life: whatever
> Leads to the seeing of small trifles ...
> Real, beautiful, is good; and an act never
> Is worthier than in freeing spirit that stifles
> Under ingratitude's weight: nor is anything done
> Wiselier than the moving or breaking to sight
> Of a thing hidden under by custom; revealed,
> Fulfilled, used (sound-fashioned) any way out to delight:
>
> Trefoil ... hedge-sparrow ... the stars on the edge at night.[11]

'Doctrine' is not a word one would usually apply to a lyric poem or to any but didactic verse. Here, though, it seems appropriate to me; for Gurney is showing the truth of the principal tenet of *Lyrical Ballads*: that 'the seeing of small trifles' increases life and frees spirit. It is an act, a process: 'the moving or breaking to sight/Of a thing hidden under by custom'. We may wonder whether Gurney was remembering Coleridge's words about Wordsworth 'awakening the mind's attention to the lethargy of custom'. But it is not a possible recollection of another poet's words that matters here, but a common vision. And what Gurney sees are things he loves, which represent his world: 'Trefoil ... hedge-sparrow ... the stars on the edge at night'. He is thinking in triads: the poet reveals a thing, fulfils it, and uses it. The use is 'sound-fashioned': well made, and made from words. Gurney connects trefoil, the small plant, with hedge-sparrow, and stars. 'The edge' is Cotswold Edge, Gurney's beloved locality perceived as edge of the cosmos. Thus, in this remarkably compact and dynamic poem, the movement connects the 'small trifle' (trefoil) with the universe and concentrates the vision in one place, Ivor Gurney's Gloucestershire.

'Most of it has never been seen', though written about a city, might also be applied to Gurney's 'The Escape', a poem that crystallizes a whole tradition of poetic seeing. Rather than being exclusively pictorial, let alone merely descriptive, this is an art that combines observation of object or thing with awareness of process, and relates the particular to the universal. It places the seeing mind in the world, and the world in the mind, but without reducing the world to the dimensions of the poet's ego. As in Gurney's poem, it enables an escape from sensory and emotional 'custom'. True poetic vision increases life and makes for spiritual freedom.

Notes

[1] Lorine Niedecker, *Collected Works*, ed. Jenny Penberthy, University of California Press, 2002, p. 184.
[2] Mary Casey, *The Clear Shadow*, Rigby & Lewis, 1992, p. 35.
[3] Richard Aldington, *The Complete Poems*, Allan Wingate, 1943, p. 16.
[4] John Riley, *The Collected Works*, ed. Tim Longville, Grosseteste Press, 1980, p, 266.
[5] Jeremy Hooker and Lee Grandjean, *Their Silence a Language*, Enitharmon Press, 1993, p. 75.
[6] *The Oxford English Dictionary*.
[7] Bellerby, *The First-Known and Other Poems*, p. 16.
[8] Geoffrey Hill, *For the Unfallen*, Andre Deutsch, 1959, p. 51.
[9] Roy Fisher, *The Long and the Short of It*, Bloodaxe, 2005, p. 37.
[10] Thomas, *Richard Jefferies*, p. 49 .
[11] Ivor Gurney, *Collected Poems*, ed. P. J. Kavanagh, Carcanet, 2004, p. 170.

Water over Stone:
REFLECTIONS ON POETRY AND SPIRIT

The relationship between poetry and spirit raises many questions, not least the question of whether a 'spiritual' poetry is possible in a secularized, materialistic culture. In this essay I do not presume to offer answers to the questions; my concern is rather with the questions themselves as they are raised by particular poems. It is thus above all an exploration based upon readings, with a view to seeing what different poems reveal of the relationship between poetry and spirit in the modern world.

In his 1802 preface to *Lyrical Ballads* Wordsworth describes 'the Poet' as 'the rock of defence of human nature', thus boldly affirming a relationship between poetry and spirituality by assimilating the poet's role to that of priest – an allusion to 'the rock' of St Peter is, surely, intended. To a sceptical reader who, like Keats, exists in doubts and uncertainties, Wordsworth's certitude here is questionable. From a sceptical viewpoint, the assurance with which Wordsworth assumes the constancy of human nature is astonishing. Another problem with the formulation that has become especially troubling since Wordsworth's time is that his identification of 'the Poet' is exclusively male. The poet, 'a man speaking to men', is rock, a hard, unyielding substance, seemingly permanent. Wordsworth uses other images and ideas that qualify this: 'Poetry is the breath and finer spirit of all knowledge'; the poet carries everywhere 'relationship and love'. Wordsworth's idea of 'the Poet', however, effectively excludes the female – both the woman poet and that in the nature of a male poet which might be regarded as female.

This emphasis upon the exclusively male would recur among modernists, such as Ezra Pound and Wyndham Lewis, with their belief in the power of the 'logos spermatikos', or seminal thought: the 'male' creative principle; the will imposing form on the chaos of the material world.[1] It is a limited, even dangerous, idea; which isn't to say that artists espousing it haven't produced great work – they have, but whether the *idea* is responsible for the work is another question. The concept of the rock of human nature risks petrifying life itself, and denying what is creative because changing, unstable, quick.

The problem with rock as a symbol for poetry is that it is insufficiently vital. When in April 1862 Emily Dickinson first wrote to Thomas Wentworth Higginson, her opening words were, 'Mr Higginson, Are you too deeply occupied to say if my Verse is alive?'[2] Confirmation that their poetry is alive is what poets desire above all.

In what sense, though, can a poem be said to be alive? To answer the question we have to consider the relation between life, breath, and spirit. According to Walter J. Ong, SJ:

> All verbalization, including all literature, is radically a cry, a sound emitted from the interior of a person, a modification of one's exhalation of breath which retains the intimate connection with life which we find in breath itself, and which registers in the etymology of the word 'spirit', that is, breath.[3]

Words are sounds emitted from within a person, a modification of breath, which means spirit. Here is one line of thought – an idea of spirit and life, which poetry renders through a variety of metaphors.

Dickinson to Higginson, again: 'Nature is a Haunted House – but Art – A House that tries to be haunted.'[4] What haunts a house if not a spirit of some kind? Emily Dickinson, we say, is a haunting poet. Her poems are haunted houses. This one, for example:

> I felt a Funeral, in my Brain,
> And Mourners to and fro
> Kept treading – treading – till it seemed
> That Sense was breaking through –
>
> And when they all were seated,
> A service, like a Drum –
> Kept beating – beating – till I thought
> My Mind was going numb –

And then I heard them lift a Box
And creak across my Soul
With those same Boots of Lead, again,
The Space – began to toll,

As if the Heavens were a Bell,
And Being, but an Ear,
And I, and Silence, some strange Race
Wrecked, solitary, here –

And then a Plank in Reason, broke,
And I dropped down, and down –
And hit a World, at every plunge,
And finished Knowing – then –

As we see here, Dickinson could be what Lionel Trilling called Robert Frost, 'a terrifying poet'.[5] Excitement, awe, and horror are compounded in her verse. She writes so concretely about dying, for example. But is this poem therefore a morbid one? Or is she using dying as a metaphor, the physical to intimate the metaphysical? Brain and Soul are described as parts of a house, floorboards creaking as mourners carry out the coffin. But the poem is really about the confines of our human 'walls', about the limits of Reason, about where Knowing ends. It haunts because it takes us to that limit, conducts us to the verge of mystery.

In another poem Emily Dickinson writes, 'One need not be a Chamber – to be Haunted –/One need not be a House –/The Brain has Corridors – surpassing/Material Place.' Her subject is strangeness: the self as a stranger to the self; nature as a haunted house; our lives situated between knowing and unknowing. This could be described philosophically as liminal ontology, 'metaphysics of the threshold'. In the words of Philip Wheelwright: 'To be conscious is not just to be; it is to mean, to intend, to point beyond oneself ... The existential structure of human life is radically, irreducibly *liminal*.'[6] To David Jones, 'man is a "borderer", he is the sole inhabitant of a tract of country where matter marches with spirit'.[7] David Jones's (and Wordsworth's) 'man' would probably have amused

Emily Dickinson. She wrote as she experienced life, on the threshold. According to the feminist theologian Sallie McFague,

> Theological constructions are 'houses' to live in for a while, with windows partly open and doors ajar; they become prisons when they no longer allow us to come and go, to add a room or take one away – or if necessary, to move out and build a new house.[8]

The metaphor is good for poems too. We can take it further. Poets make houses and move house – they can't settle in any one permanently; their insecurity, in this sense, is desirable: moving house is a constant trying out of more or less unsatisfactory arrangements – a pursuit of – what? In their poems poets pursue life that is always escaping. Emily Dickinson didn't move house in the sense of changing poetic form; her life, in fact, involved very little outer movement. We see why in this poem:

> I dwell in Possibility –
> A fairer House than Prose –
> More numerous of Windows –
> Superior – for Doors –
>
> Of Chambers as the Cedars –
> Impregnable of Eye –
> And for an Everlasting Roof
> The Gambrels of the sky –
>
> Of Visitors – the fairest –
> For Occupation – This –
> The spreading wide my narrow Hands
> To gather Paradise –

Poetry – the metaphor again is a house – is Possibility. A house with its walls and domestic interior could be such a confining metaphor. Not for Dickinson, however. For her, the house is haunted. Dwelling in the house of the poem means living with Possibility, its ultimate purpose – as here – 'To gather Paradise'.

'A House that tries to be haunted' is one metaphor for the kind of life that poetry has. A life of its own; in Walter J. Ong's terms, a life made of breath that issues in words, a life of the spirit. Human breath issuing in words expresses the interior reality of a person. This essentially is a religious perspective, grounded upon belief in the existence and value of the person. But breath is also that which we share with all living things. What, then, if we were to take breath as spirit for that which connects us not only with one another but with all creatures, in effect, all life?

This, I think, is what the new nature poetry, the poetry of ecological consciousness, does. The 'new', though, often turns out to have its roots in the past. Thus Lynn White, Jr, concluded his argument that the origins of our ecological crisis lie in Judaeo-Christian anthropomorphism by proposing Francis of Assisi as 'a patron saint for ecologists'.[9]

Thomas Hardy is a writer with a Franciscan sensibility. R. S. Thomas saw Hardy as 'just an old-stager,//shuffling about a bogus heath/cobwebbed with his Victorian breath'.[10] In fact Hardy had an ecological sensibility at least as fine as Thomas's or that of any later poet; as we see in 'An August Midnight':

I

A shaded lamp and a waving blind,
And the beat of a clock from a distant floor:
On this scene enter – winged, horned, and spined –
A longlegs, a moth, and a Dumbledore;
While 'mid my page there idly stands
A sleepy fly, that rubs its hands ...

II

Thus meet we five, in this still place,
At this point of time, at this point in space.
– My guests besmear my new-penned line,
Or bang at the lamp and fall supine.
'God's humblest, they!' I muse, Yet why?
They know Earth-secrets that know not I.

Max Gate 1899

With the words 'we five' one of the most celebrated Englishmen of his time numbers himself, without irony, as a member of a group containing a fly, a daddy-long-legs, a moth, and a bumblebee. Or he might have been intending irony until he reflected that his 'guests' know 'Earth-secrets' he doesn't know. In fact, the irony in the poem is at the poet's expense: the idle, sleepy fly may be rubbing its hands as a satire on the poet's performance; the worth of his 'new-penned line' may be signalled by the creatures besmearing it.

For Hardy, the poem may be in part an expression of his Darwinian perspective; but it accords with his native spirit, which was Franciscan, like that of the tender-hearted boy, Jude, in *Jude the Obscure*, who allowed the rooks to eat the farmer's corn. It is in line too with 'the Poetry of Humble Life', which *Lyrical Ballads* renewed at the start of the nineteenth century.[11] Broadly speaking, this poetry, which reveals the spiritual power inherent in ordinary people and everyday objects, is a major current in British and American poetry in the nineteenth and twentieth centuries. It is, among other things, an art of seeing, an art in which the poet focuses upon particulars.

Whether directly or indirectly, Christian and neo-Christian poetry is often about making. This is a large subject, which includes the Creation, and life in created forms, and poetry as making, an art that to some degree participates in the divine. Rock with its obdurate givenness is consequently a less satisfactory metaphor for poet and poetry than some others, such as light, water, and fire. Geology, however, tends to attract modern poets, and the Catholic poet David Jones finds the divine creative principle in the material world. Jones's materia poetica is culture, history, myth, and familial things. Fundamental to these, though, is the Creation, which underlies all to which he owes his making as a human being.

The Anathemata depicts the land and life in the process of creation:

> From before all time
> > the New light beams for them
> and with eternal clarities
> > *infulsit* and athwart
> the fore-times:
> > era, period, epoch, hemera.

> Through all orogeny:
> > group, system, series, zone.
> Brighting at the five life-layers
> > species, species, genera, families, order.
> Piercing the eskered silt, discovering every stria, each score
> and macula, lighting all the fragile laminae of the shales.
> ...
> > As, down among the palaeo-zoe
> > > he brights his ichthyic sign
> > so brights he the middle zone
> > > where the uterine forms
> > are some beginnings of his creature.[12]

This passage beautifully evokes geological and evolutionary processes, deploying a technical vocabulary combined with exquisite images: 'the eskered silt', 'the fragile laminae of the shales'. This is not rock as permanent substance, but rock in the process of creation; the temporal illuminated by 'the New Light ... with eternal clarities'. It is in this belief in the divine Creation that David Jones accepts the material history that so daunted Victorians such as Thomas Hardy and John Ruskin. He more than accepts it; he delights in the materials and processes, marrying a touch of humour and a Franciscan tenderness to their evocation. This is praise poetry in the fundamental sense that the creature praises God through the Creation.

David Jones perceives his Christian vision in geological processes and evolutionary science. For a non-Christian poet, however, matter can be holy because it *is*. Thus Lorine Niedecker begins her poem 'Darwin': 'His holy/slowly/mulled over/matter'.[13] Niedecker called another poem 'My Life by Water'. This is a literal description, for she lived most of her life on Black Hawk Island, a peninsula of Lake Koshkonong outside Fort Atkinson in Wisconsin.

Niedecker's poems deploy Imagist and Objectivist techniques but have a character all their own. This is manifested in extraordinary concentration, in which a few words open on vast temporal and spatial vistas, as in this section from 'Traces of Living Things':

> We are what the seas
> have made us
>
> longingly immense
>
> the very veery
> on the fence[14]

Niedecker's special sense of humour – her light touch – appears here in wordplay: 'the very veery', the veery being a kind of American thrush.[15] The perspective she creates with these five lines is staggering, as a Zen saying can be; bemusing and illuminating.

Meanings may unfold gradually, seeming to conflict with one another, or hit us all in a rush. 'We are what the seas/have made us': we are evolutionary beings, our origins in the seas, which we still contain in our blood. The seas have made us 'longingly immense' – with a longing for immensity, perhaps, a longing instilled in us by our sea-birth. But 'longingly immense' refers equally to 'the very veery', this particular thrush. Do we perhaps hear in the bird's song longing for immensity – the thrush's longing, or ours, or both: a longing inherent in all living things for their boundless origins? The very veery is 'on the fence': on the threshold, on the man-made boundary, where the longing for immensity is experienced.

These my be some of the poem's meanings, which we experience with a leap – a leap from our fenced-in condition to an immensity both outside and inside ourselves – such a leap as we make when Emily Dickinson breaks a plank in Reason. At the same time we may remain bemused by 'longingly immense' with its grammatical peculiarity. Whether we feel we understand the poem or not, however, it activates our minds and, like Dickinson's poems, gives us a sense of the kind of beings we are, with a glimpse of the vistas that haunt us. It creates a deep image, which calls to mind Cézanne's 'the immensity, the torrent of the world in a little bit of matter'.[16]

Niedecker relishes Objectivist techniques. The Objectivist movement in American poetry originating in the late 1920s and early 1930s was marked by Jewish and Marxist influences. It had other philosophical underpinnings, too. Aspects of Jacques Maritain's thought affected George Oppen, as it had David Jones. Oppen used as epigraph to his book *The Materials* (1962) Maritain's 'We awake in the same moment to ourselves and to things'. In Oppen's 'Sara in Her Father's Arms', awakening is seen as the ground of relationship and love. The poem begins by describing a biological process: 'Cell by cell the baby made herself, the cells/Made cells. That is to say/The baby is made largely of milk.' Oppen then proceeds to unfold the baby's growth into a seeing and creative being:

> Lying in her father's arms,
> the little seed eyes
> Moving, trying to see, smiling for us
> To see, she will make a household
> To her need of these rooms – Sara, little seed,
> Little violent, diligent seed. Come let us look at the world
> Glittering: this seed will speak,
> Max, words! There will be no other words in the world
> But those our children speak. What will she make of a world
> Do you suppose, Max, of which she is made.[17]

This is at once a materialist poem and a profoundly spiritual one. The poem is about making, seeing, speaking. Made, the human baby sees, and relates to others: 'smiling for us/To see'. Her making involves creating a home in the world. Despite the subject, Oppen is never in danger of sentimentality. Sara, 'little seed', is 'violent, diligent' – violence and diligence are essential human characteristics, integral to human creativity. We may think of writing poetry, which requires diligence and violence: care, and also rejection as part of choice. Out of the processes of making comes speech – speech that contributes to the making of a world. And where, we may ask, does love come from? The answer is implicit in this poem of relationship and love, which values the personal, Sara and Max, and accepts continuity and death: 'There will be no other words in the world/But those our children speak.' 'The milk of human kindness' is an unspoken phrase that haunts the poem.

Language awakens; and with language we make our world. Language liberates, but can also imprison and conceal. Women poets in particular have in recent years made us aware of language's negative capacities. And in disclosing language's tyranny they have used language to cast its tyranny off. Wendy Mulford, for example, in 'The meaning of blue':

> There are other things out there beneath the whiteness
>   besides those
> the conscious mind allows –
> sometimes a dipper's beak slitting the gleaming mud or the
> imperturbable black tilt of a staithe or
>   dancing to fulltide pools the escaped red clouds that promise
>   fine morrow
>
> or the curve of a creek round its fellow
> or a break in the horizon
> leading the eye down
> to the sea's cradle
> or the fall & fetch of the wave cleaning crabshells at our feet
> the feathering touch of highwater nudging the estuary grass –
> taking my mind beyond image
> in to silence
>
> Through density dictator language must be
> indefinitely in absence we uncover the
> real meaning of blue[18]

This has features of a recognizable kind of lyrical poem: one that works through images – Hopkins-like inscapes – to convey a sense of the natural world. It renders a tidal shore vividly. But, far from being merely descriptive, it presents a liminal situation, alerting us to 'other things', things 'beneath the whiteness', which 'the conscious mind' does not allow. It is, then, a poem that cuts down beneath consciousness, as the dipper's beak slits the mud. It is structured so as to lead the mind down, as though by steps of images. And what it leads to is 'the sea's cradle' – a fundamental sense of female being, implicit in the poem's imagery, which in a poem about Julian of Norwich Mulford calls 'woman-depths'.[19] This is not a case of the female being identified *with* nature, which patriarchy exploits. This is a woman who in her being apprehends the quick of the natural world and is open to that which lies 'beyond image', in silence. The poem overcomes 'dictator language' and works to 'uncover the/real meaning of blue'. The very form makes us work with the poem in its act of uncovering – form is active in the process of disclosure. It incarnates spirit; spirit breathes in, animates, a poem that is implicitly religious, leaving us to reflect that blue is, among its other meanings, the colour associated with the Virgin Mary.

There is tension in Mulford's poem: tension between conscious mind and what lies beneath it, between 'dictator language' and 'real meaning'. It is ultimately a poem of release, but Christian poetry, and especially poetry in the Protestant tradition, generally tends to be a poetry of tension, involving spiritual struggle, spiritual warfare, and pilgrimage. In the words of Rowan Williams: 'Conversion and repentance ... involve going down into the chaotic waters of Christ's death, so that the Spirit can move us to make "new creation", being unmade to be remade.'[20] Highly articulate as theologian and poet, Rowan Williams is keenly aware of what words cannot say, and of their capacity to obscure or distort. Stephen Prickett, in *Words and The Word*, emphasizes the Judaeo-Christian 'language of disconfirmation and ambiguity': 'Elijah on Horeb, Moses and the Burning Bush, the Incarnation itself present events so baffling as to imply quite new ways of seeing the world.'[21] When God speaks, he doesn't say what the listener expects or wants to hear: He disconfirms human expectations. All words or images purporting to represent God are at best inadequate, so that Christian poets, exercising this knowledge, are iconoclasts as well as image makers. 'God himself', Rowan Williams says, 'is the great "negative theologian", who shatters all our images by addressing us in the cross of Jesus.'[22]

Other religious and philosophical traditions, such as Buddhism and Taoism, untie knots that Christianity holds fast. Chuang Tzu, for example, the ancient Chinese philosopher, celebrates spontaneity and freedom. In a version by the Christian monk Thomas Merton, Chuang Tzu speaks of a draftsman who

> Could draw more perfect circles freehand
> Than with a compass.

> His fingers brought forth
> Spontaneous forms from nowhere. His mind
> Was meanwhile free and without concern
> With what he was doing.

The draftsman keeps his mind 'perfectly simple'. Self-forgetfulness is the way:

> So, when the shoe fits
> The foot is forgotten[23]

In his introduction to *The Way of Chuang Tzu* Merton speaks of Master Chuang's preaching of '"cosmic" humility of the man who fully realizes his own nothingness and becomes totally forgetful of himself'. Not surprisingly, Merton connects Chuang's thought to his own Christian tradition, saying 'cosmic' humility 'manifests itself everywhere by a Franciscan simplicity and connaturality with all living creatures'. This may be so, but it is also what Thomas Hardy showed when entertaining his insect guests.

Merton observes that 'the true inheritors of the thought and spirit of Chuang Tzu are the Chinese Zen Buddhists of the T'ang period'.[24] The American poet Gary Snyder, closely associated with Jack Kerouac and Allen Ginsberg in the Beat movement of the 1950s, spent many years in Japan immersing himself in Zen Buddhism. Snyder is also a leading ecological thinker, identified with what he calls, in the title of one of his books, 'The Practice of the Wild'. The unity of his commitments can be seen, early on, in 'Piute Creek', which begins,

> One granite ridge
> A tree, would be enough
> Or even a rock, a small creek,
> A bark shred in a pool.
> Hill beyond hill, folded and twisted
> Tough trees crammed
> In thin stone fractures
> A huge moon on it all, is too much.

The mind wanders. A million
Summers, night air still and the rocks
Warm. Sky over endless mountains.
All the junk that goes with being human
Drops away, hard rock wavers[25]

Influences converge here. The name Piute Creek calls up the life-world of the Native Americans, which Snyder honours, and which in spirit he shares. His passion for the wilderness recalls Thoreau and Thoreau's sense of the real – rock, water, trees – and admiration for the Native American way of life. We may remember Thoreau on Mount Ktaadn:

> Talk of mysteries! Think of our life in nature, – daily to be shown matter, to come in contact with it, – rocks, trees, wind on our cheeks! The *solid* earth! The *actual* world! The *common sense*! Contact! Contact! *Who* are we? *where* are we?[26]

'Piute Creek' is thus a very American poem of the West Coast in its feeling for the primordial New World wilderness; as it is also in looking towards Asia and drawing upon Buddhist thought, rather than towards Europe and the Judaeo-Christian tradition. This poem, too, is about 'seeing'.

A clear attentive mind
Has no meaning but that
Which sees is truly seen.

The seeing it practises, however, differs significantly from that of English Romanticism with its emphasis upon the observing self. The reference here is to the concept of 'original true mind, seeing the universe freshly in eternity; yet any moment'.[27] The Buddhist idea has a direct bearing on the vexed notion of self-expression, which poets such as T. S. Eliot and David Jones condemn. In the same interview quoted above, Snyder says,

> a great poet does not express his or her self, he expresses *all*

of our selves. And to express *all* of ourselves you have to go beyond your own self. Like Dogen, the Zen master, said, 'we study the self to forget the self. And when you forget the self, you become *one* with all things'.²⁸

'And', Snyder adds, 'that's why poetry's not self-expression in those small self terms.'

Poetry that encounters sacred reality expresses a sense of awe. It is a different sense in Snyder's Buddhist poetry from that which we find in poetry in the Judaeo-Christian tradition. We may consider, for example, 'Tell Us', one of R. S. Thomas's later poems, in which he brings to theology modern science's perspective upon the universe:

> We have had names for you:
> The Thunderer, the Almighty
> Hunter, Lord of the snowflake
> and the sabre-toothed tiger.
> One name we have held back
> unable to reconcile it
> with the mosquito, the tidal-wave,
> the black hole into which
> time will fall.

The poem is about our names and images for God and their inadequacy. What is the name we have held back 'unable to reconcile it/with the mosquito, the tidal-wave,/the black hole into which/time will fall', as if these destructive phenomena exacerbate the age-old problem of theodicy? The answer is 'love': 'the image of yourself/on a hewn tree,/suffering injustice, pardoning it'. The poem concludes,

> Ah, love, with your arms out
> wide, tell us how much more
> they must still be stretched
> to embrace a universe drawing
> away from us at the speed of light.²⁹

One interesting thing about this poem is that it differs from biblical and metaphysical poetry in which God frequently does speak and what he says disconfirms human presuppositions and expectations. Here, though, it is as if human ideas, scientific theories, challenge God. The result is a powerful poem, though it may be questionable theology and lend some support to those who see Thomas as an atheist manqué.[30]

From our present point of view, however, it is the treatment of space in the poem that is most interesting. The Buddhist Snyder is at ease with the temporal and spatial vistas encountered in the wilderness; he even relishes them, feeling a thrill at 'the junk that goes with being human' dropping away. Thomas, on the other hand, belongs to the Protestant tradition exemplified by Pascal with his terror at the spaces between the stars and Kierkegaard with his vertiginous feeling of stepping out over 70,000 fathoms. Snyder, we feel, could share Niedecker's joke about the very veery on the fence. Not so Thomas – black hole and speed of light provoke horror not awe: horror at the possibility of the soul's – and the universe's – total abandonment by God.

How different from David Jones and from Gerard Manley Hopkins's 'The Blessed Virgin Compared to the Air We Breathe':

> Wild air, world-mothering air,
> Nestling me everywhere,
> That each eyelash or hair
> Girdles; goes home betwixt
> The fleeciest, frailest fixed
> Snowflake; that's fairly mixed
> With, riddles, and is rife
> In every last thing's life;
> This needful, never spent,
> And nursing element

For Hopkins, air, with its likeness to the Mother of God, is a maternal element, 'world-mothering'. Poets can have similar feelings about air and other elements without being Christians. Lorine Niedecker records how 'Early in life I looked back of our buildings to the lake and said: "I am what I am because of all this – I am what is around me – those woods have made me".' Commenting on this, Joseph M. Conte writes, 'This espousal brings to mind Pia in Dante's *Purgatorio*, who introduces herself by saying "Siena mi fe" [Siena made me], an acknowledgment of a bond to a place so strong and so intimate that it can only be considered maternal.'[31] Niedecker's own words, in 'Paean to Place', give poetic expression to the sense of belonging:

Fish
   fowl
      flood
Water lily mud
My life
in the leaves and on water[32]

Niedecker refers her sense of belonging to the experience of being *made*.

R. C. Zaehner, discussing Richard Jefferies' sense of a force pervading nature, likens the force to the Hindu '*prana* which means "breath"'. To the Hindus this is 'the spirit which animates the universe and which breathes in man'.[33] In the Upanishads Brahman, the 'ground' of the universe, appears simply as prana, 'breath'. Here, we may recall John Ruskin's *The Queen of the Air* (1869), in which he describes Athena as 'air as the spirit of life'; 'whenever you throw your window wide open in the morning, you let in Athena, as wisdom and fresh air at the same instant; and whenever you draw a pure, long, full breath of right heaven, you take Athena into your heart, through your blood; and, with the blood, into the thoughts of your brain'.

Ruskin may have been conducting a losing battle to protect the vitality of myth from Victorian rationalism. But that we breathe and live isn't myth. David Abram, in *The Spell of the Sensuous*, discusses belief in the air as 'a singularly sacred presence', both in ancient Mediterranean cultures and among the Lakota and Navajo:

As the experiential source of both psyche and spirit, it would seem that the air was once felt to be the very matter of awareness, the subtle body of the mind. *And hence that awareness, far from being experienced as a quality that distinguishes humans from rest of nature, was originally felt as that which invisibly **joined** human beings to the other animals and to the plants, to the forests and to the mountains.* For it was the unseen but common medium of their existence.[34]

This may recall Walter J. Ong's idea that breath as life expresses the spirit of the person. But Ong is expressing the Christian idea of human uniqueness, which is challenged by ecological thinking, such as Abram's, which stresses the shared nature of life, in the belief that spirit pervades nature, joining humans to all that lives. As I understand it, this is an underlying belief of the new nature poetry, which avails itself of resources drawing upon ancient religious practices, such as shamanism, as well as new scientific thinking, such as David Bohm's *Wholeness and the Implicate Order*, which emphasizes flow as being 'in some sense, prior to that of the "things" that can be seen to form and dissolve in this flow'.[35]

Theories are probably best viewed by poets as theatres – Bohm reminds us that the words 'theory' and 'theatre' have the same root. Poetry, viewed thus, is a theatre of exploration. Our new sense of kinship with the natural world, including revelations of reality at macro and micro levels, invites exploration, presents new opportunities for extending a poetry of relationship and love. Human nature, whether or not we see it as exclusively part of nature, is not as rock-like, or as stable, as Wordsworth thought. Poets are explorers and questioners, and they are implicated in what they explore and question. It is not the ego only that is involved, but the very ground of their being. Poets are aware that 'the existential structure of human life is radically, irreducibly liminal'; they are conscious of living on the 'border', 'where matter marches with spirit'. This is haunted country, in which we meet ourselves as strangers; in the words of R. S. Thomas, 'We are our own ghosts, haunting/and haunted'.[36]

Theologians speak of 'shaking-power', the power of God to disconfirm our ideas, unsettle us, and shatter the images we make of him. As Bernard Green writes: 'God cannot be confined by the littleness of our imagination ... God must be sought beyond the limits of our minds and the whole created order. We must reach out into the darkness, beyond our knowing, to the God-beyond-our-grasp.'[37] This is not a view that negates the imagination; it accords, rather, with a humbling of ideas of human power, including imaginative power, which is closer to Keats's idea of negative capability than to stable certainties. For all the domineering assurance of some of Wordsworth's pronouncements about 'the Poet', Wordsworth's greatness, too, shows in the way in which his imagination thrives on humble receptivity.

Matthew Arnold thought Wordsworth the last sacred poet. This was certainly premature. Major twentieth-century Christian poets in English – poets who express a sense of the sacred – include Eliot, Auden, and David Jones. Christianity is also very much alive as an inspiration in the work of a number of important women poets, such as Elizabeth Jennings and Kathleen Raine. But we can't identify the spiritual exclusively with religion, let alone Christianity. Richard Jefferies may be taken as representative of those who do not believe in God, but are, nevertheless, mystics. His iconoclasm took the form of rejecting all ideas of life, being, and divinity. It was in this very rejection – this breaking of ideas and images – that his work opens to the vital force; the force that Zaehner identifies with prana, 'the spirit which animates the universe and which breathes in man'. Jefferies might not have accepted this identification; he might have rejected it as an idea imposing another limitation. Jefferies' iconoclasm bespeaks an imaginative energy, which in turn relates to a way of seeing nature – the life in things – that no word or image can hold. It is a mysticism that ultimately gives priority to sensation, and to perception rather than conception. Poetry, whether religious or not, tends to identify the feeling of life as a spiritual reality. Boris Pasternak spoke of 'the joy of existence', of the poet's work enabling people centuries later 'to come close to the living, personal form of his original sensations'.[38]

The present is radically a time of unmaking, not only politically, but in terms of ideas of gender, the self, the scientific picture of the universe. It isn't only Wordsworth's idea of the Poet as a man, and as 'the rock of defence of human nature', that has fragmented. In the words of my poem 'Groundless She Walks':

> The child I carry
> will crawl into the world.
> What ground will he stand on?
> What humus or piece of debris
> hurtling from the supernova,
> the giant star that once was man?[39]

What certainties are not shaken by that explosion? Moreover, it isn't only old certainties that are shaken; modern ideas are exposed to ancient challenges – by the spiritual values of aboriginal cultures, for example. As Lame Deer, the Sioux holy man, said: 'We Sioux spend a lot of time thinking about everyday things, which in our minds are mixed up with the spiritual. We see in the world around us many symbols that teach us the meaning of life. We have a saying that the white man sees so little, he must see with only one eye.'[40]

This should be an exciting time to be a poet. Viewed positively, a time of unmaking, of instability, opens upon possibility. And Possibility, as Emily Dickinson affirmed, is a fair house to dwell in.

Notes

[1] Richard Humphreys discusses this concept in 'Introduction', in *Pound's Artists*, Tate Gallery, 1985, p. 19.

[2] Emily Dickinson, *Selected Letters*, ed. Thomas H. Johnson, Harvard University Press, 1971, p. 171.

[3] Walter J. Ong, SJ, *The Barbarian Within*, Macmillan, 1962, p. 28.

[4] Dickinson, *Selected Letters*, p. 236.

[5] Quoted in Richard Poirier, *Robert Frost: The Work of Knowing*, Stanford University Press, 1990, p. 3.

[6] Philip Wheelwright, *The Burning Fountain*, Indiana University Press, 1968, pp. 18–19, emphasis in original.

[7] David Jones, *Epoch and Artist*, Faber & Faber, 1959, p. 86.

[8] Sallie McFague, *Models of God: Theology for an Ecological, Nuclear Age*, Fortress Press, 1987, p. 27.

[9] Lynn White, Jr's essay 'The Historical Roots of Our Ecological Crisis', first published in *Science*, 10 March 1967, is reprinted in Cheryll Glotfelty and Harold Fromm (eds), *The Ecocriticism Reader: Landmarks in Literary*

Ecology, University of Georgia Press, 1996, pp. 3–14.
[10] R. S. Thomas, 'Taste', *Laboratories of the Spirit*, Macmillan, 1975, p. 35.
[11] See Stephen Gill, *Wordsworth and the Victorians*, Oxford University Press, 1998, Chapter 4 et passim.
[12] David Jones, *The Anathemata*, Faber & Faber, 1952, pp. 73–4.
[13] Lorine Niedecker, *Collected Works*, ed. Jenny Penberthy, University of California Press, , 2004, p. 295.
[14] Ibid., p. 240.
[15] For relevant information about the veery, see Richard Caddel, 'A Note', in *The Full Note: Lorine Niedecker*, ed. Peter Dent, Interim Press, 1983, p. 88.
[16] Quoted in Tony Tanner, *The Reign of Wonder*, Cambridge University Press, 1965, p. 196.
[17] George Oppen, *New Collected Poems*, ed. Michael Davidson, New Directions, 2002, p. 51.
[18] Wendy Mulford, *and, suddenly, supposing: selected poems*, etruscan books, 2002, p. 15.
[19] 'Palimpsest: Of Julian the Woman', in Sara Maitland and Wendy Mulford, *Virtuous Magic*, Mowbray, 1998, p. 298.
[20] Rowan Williams, *The Wound of Knowledge*, Darton, Longman & Todd, 1990, p. 8.
[21] Stephen Prickett, *Words and The Word*, Cambridge University Press, 1986, p. 224.
[22] Williams, *The Wound of Knowledge*, p. 149.
[23] Thomas Merton, *The Way of Chuang Tzu*, New Directions, 1965, p. 112.
[24] Ibid., p. 15.
[25] Gary Snyder, *A Range of Poems*, Fulcrum Press, 1966, p. 13.
[26] Henry David Thoreau, *The Maine Woods*, quoted in Max Oelschlaeger, *The Idea of Wilderness*, Yale University Press, 1991, p. 149, emphases are Thoreau's.
[27] Gary Snyder, *The Real Work: Interviews & Talks 1964–1979*, New Directions, 1980, p. 72.
[28] Ibid., p. 65.
[29] R. S. Thomas, *Mass for Hard Times*, Bloodaxe Books, 1992, p. 46.
[30] See chapters by John Barnie and John Pikoulis in Damien Walford Davies (ed.), *Echoes to the Amen: Essays after R. S. Thomas*, University of Wales Press, 2003.

[31] Joseph M Conte, 'Natural Histories: Serial Form in the Later Poetry of Lorine Niedecker', in *Lorine Niedecker: Woman and Poet*, ed. Jenny Penberthy, National Poetry Foundation, 1996, p. 346.

[32] Niedecker, *Collected Works*, p. 261.

[33] R. C. Zaehner, *Mysticism, Sacred and Profane*, Oxford University Press, 1961, p. 48.

[34] David Abram, *The Spell of the Sensuous*, Vintage Books, 1997, p. 238, Abram's emphases.

[35] David Bohm, *Wholeness and the Implicate Order*, Routledge, 1995, p. 11.

[36] R. S. Thomas, untitled poem printed as epigraph to his lecture 'Time's Disc Jockey: Meditations on Some Lines in *The Anathemata*', in *David Jones: Diversity in Unity*, ed. Belinda Humfrey and Anne Price-Owen, University of Wales Press, 2000, p. 153.

[37] Bernard Green, in a review, *The Tablet*, 27 July 2002, p. 19.

[38] Quoted in 'Introduction', Boris Pasternak, *Selected Poems*, trans. Jon Stallworthy and Peter France, Allen Lane, 1982, p. 20.

[39] Jeremy Hooker, *Adamah*, Enitharmon Press, 2002, p. 45.

[40] Quoted in Paula Gunn Allen, *The Sacred Hoop*, Beacon Press, 1986, p. 69.

'Tending Words and Sheep'
THE POETRY OF LES ARNOLD

'Dervish of energy' is a phrase that quickly comes to mind when I think of Les Arnold or read his poetry. A friend with whom he had taught at a university in Canada used it of him after his death.[1] It was certainly true of the man I had known, and it is true of his poetry. But is there, I wonder, a contradiction between this and the fact that his poetry is haunted by the omnipresence of death? Once the immediate grief of loss is past, one temptation in reading the work of a poet who was a friend is to find it not only death-haunted, but shadowed by premonitions of his own mortality.

'Running' is a poignant example:

> My heart crows along this morning
> road. Running zippy zappy through
> the day, blue-frost, ice-sun, hearing
> only thud of distant blood, my body
> fell from a great height.
>
> I merge with the road's indirection.
> I can't die. I can only go on like
> this, amplifying the world's pulse
> under a clear sky, drawing after me
> the trees, the early flowers, sleight
> of fox & deer in celebratory
> silent marathon.[2]

It is impossible after the poet's death not to detect a sliver of ice at the heart of such a poem. In the case of Les Arnold, however, the premonitory shiver was not morbid. Rather, as 'Running' reveals, it was inherent in his acute sense of physical, even athletic, life. He had a dynamic vitality, a sense of natural existence as a dance of energies, which was sharpened by his knowledge that death is an ever-present possibility within the moment.

While living in Canada, Les wrote poems that were marked by the informality and expressiveness of Beat generation influences and also showed his abiding interest in modernist painting. His most enduring influence, however, was William Carlos Williams. I say 'influence', but it is hardly the right word for the ways with poetic language and form which set Les free to develop a style true to his own apprehension of life. The Les Arnold who appears in the poems he wrote after he settled with his family on a smallholding in Gloucestershire in 1978 is a distinctively English poet. He and his wife Sandra had kept sheep in Canada, but now his subject is sheep-keeping and the life of the Cotswolds. 'The Brassrubbing' is a witty representation of this phase of his work:

> The Unknown Sheepman of Northleach
> and his Unknown Wife have been sleeping in
> the same stone bed for more than 400
> years Both are fully clothed He is always
> the perfect gentleman Sheep explain
> his success His unknown wife
> lies perfectly still with hands crossed
> in prayer But he cannot touch her
> Lord I have covered her body with paper
> rubbing until nipples again shine through
> in the exhausted cold at Northleach
> we go about our business Whilst the
> sheepman dreams of the brass he has made
> and the fleecing that remains to be done.

One may see a kinship to poems by George Herbert in the 'shape' of this poem, with its resemblance to a commemorative brass, but, rather than having a pious intention, the shape serves to make ironic and witty comment on the sheepman dreaming 'of the brass he has made'. The poem is alive, whereas the sheepman with his dream of material gain is dead. Vitality, in more than one sense, characterizes Les Arnold's poems.

When I read his poems in *Joy Riding*, and in his second and last posthumous volume, *Shaker City*, words that come to mind are those which Mike Weaver in *William Carlos Williams* applied to the modern poet who meant most to Les. 'For Williams the image of reality was a river of pleasure running through a man's body.' Weaver, quoting a Shaker source, also says the Shakers 'affirmed "the generous soil of North America" in song and dance'.[3] Les Arnold's self-renunciation had a similar effect upon the world outside himself.

Yet the emphasis upon physical pleasure, while this applies to Les, also needs to be qualified in his case. For one thing, his poetry manifests the bodily and mental and spiritual discomforts stemming from a puritan conscience. For another, he has a strong sense of the reality that manifests itself when the familiar world dissolves and the self is deeply shaken. Without intending any pun, the latter can be related to his interest in the Shakers, to whose beliefs and way of life the title poem-sequence of his last book is devoted. Before explaining more fully what I mean by this, I should say that I see the radical insecurity of Les Arnold's sense of self and world as one of his main sources of strength as a poet.

Les's earliest native stone was sandstone, and in a poem titled 'Sandstone' he wrote, 'Love's discomfort reminds you of//the gritty surface of things so/that the eyes can be sanded down//& made ready for sight.' In another poem from the 'Imprints' section of *Shaker City*, 'The Fell Runner'[4] (with a probable pun on the 'fell Sergeant'), he invokes his original northern landscape to reject 'southern comfort of the soul'; but, rather than conventionally posing a rugged northernness against the soft south, the poem dramatizes a guiltily divided sense of self. In 'A Poem Like a Lemon', he speaks of his desire to write a poem that 'will/bring tears to the eyes of the moment//for washing out sleep and rheum'. Les Arnold was acutely sensitive to the pain and disorder in the world, and this, together with his lack of egotistic complacency, alerted him to revelatory instants, when human defences break down, exposing what lies behind them.

Moments in which the familiar world dissolves, or in which it is threatened from without (as wind drives against the windows of human habitations), recur in poems in 'Imprints'. In 'Her Head Turns', for instance, a woman is startled by catching through the window 'a silent clattering of wings'.

> When she turns back inside
> the room she'll say Oh so that was it.
>
> That's what it was after all!
> And name it 'Owl' unbroken now
>
> by flight. She'll soon be back
> to her old self, composed and coveting
>
> the same. But for the moment
> she does not know what possesses
>
> vision this random day.

This is an 'unguarded moment', a moment when, being taken out of 'her old self', the woman loses her sense of 'possession' and is open to 'vision' as a way of seeing (and being seen) shaken free of ego-centred ('composed and coveting') assumptions.

Parallels to both Ted Hughes and Gary Snyder suggest themselves, though Les Arnold is distinct from both. As a poet concerned with seeing, who set many of his later poems in Cotswold landscapes, he was recognizably an English poet, a poet in the tradition of the aim that Coleridge, in *Biographia Literaria*, ascribed to Wordsworth, of 'awakening the mind's attention to the lethargy of custom', and of Ivor Gurney's 'nor is anything done/Wiselier than the moving or breaking to sight/Of a thing hidden under by custom'. Les's concern, however, was with newness. 'Snow', one of his finest earlier poems, begins,

> What is promised
> is a new day when a man
>
> by walking first

into stunned white

can become himself again

One of the epigraphs to *Shaker City* is Williams's 'A New World is only a new mind'. In many respects, Les was close to Williams in spirit, as quotations from his doctoral thesis on the American poet show. For Les too, writing was 'a complete openness to all kinds of experience'. Like Williams, he recognized the need to 'keep intact what the understanding touches'. He shared Williams's interest in the Shakers and sought in his poems a structure analogous to that of Shaker furniture, 'in which only what was essential to the demands of the composition was retained'. In my view, Les's most substantial work, 'Shaker City', is a major poetic sequence. It is a work in which his joy in life and his sharply intelligent moral sense, his sensuousness and his asceticism, powerfully interact, and in which he combines his native wit and sensibility with the formal liberation that he found in the Americans. The care he showed for the essential detail in a poem was closely associated with the care he bestowed upon people and the natural world. It was after Les and his family had returned from Canada to England in 1977 that a contributor's note to the Canadian magazine *Grain* said, simply, 'Les Arnold tends words and sheep in England.'

With his interest in newness, Les was concerned less with history in landscape than with original perception and the way it affects the relationship between self and world. He had been influenced by his years in Canada, which enhanced his sense of the elemental. Often, in his poems set in southern England, the landscapes are shadowed by other, more abrasive, landscapes, whether the north of 'The Fell Runner' and 'Sandstone', or the Mediterranean world of 'A Poem Like a Lemon', or the Canada of his Cotswold snowscapes. Part of the appeal of the Shakers for him was, no doubt, the movement of the founder, Ann Lee, from Manchester to America. He was also, as I have suggested, radically unsettled when most at home, partly because of the way he saw things, and partly because he was at odds with the kind of self-composure (in the sense of settled, if troubled, selfhood) that characterizes mainstream post-war English poetry.

Les's quick nervous openness to impression, sensation, and idea is reminiscent of Black Mountain poetics, while his insistence on sincerity as integral to the poem recalls George Oppen.

It was, perhaps, his rejection of conventional 'composure' that drew him to the Shakers. 'It is in the coherence of their lives', he wrote, 'that the Shakers serve as images of wholeness.'[5] Yet their coherence was close to the form of ecstatic dance (one of their principal forms of communal and spiritual expression) and did not resemble the 'order' of bourgeois society, and they rejected the World and its materialism. Les Arnold's interest in their craftsmanship also cohered with his love of a kind of imagistic plainness, writing crafted to serve the occasion, but without ornament or embellishment. Ecstatic unworldliness, on the other hand, appealed to the dervish in him, while the 'brothers' and 'sisters' spoke to his egalitarianism. An additional attraction was insecurity – the very source from which he derived his poetry. In 'Entries from Mother Ann's Journal', for example, we see the sense of the real that ensued when Ann Lee 'gave up everything'. Here, she speaks of the voyage to America:

> I am glad to be between.
> To have neither knowledge nor
>
> desire, exiled from before
> and after, without language or
>
> image, a perfect stranger
> even to myself ...

There is something provisional about 'Shaker City'. Les would almost certainly have revised it before publishing it had he lived. In the event, however, the lack of perfect finish fits the subject, as well as being true to the poetic. The world of the poem is, as it were, shaken, as the subversive and disruptive Shakers shook their fellow townspeople when they came

> stamping through
> streets where we're all on the point of surrender

with nothing to light our way and our neon signs

flagging in an air where whips and whoops! are the only
signs of a life we never knew until too late.

The poem continues with the brothers and sisters breaking 'shop-front windows with their singing'. Les was like them, metaphorically speaking. He had an acute sense of the provisional nature of human order, and frequently saw the window as the fragile division between the accommodations we make with the world, and the reality we do not see. He did not have a monolithic view of the latter, apprehending it sometimes as death and sometimes, in the language of the Shakers, as 'a free circulation of the gifts of God'. In either case, his perception was sharpened by his sense of what lay outside the window.

A certain plainness of diction in 'Shaker City' reflects both the subject and the poet's honesty, but plainness is far from meaning dullness. Les was a man who, like the Shakers, loved to dance. Quickness of movement, including speed of perception, distinguishes all his most vital poems. Dancing, as we see in the following lines from 'The Instruments', a section of 'Shaker City', was for Les, as for the Shakers, an expression of wholeness:

Feel me shake. You may call it
dancing but it does not pass
from me but stays about me,
even when stilled.

If trees had names
what would they call this passing

in which wildwood is joined root
trunk branch & leaf in trembling.

'Shaker City' is the most complete expression of what our friend and colleague Colin Edwards has called 'Les's sense of domestic order: the powerful and increasingly important anti-materialism, the almost loving attention to objects with use-value'. The poem also expresses the poet's (as well as the Shakers') joy in life. 'Shaker City' dances with energy.

A reviewer of *Joy Riding*, Ivor Thomas, writes of discovering 'that this poet is now dead and I'm saddened to lose a friend I've only just made'. Others will feel the same. I found one of Les's gifts to me, for the first time, on a rainy day in April when I was looking through his papers for writings that might be used in a collection of his unpublished work:

Moving in

for Jerry

Leaning today
into spring's first wind – cold

furrow in greening air –
I thought of you &

your new home. How again
you were rebuilding. Books to

furnish a living space,
a typewriter to displace fears of

other emptied places. Around
this house long unframed

memories. Your desk aches
with absence. Aga's dead & won't

light until Mieke hauls you up
to shop. To stock up. Now

phone installed, gas turned on,
may this ordinary be your home,

spring rains your remembrancer
of pain. And may pain become

a window through which you
celebrate the weather

beating a path to your door

Why hadn't he shown me the poem? Perhaps he didn't think it good enough, yet it is, I think, a good poem. In his judgement, though, it may not have been good enough for friendship, or to meet the severe demands he made of a gift. Now, it is the intactness of the understanding in his poems that I continue to learn from Les and about him; no longer from the man outside the poems, but from the touch of his mind and being in every detail of their composition. There are poets who set out to teach us something in their poems, and they are usually best avoided. And there are poets for whom experience itself contains the need to see and understand. Les Arnold was the latter kind. From such it is a pleasure to learn.

Notes

[1] Stan Dragland, 'Les Arnold in London (Ont)', in Les Arnold, *Uncollected Writing*, ed. Jeremy Hooker, Plain Sailing Press, 1995, p. 93.
[2] Les Arnold, *Joy Riding*, Taxus Press, 1993, p. 32. Except where otherwise stated, all quotations from Les Arnold's poetry are from this book.
[3] Mike Weaver, *William Carlos Williams: The American Background*, Cambridge University Press, 1971, p. 59.
[4] Les Arnold, *Shaker City*, Stride, 1998, p. 37.
[5] Arnold, *Shaker City*, p. 69. All 'Shaker City' quotations are from this edition.

Reflections on 'Ground'

1

My feel for 'ground' as *matter* – earth, stones, and growing things, as the *life of place* – must have been laid down from the start. Indeed, I think of it as familial, ancestral, a feeling deriving from people who worked on the land as labourers and gardeners mainly in the south of England. In these fundamental things, however, original feeling becomes hard to distinguish from later imagination, from the stories one tells oneself or is told; so, too my own memories as a child became linked with my parents' memories of their childhoods, thus reinforcing my sense of belonging to a particular area over a period running back into the past, before I was born. The conventional word for the resulting sense of belonging is 'roots': a word I would come to distrust because it converts a complicated history into a natural process. But this would come later. As far as I am aware, my original feeling for poetry was closely associated with 'ground' as the elemental life of place.

The poems my mother loved, and which she read or recited to me when I was a boy, came mainly from *Laureata: A Book of Poetry for the Young*, which she had studied in school at the time of the First World War. This anthology, not unlike Palgrave's *The Golden Treasury*, was particularly rich in lyrical and narrative poems, and among my favourites were 'Horatius', 'After Blenheim', 'The Deserted Village', 'The Forsaken Merman', and poems by Tennyson, such as 'Break, Break, Break' and 'The Brook'. After years during which the word 'ground' has undergone complex changes of meaning in my mind, I was startled when I came recently upon another favourite poem from *Laureata*, Pope's 'Ode to Solitude', in which the word probably first resonated for me:

> Happy the man whose wish and care
>   A few paternal acres bound,
> Content to breathe his native air
>   In his own ground.

It was a shock to recognize the sentiment of basic attachment that must have originally drawn me to the word. But it's salutary to be reminded of the simple things from which one's poetry springs: from sensations such as the feel of earth underfoot, or soil crumbled in the hand, or the experience of simply being in a place that one loves; from a liking for particular words.

Many of the Victorian and earlier poems in *Laureata* conveyed a sense of place. Thus, for me, Tennyson was associated with West Wight, which we could see across the Solent; Thomas Hardy (though not in *Laureata*) with Dorset, as was William Barnes. Richard Jefferies, whose essays, when I read them first at about the age of twelve, opened my eyes to nature, was identified with Wiltshire, ancestral ground, and country that I knew from visits. Some years later I read Edward Thomas, who was closely associated with my home county of Hampshire. From the beginning, then, my feeling for poetry was bound up with a feeling for the land. This is probably why I experienced no discontinuity – at least, no radical break – between love of *Laureata* poems and the modernist poetry I began to read when I was about eighteen (some, earlier). There are, of course, enormous formal and linguistic differences between, say, Tennyson's lyrics and the Imagism and fragmentation of Eliot and Pound. Yet both Victorians and modernists ground their poetry in a feeling for the elements – for soil and sea and winds – and for elemental places. For me, then, though I know why modernists felt the need to break with their immediate predecessors (a break that, in some respects, seems less radical now than it did at the time), the transition from traditional English lyricism to *The Waste Land* and *The Cantos* wasn't a difficult one.

2

It is possible that revolutions in one's idea of poetry may involve a return to original sources, rather than being complete transformations. To some extent, this, I believe, is what happened to my thinking about 'ground' in the years following my move to Wales in 1965. Initially, I was drawn to London as the 'centre' where I hoped, as a young poet, to publish and make a name. At the same time, I had a vague idea of poetry as self-expression, or the expression of states of mind. All this began to change when I encountered modern Welsh poetry in translation, especially poems by Gwenallt and Waldo Williams, which spoke out of the crisis of their culture in the twentieth century and gave voice to a body of shared experience. More influential was the writing of David Jones, which I began to read in 1970.

The idea I developed at this time was that poetry should be written not *about* but *from* place. This, at any rate, was what I aspired to do. In some respects, as I realized later, it was a nostalgic desire, arising from the fact that, living in Wales, I could see the place I had come from, where I felt I belonged. I identified closely with David Jones's words in the preface to *The Anathemata*: 'one is trying to make a shape out of the very things of which one is oneself made'.[1] This was a definition of poetry that gave priority to the poet's *matter*, to all that shaped him in terms of culture, history, family and ancestry. At the same time it defined poetry by implication as essentially exploratory, since one has to discover the things of which one is made in the process of making a shape of them. Now, my idea of 'ground' became the whole 'matter' of place: the geological and historical shaping forces, the ecology, and family and ancestry, as well as personal experience. All this I could see as one cannot see what one remains part of.

John Matthias wrote perceptively of my poetry at this time, in for example *Solent Shore* (1978), that I would like it to be of use in the place: 'as essential as the necessities unladen in the harbor'.[2] Donald Davie described the whole of *Solent Shore* as suffused with 'the emotion that we have when we recognize some particular terrain as "home"'.³ What is clear to me is that the light in which I saw things was sharpened by the experience of growing up during and after a world war and under the shadow of the Bomb. As a sense of place is quickened by the encroachments of uniform placelessness, so it is greatly intensified by awareness that all may be annihilated.

One effect of thinking about poetry as, in a sense, voicing the life of place was that I conceived my work in terms of sequences, and as working with and through what I now consciously thought of as 'ground'. I perceived a continuity between natural and non-human constituents of place – geological processes and materials such as chalk and flint, shingle and clay – and historical, human experience; I made formal connections between poetry and place, which I described in an essay, 'A Poem like a Place', included in my book *Master of the Leaping Figures* (1987):

> Entering a place that is new to us, or seeing a familiar place anew, we move from part to part, simultaneously perceiving individual persons and things and discovering their relationships, so that, with time, place reveals itself as particular identities belonging to a network, which continually extends with our perception, and beyond it. And by this process we find ourselves, not as observers only, but as inhabitants, citizens, neighbours, and locate ourselves in a space dense with meanings.⁴

The connection I was seeking was similar to that which I found in the Welsh poets. It defined a poetic function, a way of speaking beyond the isolated self, as a voice of community.

3

The thing I was not initially prepared to recognize was the extent to which my perception of home ground depended upon distance: that if I could see where I had come from, it was because I was no longer living there. But seeing had long been one of my preoccupations. It originated in my reading of Jefferies, who opened my eyes to the life in nature, vibrant in every ditch and hedge. It owed a great deal to the fact that my father was a landscape painter, although it wasn't until I was in my twenties that I *really* looked at his paintings and appreciated his sense of colour, of dynamic movement, of water and light, shadow and cloud. When I saw these things, I knew them in myself too, in my perception of the world. His work helped me to make a personal connection between the tradition of English landscape painting and the literary tradition that descends from William and Dorothy Wordsworth through John Ruskin and the Victorian 'poet-naturalist' Jefferies to Hardy and Edward Thomas and Ivor Gurney: a tradition in which accurate observation is integral to moral and visionary 'seeing'.

It was as I began to recognize factors that complicate the 'art of seeing' that I came – following an earlier admiration for William Carlos Williams – to read the American Objectivists, especially George Oppen and Charles Reznikoff. In one sense, my 'discovery' of these poets was not a complicating factor. On the contrary, Oppen confirmed my feeling for Imagism as a root of modern poetry, and as a technique for transcending momentary perception and for building sequences and long poems. The 'mosaic' form, which I adopted in some poems, owed something to the example of Reznikoff's *Jerusalem the Golden*. The Objectivists' close attention to the things of a 'common' world reinforced what I had long been drawn to in the tradition of *Lyrical Ballads*, thus enhancing my sense of connection between the vision of English Romantics and naturalists and a key element in American modernism. But it was also Oppen who wrote, '"Whether, as the intensity of seeing increases, one's distance/from Them, the people, does not also increase"/I know, of course I know, I can enter no other place.'[5] Place itself, in this sense, becomes distance from others, instead of a space of shared meanings. Lost in this distance, the poet can become a solipsist leading what Martin Buber calls 'the life of monologue'. Looking back, I can see that this was the risk I became most aware of after completing some of my most 'rooted' poems.

It was in Buber that I discovered new possibilities of relationship: 'We do not find meaning lying in things nor do we put it into things, but between us and things it can happen.'[6] I had struggled as a poet to write a convincing experiential poetry using the first-person singular. Indeed, in the first sustained work that seemed to me authentically mine I had adopted as a persona the chalk giant of Cerne Abbas, which had enabled me to explore relations between self and other, male and female, and life-engendering and destructive forces. I should have learnt from this that poetry for me is essentially exploratory – that I have no real interest in rendering 'completed' experience, but only in using the known to reach towards the unknown, and to find in the familiar the strange, the other.

Emily Dickinson said it perfectly: 'Nature is a Haunted House – but Art – a House that tries to be haunted.'[7] The perfection of the saying inheres in its mystery, which different readers will understand differently according to their needs. As I understand it, it refers to the artist – the poet – as one who works at the limits of the sayable; or rather as a maker, one who shapes objects that are open to mystery. We can't be certain that spirit will animate our poems; we can only make them so that they are open to spirit, not closed within the confines of one's ego.

4

It was Lee Grandjean, the sculptor and painter, who said to me, 'We must break our taste.' We had met in 1981 at Winchester School of Art, where we both held residencies. It was in the following decade, however, that we began to work together collaboratively, producing a book, *Their Silence a Language*, consisting of poems and prose, and drawings and photographic images of sculptures, and *Groundwork*, an exhibition of sculptures and poems. Meeting Lee and seeing him at work renewed my original feeling for the sculptural. In *Welsh Journal*, in an entry made in 1972, I wrote, 'Last night, looking again at pictures of Henry Moore's sculptures, I realized once more that my instinctive feeling for things and for landscapes is closer to the feeling of sculptors like Moore and Barbara Hepworth, and of certain painters, than to that of most writers.' I was thinking of earliest impressions: of the rhythms and shapes of downland, of scalloped ploughland, of sea walls, shingle beaches, and mudflats. I was aware, too, of the texture of my father's oil paintings. It was important that

Lee and I felt similar needs as image-makers, yet were practising different arts, so that our differences were at least as imaginatively stimulating as our similarities.

Working with Lee helped to confirm my sense of ground as both material and shaping force. But also, when he spoke of breaking our taste, challenging us to 'make it new', the idea harmonized with my conviction that poetry is both image-making and image-breaking. That is to say, the poet needs to be iconoclastic towards his or her own work, knowing that every image is provisional, and reality larger, stranger, and more mysterious than any word or image. This is not a philosophical position, but a fundamental instinct springing ultimately from my earliest sense of what I would learn to call particularity and personhood; from life as Henry Vaughan apprehends it: 'A quickness which my God hath kissed'.

5

Writing the foreword to a selection of Rutger Kopland's poems in English translation, in 1991, I described Kopland as 'distinctively a Dutch poet, and therefore a European poet', and explained that by this I meant 'that he, in common with other European poets and artists, conveys a strong sense of the special material and spiritual qualities that make his country unique'.[8] My experience of living in the Netherlands for four years during the 1980s enhanced my sense that, as I wrote in my journal, 'real poetry incorporates a feeling for native land'.[9] I had earlier felt something similar about R. S. Thomas and Welsh-language poets, and about other British and Irish poets. It was living in continental Europe, however, that sharpened my sense of common differences among poets in whose work a country or a region was a presence, a source of the imagination, feeding the senses, enriching with personal and historical associations, and giving a body to the apprehension of life.

The highly visual culture of the Netherlands, together with the largely man-made nature of the land, helped to make me yet more aware of the material world. But there is also in Dutch art, as Svetlana Alpers has shown in her remarkable book *The Art of Describing*, a sense of 'the world prior to us made visible',[10] and of representations of people and things as 'ungraspable'. Thus, if Rutger Kopland is indeed 'distinctively a Dutch poet', it is because he is not a naïve realist, but a poet who 'knows that the world is beyond him, and the reality of life eludes his words'.[11] Along with this elusive spirit in Dutch art, and in the most material, manhandled landscapes, I found that living in the Netherlands — and not just visiting a wartime transit camp or travelling to Verdun or Berlin — impressed upon me our human subjection to historical forces. Alpers writes that Vermeer in his paintings of women 'recognizes the world present in these women as something that is other than himself and with a kind of passionate detachment he lets it, through them, be'.[12] Can poetry too be an art of letting be? It is to my time in the Netherlands that I date an increased aversion to 'mastery' in any shape or form, including 'mastery' over language.

6

A poet risks becoming fixed in his or her ideas. No doubt this was the case with me when I was preoccupied by 'poetry of place' and a concept of 'belonging'. One day my friend Anne Cluysenaar said to me, 'You have never accepted being a stranger,' and I knew she spoke the truth. Or rather, it had been the truth, and it had determined my earlier thinking. For some time now, however, I had known what it means to be a stranger. The reference wasn't especially to any form of 'alienation'. It had more to do with recognition of 'not knowing', and of the perception that, as Philip Wheelwright says, 'The existential structure of human life is radically, irreducibly *liminal*.'[13] In my critical writing I had become increasingly concerned with the relation between poetry and the sacred, continuing work begun on David Jones in the 1970s but also focusing upon Henry Vaughan and Thomas Traherne, and modern and contemporary poets who attempt to express a religious sensibility in a language imbued with secular values. I had come to think of ground in a religious sense; but what I was most aware of was its instability.

There was a sense in which this took me back to the beginning, but with a new awareness of the question of underlying reality. In my experience the actual shore close to where I had been brought up was, from my first sight of it, dangerously and excitingly unstable – the path along the sea wall eroded; the detritus of war, which might have been booby-trapped, washed up and mixed with natural flotsam. The world inland from the shore extended the instability, with razed buildings, bomb craters, layers upon layers of the past exposed. All this influenced my sense of language, and therefore of identity. I'd always felt a disparity between the definition of names and the mystery of identity – the self-feeling that descends into being. In poems in *Adamah* (2002), especially 'Seven Songs', I explored this instability, which could also be called a sense of wonder at the strangeness of existence, which precedes all concepts and categories but also continues *behind* them and as a kind of under-life in words.

Writing of 'Seven Songs' in *Adamah*, I described them as characterized by 'fluidity', and said their voice 'is conceived as being female, not in the form of a woman persona, but as a kind of androgynous space, in which I attempt to transcend the limitations of both male and female egos'. I had reached this position, not by rejecting the materiality of ground, but through a greater awareness of 'groundlessness'. This has its negative aspects, but, positively, 'it is associated with possibility, with loss of ego boundaries in an enlarged sense of being, and with imaginative energy that both makes and breaks images, in an attempt to intimate the power beyond images, on which all life depends'.[14]

In these reflections on 'ground' I have described some of the things that I think I can see when I consider my present writing and look back over my work as a poet during some forty years. One thing is certain, however. As I wrote in 'At the Edge', the afterword to *Their Silence a Language*: 'I think of poetry as an art of seeing, an art by which, in my blindness, I learn to see.'[15]

Notes

[1] David Jones, Preface, *The Anathemata*, Faber & Faber, 1952, p. 10.

[2] John Matthias, *Reading Old Friends*, State University of New York Press, 1992, p. 84.

[3] Donald Davie, 'Hard Squares', *P N Review*, Vol. 6, No. 1, 1980, p. 57.

[4] Jeremy Hooker, *Master of the Leaping Figures*, Enitharmon Press, 1987, p. 76.

[5] George Oppen, 'Of Being Numerous', *New Collected Poems*, ed. Michael Davidson, New Directions, 2002, p. 167.

[6] Martin Buber, *Between Man and Man*, Fontana Library, 1961, p. 56.

[7] Emily Dickinson, *Emily Dickinson: Selected Letters*, ed, Thomas H. Johnson, Belknap Press of Harvard University Press, 1971, p. 236.

[8] Rutger Kopland, *A World Beyond Myself*, Enitharmon Press, 1991, p. 9.

[9] Jeremy Hooker, *Openings: A European Journal*, Shearsman, 2014, p. 239.

[10] Svetlana Alpers, *The Art of Describing*, University of Chicago Press, 1983, p. 70.

[11] See Jeremy Hooker, 'Foreword', Rutger Kopland, *A World Beyond Myself*, Enitharmon Press, 1991, pp. 9–12.

[12] Alpers, *The Art of Describing*, p. 224.

[13] Philip Wheelwright, *The Burning Fountain*, Indiana University Press, 1968, pp. 18–19.

[14] Jeremy Hooker, *Adamah*, Enitharmon Press, 2002, p. 107.

[15] Hooker and Grandjean, *Their Silence a Language*, p. 75.

Reflections on the Lyric 'I'

Hast thou ever raised thy mind to the consideration of EXISTENCE, in and by itself, as the mere act of existing? Hast thou ever said to thyself, thoughtfully, IT IS! Heedless in that moment, whether it were a man before thee, or a flower, or a grain of sand? ... [I]f thou hast indeed attained to this, thou wilt have felt the presence of a mystery, which must have fixed thy spirit in awe and wonder.
Samuel Taylor Coleridge, *The Friend*, 1809

Am I a man who dreamed of being a butterfly, or am I a butterfly dreaming myself to be a man?
Chuang Tzu (fourth or third century BCE)

Lyric poetry, in the form with which I am concerned, is an exploratory art. The poem must first surprise the poet, enlarging his or her sense of being. Accordingly, I stumbled upon the central idea of my work in progress – seeing with a stranger's eye – when rereading a poem I had written for an American photographer who makes studies of former coal-mining areas in South Wales:

The unimaginable is what he sees with a stranger's eye –
lives made shaping and re-shaping
material ground ...

Ray Klimek's post-industrial landscapes convey a sense of what cannot be seen or imagined – the reality of working lives 'made' in shaping the material ground. A sense of lives made through work – initially the lives of my agricultural forebears – has inspired me from the outset as a poet, strongly affecting the way in which I saw my first landscape in the south of England.

Ditch Vision

In poems set in Hampshire, Wiltshire, and Dorset I wrote about places that were, in part, familial and ancestral. These poems involved different kinds of knowledge – geological, ecological, historical, personal. But they involved also an awareness of mystery, of what cannot be known about other lives, and a sense that reality is more, and other, than human concepts and perceptions.

As a boy, I responded keenly to Richard Jefferies' belief in 'unlearning, the first step to learn'. In words that impressed me deeply, he wrote, in 'Nature and Books', 'Then to unlearn the first ideas of history, of science, of social institutions, to unlearn one's own life and purpose; to unlearn the old mode of thought and way of arriving at things; to take off peel after peel, and so get by degrees slowly towards the truth – thus writing as it were, a sort of floating book in the mind, almost remaking the soul.' Unlearning for Jefferies was a way of 'coming to have touch of that which is real'.

The iconoclasm born of Jefferies' nature worship spoke directly to my instinctive sense of things – to a way of seeing that was also an apprehension of language. Quite simply, I might look at a tree, or any living thing, and know that its reality would always be beyond my words. Jefferies was an early influence that would prepare me for my later encounter with Martin Buber's philosophy of 'otherness', and with apophatic theology. From early on, I did not despair of poetry, but thought of it as a way of approaching the unimaginable.

What is at issue here is an apprehension of existence before it is an idea. Many years after reading Jefferies, and discovering Buber, I read, in Czeslaw Milosz's *Native Realm*,

> Poetry is a constant self-negation; it imitates Heraclitian fluidity ... [P]oetic discipline is impossible without piety and admiration, without faith in the infinite layers of being that are hidden within an apple, a man, or a tree; it challenges one through becoming to move closer to what *is*.[1]

A 'poetry of place' suggests something different from a poetry of unlearning, not-knowing, self-negation. It suggests rootedness, belonging, stable identity. It is true that in earlier poetry I harboured a sense of belonging. Ironically, though, this sprang largely from distance, even from hiraeth, longing to return to my original home ground in the south of England. My aspiration was to write not about but *from* place, as a participant in its life, rather than as a detached observer. This was influenced by the experience of living in Wales and by the example of certain Welsh poets, individuals who were voices of their communities, expressing deeply shared social and historical experience. This, at any rate, was my partly romanticized view, influenced also by rejection of what I regarded as facile forms of alienation, by which a poet becomes his or her only subject, isolated from people and place. When conveying an impression of belonging, however, I was writing not as a participant, but with the perspective distance affords.

I now realize that I have been finding my way back to an original apprehension of reality by a roundabout route. It was my friend Anne Cluysenaar who made me think again about being a stranger and redirected me to consider the strangeness of existence. I saw again what I had once known, thus confirming the truth of lyric poetry as I have experienced it – a truth expressed by the Palestinian poet Mahmoud Darwish as 'the stranger-in-oneself'.[2]

One product of this realization is an ongoing series of prose poems in which I look at the area of South Wales in which I now live, on the outskirts of a former pit village. Here, with the demise of the coal industry, a way of life has ended, and what is replacing it is uncertain. It is an area deeply marked by tragedy, in which one feels acutely the inadequacy of words and images to convey a sense of what has been endured. Here, the poet as stranger looks at a landscape charged with the 'presence' of an overwhelming history, but in which memory and new uncertainty coexist, creating a kind of 'historical other world'. It is hard to know just what one is seeing, or what ground there is for the onlooker to stand on.

One problem with Wordsworth's famous definition of poetry as originating from emotion recollected in tranquillity is its tacit assumption of a stable ego in the act of recollection. What we know of the Romantic poets in their age of change and uncertainty tells us that this could not be true of them. Indeed, rather than being grounded upon a sure sense of self, they were closer to modern poets experiencing radical uncertainty in both self and world. Keats was nearer the mark when he called the world 'the vale of Soul-making', an idea in harmony with his concept of negative capability, 'when man is capable of being in uncertainties, Mysteries, doubts, without any irritable reaching after fact and reason'.[3]

The unlearning of the poet-naturalist Jefferies, 'almost remaking the soul', as a way of 'coming to have touch of that which is real', and Keats's 'Soul-making' may be contrasted with David Jones's intention in *The Anathemata*: 'One is trying to make a shape out of the very things of which one is oneself made.'[4] Each involves self or soul as more process than fixed entity, as something that one works with, and realizes in the making. For David Jones, the process required discovering what 'the things' were. For him, as a Roman Catholic, they were ultimately founded upon his belief in God as Ground of Being. For most modern poets, existence inheres in 'uncertainties, Mysteries, doubts'.

T. S. Eliot famously wrote that poetry 'is not the expression of personality, but an escape from personality'. This may be misunderstood. In Jacques Maritain's view, Eliot himself misunderstood it, since he missed the distinction 'between Creative Self and self-centered ego'.[5] In modern poetry, in Eliot, Pound, and Yeats, strategies of impersonality, such as the use of personae or masks, aimed not to escape the personal, but to reach a deeper level than isolated self-consciousness. This may be conceived in terms of 'the stranger-in-oneself'. The modernist poets, in different ways, had a belief in ultimate reality, in what Milosz calls 'the infinite layers of being', in which, in some sense, the Creative Self could participate.

The Imagist root of modern poetry had a mystical bent. The good Imagist poem – Pound's 'In a Station of the Metro' for instance – is, as Andrew Welsh says in *The Roots of Lyric*, 'not simply a pictorial description but a discovery, a way of seeing that leads to a new way of knowing'.[6] For Pound, the Image was 'the word beyond formulated language'. The Objectivist poetry that developed from Imagism was, no less than Wordsworth's, essentially a poetry of 'relational consciousness'. This, in the words of David Hay in *Something There: The Biology of the Human Spirit*, 'is experienced as drawing us into closer contact with the reality of our environment. It is the reverse of alienation. Spiritual insight shows us directly at the profoundest level that we are not isolated but deeply and inextricably continuous with manifold reality.'[7] Discovering the poetry of George Oppen and other Objectivists in the 1970s increased my dissatisfaction with the limits of both the 'confessional' mode and the idea of reality that the dominant strain of post-war English poetry had settled for. At the same time, it took me back to a powerful impetus within the English tradition, represented supremely by Coleridge in the words that I use as an epigraph.

Modern Western culture is sometimes described in ugly terms as 'personalitied'. In the sense intended, 'personalities' are conventional: commodities constructed out of stereotypes. D. H. Lawrence's words about the novelist's necessary sensitivity to change are salutary in this situation, and apply especially to the lyric poet:

> In all this change, I maintain a certain integrity. But woe betide me if I try to put my finger on it. If I say of myself, I am this, I am that! – then, if I stick to it, I turn into a stupid fixed thing like a lamp-post. I shall never know wherein lies my integrity, my individuality, my me. I *can* never know it. It is useless to talk about my ego. That only means that I have made up an *idea* of myself, and that I am trying to cut myself out to pattern.[8]

We hear a great deal nowadays of the desirability of 'accessible' poetry. Accessibility is a virtue, in satire, for example, or in verse marking public events or key moments in human lives. In my view, inaccessibility is not a virtue! The danger in insisting that poetry be accessible, however, is that the resulting poetry expresses only the stereotype and produces a verse that tells us what we already know, as opposed to taking us out of ourselves or deeper in, to a further sense of reality. It isn't necessarily by the 'I' that we know the world, or our inner being. The 'I' can be the very skin we need to shed. It can be imprisoning, suffocating, deadening. It can make the poem static – a stage for dramatizing past experience, a narrow ego-space pinched out of life. Lyric poetry as a way of seeing should reach beyond both 'I' and eye. As Wordsworth said, realizing a truth of all times and places, it should see into the life of things. Learning to speak as 'the stranger-in-oneself' is difficult. The hope is that, when achieved, it speaks to the inner life in others.

'Painting is self-discovery. Every good artist paints what he is.' Jackson Pollock's words[9] are true of every good lyric poet, too. This needn't mean a callow existentialism that isolates the poet as an autonomous self. The *what* includes all the poet is part of. It descends into Being, the poet's sense of *what is*. Language is implicated in every aspect of this. We know a poet by his or her words, by uses of language that convey a particular sense of existence. This includes an apprehension of language itself, of its capacities and limits, and ultimately of its relation to the silence that underlies everything.

A lyric poem springs from personal feeling – what other kind is there? – but fails if its subject is a sense of finished self, the illusion of self as a closed entity. This is the danger of an obsession with personality, and accessibility, and the idea of recreating experience, as distinct from openness to the whole 'make' of the person, existence in relation to all one is part of – nature, history, culture, matter, and spirit.

From early on, in the poems in *Solent Shore*, written during the 1970s, I was aware of the temptation of nostalgia, and resisted it. The 'sludge of nostalgia', as I called it, was a form of fixity, both self and world stuck in a former state, with the illusion of permanence. My resistance was to the Edenic myth, to dwelling on an idea or image of some former condition, felt to be complete, which one can only yearn for. A world without the complications of adult life, outside the relationships by which one lives. Nostalgia, thus understood, denies the fluidity of existence and makes a fixed idea of the self, like Lawrence's lamp-post. The backward-looking stance is perhaps especially a temptation for poets brought up in a post-imperial nation, with a culture prone to a good deal of morbid retrospection.

I was particularly aware of the temptation in writing poems that returned to my original home ground, and above all in 'Saltgrass Lane', a poem drawing on memory. This meant going back imaginatively to a place associated with some of my past experiences; but the challenge was to return in the reality of my present condition – not just older, but with a disability that prevents the active life – walking, in particular – from which, as a poet, I have drawn so much. The last thing I wanted was maudlin reminiscence, or to write a familiar poetry of loss. Instead of merely recreating past scenes, I wanted to see and think anew, as the older, disabled man I now am, with the 'things' of that liminal place – things including the powers that drive existence.

Having written 'Saltgrass Lane', I came upon the lines in *Paterson* in which William Carlos Williams speaks of memory as 'a sort of renewal', 'an initiation, since the spaces it opens are new places'.[10] This was exactly what I needed: the idea of the poem creating a 'new place'. Memory provides materials with which the lyric 'I' works, but as a relational self, discovering itself through the things of which it is made. It awakens to 'the stranger-in-oneself', to an enlarged sense of being in relation to the world known anew. The process is one of unlearning habits of seeing and conceiving. By contrast, a poetry of known self, of assumed stable identity, possesses a fixed world, which shows us what we already know. Recognizing an idea of ourselves, together with a familiar model of reality, may move us. But we are not surprised into discovering anything new about the world, or about ourselves.

Notes

[1] Czeslaw Milosz, *Native Realm*, Penguin Books, 1988, p. 280.

[2] I came upon this in Susan Ireland's review of Mahmoud Darwish, *La Palestine comme metaphore*, in *Modern Poetry in Translation*, No. 14, 1999, p. 217.

[3] Letter to George and Thomas Keats, 22 December 1817.

[4] Jones, *The Anathemata*, p. 10.

[5] Jacques Maritain, *Creative Intuition in Art and Poetry*, Harvill Press, 1954, pp. 120–1.

[6] Andrew Welsh, *Roots of Lyric*, Princeton University Press, 1978, p. 69.

[7] David Hay, *Something There: The Biology of the Human Spirit*, Darton, Longman & Todd, 2006, p. 180.

[8] D. H. Lawrence, 'Why the Novel Matters', in *Selected Literary Criticism*, ed. Anthony Beal, Viking Press, 1956, p. 106.

[9] Quoted from a late interview in, for example, Ellen G. Landau, *Jackson Pollock*, Thames & Hudson, 1989, p. 119.

[10] William Carlos Williams, *Paterson*, New Directions, 1963, p. 77.

Revisiting 'God's Houses'

In my writing and thinking in recent years I have become increasingly concerned with a sense of the sacred, and how it can be expressed in a language imbued with the values of a secular culture. In a feature for radio, *Daring the Depths*, and in a number of essays, I have studied this subject in the work of other poets. At the same time, I have addressed the question in my own poetry, especially in *Scattered Light* (2015), which includes the sequence of seventeen poems called 'God's Houses'. Here, I wish to discuss the spirit of this sequence and to place it within the larger context of my work. I begin with three quotations from the book. The first quotation is from the opening poem, 'Brother Worm', which celebrates Charles Darwin. The poem begins by likening Darwin's experience of an earthquake in Chile, which shook his ideas of security, to what an earthworm feels when it senses a bird or mole about to strike. The second part of the poem focuses upon Darwin's study of earthworms and ends with a tribute to both Darwin and these creatures:

> Such are the powers
> beneath notice, one
> observed that steadies
> the observer, makes possible
> also the unsteady world
> in which he moves,
> breathing through the skin.

Darwin was a prime exemplar of what I call 'art of seeing'. He shared observation of 'powers beneath notice', the least regarded manifestations of life, with other naturalists, with British poets in the tradition of *Lyrical Ballads*, and with American Transcendentalists and Objectivists. A Franciscan spirit in these writers makes at first surprising connections. Both Thomas Hardy and William Carlos Williams have been thought of as 'Franciscan' poets, a designation that refers especially to the quality of tenderness in their observation of generally little regarded human and non-human phenomena.

The second quotation is from 'Like Thistledown', which begins,

> As a word surprises you
> sprung from the language net
> drifting across the mind
>
> you don't know where it came from
> you don't know what will come of it
>
> but there it is

Poetry as I practise it has no pre-planned or didactic intent. Words spring surprisingly from 'the language net' and the mind follows their drift. The process is exploratory, not random: words belong to the language; they are not a poet's private possession although for each poet they express his or her spirit.

The third quotation is from the last part of 'An Unfinished Portrait', a poem in memory of my friend Gerard Casey, who was a poet and a great religious thinker:

> He would quote Boehme,
> 'the great deeps of this world'.
>
> In the light of unknowing
> every possible end is a beginning,
> every image is a rock to break open
> in search of the mica sparkle
> which at once dulls, if found.

As these lines imply, my poems honour the modernist discipline of Imagism but resist its limitations. Images are provisional; they are for making and breaking: 'the mica sparkle' of ultimate reality is unknowable. 'The great deeps of this world' may be sensed but not fathomed.

I have chosen to begin with these quotations because they point to a particular 'art of seeing', to the poem as an adventure in language that surprises the poet, and to 'the light of unknowing'. They may serve as a rough guide to *Scattered Light* and the sequence 'God's Houses'.

'One is trying to make a shape out of the very things of which one is oneself made.'[1] These words of David Jones's preface to *The Anathemata* have become talismanic for me. I interpret them as a credo for an exploratory poetry, since 'the very things' are not simply given, but must be discovered through the process of writing. Earlier I would have identified the things with 'place' conceived in terms of all its formative elements, both material and cultural. Later I would call this 'ground', a word that still refers to the formative elements of place, but now asks fundamental spiritual questions, shadowed by 'Ground of Being'. The shift from 'place' to 'ground' marks a deepening of my preoccupation with the basically religious question of the foundations of ultimate value, of what we can hold sacred in a secular culture.

I have written poetry from my youth. From the first, my mother had introduced me to English poems in the lyrical and dramatic modes, from Shakespeare to Tennyson. Even before I could read, poetry moved and excited me. My mature work, which began in my mid-twenties, owes a great deal to my life in Wales, which introduced me to a society, a culture, and landscapes that were quite different from my original home ground in the south of England. At the same time, Wales enabled me to see where I had come from with special intensity, and with the emotion of hiraeth. Many of my poems are located either in Wales or in the area of southern England situated between the New Forest and the coast.

I have come to think of lyric poetry as a poetry of being that works through suggestion. The eleventh-century Wei T'ai expressed this beautifully:

> Poetry presents the thing in order to convey the feeling. It should be precise about the thing and reticent about the feeling, for as soon as the mind responds and connects with the thing the feeling shows in the words; this is how poetry enters deeply into us.[2]

A poet true to the modernist root in Imagism might have written these words.

Here, again, the emphasis falls upon 'things'. Seeing things in nature began for me as a boy and was influenced by reading the poet-naturalist Richard Jefferies' essays and *Wild Life in a Southern County*. This was followed by reading other writers from my home region: Thomas Hardy, Edward Thomas, and, later, the Powys brothers. Love of nature and of these writers has never left me. With these influences, and the freedom of country in which the spirit of Jefferies and Thomas could still be felt, it was only in growing up that I became conscious of living in different, radically changed times. I read T. S. Eliot and Ezra Pound and other modern writers and felt the necessity for a poet to 'make it new'. My earliest memories are of the Second World War, and as a youth I became intensely aware of the Cold War and the threat of nuclear annihilation. I captured the feeling in 'And Shall the Spring Be Desolate?', a poem that I published in the school magazine, which ends with the lines:

> Oh, shall life be a blackened husk
> ere the ears were ripe?
> And shall the cuckoo call no more?
> And shall the spring be desolate?
> Oh! Shall the spring be desolate?

It seemed to me that the idea of light itself changed on 6 August 1945 with the dropping of the first atom bomb. Henceforth all things loved and known would shine with preternatural clarity, framed against the blinding light and the darkness that followed it.

Awareness of living in the nuclear age affected my sense of both things and language. The naming or metaphorical expression of things demanded special care lest words become agents of the destructive milieu. Had I known them then, some words from Wordsworth's 'Essay on Epitaphs' would have spoken to me forcefully:

> Words are too awful an instrument for good and evil, to be trifled with; they hold above all other external powers a do-

minion over thoughts ... Language, if it do not uphold, and feed, and leave in quiet, like the power of gravitation or the air we breathe, is a counter-spirit, unremittingly and noiselessly at work, to subvert, to lay waste, to vitiate, and to dissolve.

Language according to this understanding is a spiritual power that resists powers of dissolution.

In the 1970s I encountered the poetry of George Oppen and other American Objectivists and their 'poetics of resistance', which Burton Hatlen describes thus:

Resistance against centralizing cultural hegemonies, against the financial and media oligarchies that were and are steadily consolidating their control over our lives, against the pressure of a language that lulls the reader into a comfortable or despairing acquiescence to these powers.[3]

The American poets with their moral witness confirmed my sense of the importance of subject, of respect in naming the reality of things. Oppen's emphasis upon the importance of the substantive, of naming what we are actually talking about, the things we value, spoke to me powerfully. It represents care, a quality of attention that resists vagueness and abstraction, which serve manipulative political forces. This accorded with my experience in Wales as I became more deeply involved with Welsh poets, in both languages, who are voices of resistance to the powers, including Anglicization, hostile to the survival of their culture.

From the late 1960s into the 1970s I was discovering in modern American and Welsh poetry, the latter unfortunately only in translation, a seriousness about living in the nuclear age and a value placed upon community which spoke to me. In Waldo Williams for instance, and in Gwenallt's 'Rhydcymerau',[4] with its image of saplings planted in his rural Welsh homeland 'to be trees of the third war', I met a poetry that took the measure of the times as I felt little in contemporary English poetry did. Charles Olson's 'All's now is war', as Stephen Fredman observes, announces that 'everything has changed ... what it means to be a human being is something new and newly terrifying'.[5] In this situation, 'Oppen and Olson began to write a new poetry'. In 'World, World –', George Oppen wrote,

> The self is no mystery, the mystery is
> That there is something for us to stand on.[6]

I interpret this to refer to a democratic grounding, and read it as an affirmation of our common humanity. It also means that we stand in the presence of mystery – a mystery that is 'Other', which the poet regards with awe. Oppen, the Marxist, shared with fellow Jewish Objectivists the sense 'that the world is not only real but also Other – and inherently numinous'.[7]

From early days, I have been conscious that life is sacred. This may be understood as what Paul Evans calls 'an ordinary, vernacular kind of sacred', a 'knowing of how Nature matters ... a recognition of a sacredness in Nature which is indifferent to us'. It is 'a feeling' that 'comes from love'.[8] My sense of the sacred was also bound up with religion. In the 1940s and 1950s it was a matter of course for most village children to attend Sunday school and church on Sunday. I record what the experience meant to me in 'St Mark's, Pennington', which ends with the lines:

> But it was there solemnity claimed me.
>
> Shining brass plaques with heroic names.
> Language rolling among the pews
>
> like sea in a cave, and above all
> my father singing,
> his voice raised above all the rest.

In our village church, where I first heard 'language rolling among the pews', I found things to love and things to respect: the building itself, which was an important part of the place where I belonged; the memory of 'heroic names'; poetic words; and song. Later, in part through the church, I also found something to resist. 'Churchiness', as Thomas Hardy called it, is an element in modern British poetry.

Often it takes an elegiac form, and it is prone to nostalgia. One thinks of poems by John Betjeman and Philip Larkin, and Hardy himself, for whom the village graveyard was a place of 'friends beyond' and an extension of the living community. As a boy, I was attracted to the morbid lyricism of poems such as Southey's 'After Blenheim' and Tennyson's 'Break, Break, Break', and of the prayer with which our vicar concluded Evensong:

> O Lord, support us all the day long of this troublous life until the shades lengthen, and the evening comes, the busy world is hushed, the fever of life is over, and our work done. Then, Lord, in Thy mercy, grant us a safe lodging, and a holy rest, and peace at the last. Amen.

The words chimed in my mind with my favourite hymn, Isaac Watts's 'Our God, Our Help':

> Time, like an ever-rolling stream,
>   Bears all its sons away;
> They fly forgotten, as a dream
>   Dies at the opening day.

We believed the prayer was medieval, composed by a monk at nearby Beaulieu Abbey. In fact it was by Cardinal Newman. Both prayer and hymn breathed what I would come to think an insidious air, offering a deathly sort of 'peace'. This toxic emotional atmosphere fed into my sense of the past and encouraged the feeling that Christianity is *only* historical, as in Larkin's 'Church Going', in which the church is 'a serious house on serious earth': a building 'which, he once heard, was proper to grow wise in,/If only that so many dead lie round'.[9]

Philip Larkin has been the master of many English poets of his generation and mine. I am moved by his lyricism, but resist the retrospective emotion and end-stopped thinking of a poem such as 'Church Going', which is dead to the existential challenge of Christianity. Geoffrey Hill has spoken of 'the floating of nostalgia: there's been an elegiac tinge to the air of this country ever since the end of the Great War'.[10] I have long felt the truth of this, and in an early poem wrote of 'the sludge of nostalgia'. It constantly threatens to drag me back, like boots stuck in the mud. Feeling and resisting it set up a tension in 'God's Houses', but also provided an energy. The churchgoer in these poems is not just a visitor. He is one of the people invoked at the end of 'Cathedral' who 'come with questions they seek to answer.//Questions that are themselves'.

R. S. Thomas was not a church visitor; he was an incumbent, often on his knees, a priest for whom the presence (or present absence) of God was central. We see in his poems how the question of God involves the validity of religious language, and the survival of sacred poetry in a post-Christian culture. I respond keenly to Thomas and the dilemma he confronted. At the same time, my admiration of his poetry is touched by a sense of every poet's inevitable limitations:

> Lord, forgive
> your poets their pride.
> Even the greatest,
> the man on the stone beach,
> is a frail craft,
> a stuttering probe,
> an obstructed channel
> giving shape to a drop
> of the life that made him.
>
> ('Eglwys Hywyn Sant, Aberdaron')

The poem ends affirmatively, envisaging visitors to Thomas's former church at Aberdaron as 'pilgrims' who 'will imagine him/committing his prayers/to the airways and the waters,/probing the darkness/that is now, because of him, more nearly their own'.

I share the painter David Tress's love of ancient churches, which he sees as 'literal, physical embodiments of a relationship between the spiritual, the people that lived there, and the land around them, over a long, long time'.[11] 'God's Houses' arose in part from a similar feeling. Like Tress, I approach the subject anxious to avoid spiritual voyeurism, and with a sense of history, of the age-old relationship between worshippers, the building, and the land.

My family descends on both sides from generations of agricultural labourers, from whom I have inherited a feeling for the land which is inseparable from work on the land: toil, but also rural crafts, building, and the arts of medieval masons, painters, and sculptors – worshippers who also made and adorned the churches in which they worshipped. The first poem in the 'God's Houses' sequence, 'St Faith's, Little Witchingham', celebrates a Norfolk church known for its fourteenth-century wall paintings. Decommissioned, the church is an empty shell, in which the painter's work, interrupted by the Black Death, is fragmentary, but intensely dramatic, alive:

> a man's leg twisted violently
> as he braces himself to deliver the scourge,
> a ladder, placed as it might be
> against a house wall to bring down the body from the cross.

The painter lives in his work; the Christian story is alive in its telling. What, then, is 'finished'? Here, it can be said, 'Nothing is missing /though so much has gone'.

'Kilpeck' brings together the church with its famous Romanesque carvings and the historical, 'border' landscape in which it was built. The Normans made this area a site of slavery. It was where two kinds of making and two kinds of mastery interacted:

> All praise to the master
> with strength and delicacy in his hands
> imagination at the tips of sense
>
> knower of man and woman
> falcon and deer, fish dog and boar
>
> God's creatures, his inventions ...
> ...
> Falcon and deer, fish dog and boar
> creatures of the chase,
> quarry of lords

who harried this land,
masterful men
who grasped creation in their hands.

The sculptor (or sculptors) depended upon the lord's power, but his work represents a different order of creation. The building in its landscape holds the tension between related but ultimately opposing powers. The poem thus observes, implicitly, the question, posed by Coleridge and others, that is central to the Christian idea of the imagination: what is the relation between human creativity and God's Creation? 'God's creatures, his inventions' implies the question, but does not presume to answer it. This is a place of tense interrelated powers. The figure of the maker – mason, sculptor, painter, poet – belongs to the church and depends upon the Christian claim that the church represents. Kilpeck is in 'border country', in more than a geographical sense. This is the 'location' of which David Jones spoke:

> man is a 'borderer', he is the sole inhabitant of a tract of country where matter marches with spirit, so that whatever he does, good or bad, affects the economy of those two domains.[12]

'Kilpeck' describes a 'border' embroiled in conflict.

The act of making and the figure of the maker are central to 'God's Houses'. They are themes involving ideas of self and memory, which I explore through personal experience. 'Boldre Church Revisited' draws explicitly on childhood and later experience. It begins with painters, my father and his cousin, outside the church committing their visions of the building to canvas. The interior contains remembrance of a tragic and violent history: the sinking of HMS *Hood* in May 1941 with the loss of 1415 men. At a different level, the church holds childhood memories for me. Memory, though, is untrustworthy:

Reminiscence tempts –
a recital of decomposed memory
sprouting half-truths,

ways of the little self,
a bubble of identity,
the whole river
that powers on, forgotten.

It is life to which the self belongs, life 'that powers on', the creative force flowing from the past through the present and into the future, not just bearing all its sons away. Churches are not, or should not be, museums. 'Cathedral' carries an epigraph from the twentieth-century Russian religious thinker Nicolas Berdyaev, who wrote in *The Divine and the Human* (1949),

> The greatest error of historical Christianity is linked with the fatally limiting idea that the revelation is finished, and that nothing more is to be expected, that the building of the Church is completed and the roof laid on it.[13]

Ancient churches in the landscape look as though they belong entirely to the past, roofs laid on long ago, so that not only the building is 'finished', but also what it represents. Churches originally stood for the eternal entering time. If we respond to the claim they made we are challenged with an ever-new sense of possibility. Churches address us with questions about the nature of reality and the meaning of human life. Berdyaev's meaning, as I understand it, is not impossibly remote from the quotation from Richard Jefferies that I use as epigraph to 'Salisbury Cathedral: The Bust of Richard Jefferies': 'I look at the sunshine and feel that there is no contracted order: there is divine chaos, and in it, limitless hope and possibilities.'

'Brother Worm' celebrates Darwin in Franciscan mode. Jefferies was another who perceived in nature 'powers beneath notice', on which life depends. I learned from Jefferies at an early age to see the mystery and magic of common things that are easily overlooked, such as the rushes he describes in 'The Pageant of Summer'. It is a way of seeing 'Wild England', 'in ditch and field corner', that I call 'ditch vision'.

Jefferies was an iconoclast, who broke down all forms of knowledge to reveal the real mystery of life:

as I felt the wind blowing
through his words,
breaking images,
leaving knowledge
a heap of ruins, driving me
back from the known.

('Salisbury Cathedral: The Bust of Richard Jefferies')

The sense of wonder that Jefferies first articulated for me was a way of *unlearning*: a form of defamiliarization, not so much 'making strange' as *seeing* the being of things as a mystery we can sense but never wholly know. I think this 'unlearning', through which he perceived the divine, 'and, in it, limitless hope and possibilities', is not entirely incompatible with an apophatic theology.

Churches are to me places of powerful cross-currents – pun intended – where matter and spirit, life and death, historical time and the timeless, come into tension and seek reconciliation. The buildings have a resonance that comes from ages of prayer and worship, humble need and spiritual illumination. They are at once products of human making and channels of complex spiritual and imaginative energy. I think of myself, metaphorically speaking, standing in the doorway, drawn towards the altar, while feeling the pull of the natural world outside.

For me, the poem is a fluid form, which explores, but can never fully express, the mystery of being. I have described poetry as 'an art of seeing, an art by which, in my blindness, I learn to see'.[14] This implies that, beginning a poem, I don't know where it will go or how it will end, let alone whether it will work! An idea of 'open field' poetics attracts me – a poetry open to process and resistant to closure. If the result is a real poem I shall learn something from it. 'St Bride's, Llansantffraed' was a prime example of this. 'Two stone heads' are all that remain of the church building in which Henry and Thomas Vaughan worshipped, yet for them, in Thomas's words, the world was 'God's building', 'full of Spirit, quick and living'. Henry Vaughan's grave in the churchyard draws visitors, but in what sense is the material place 'sacred'?

> This, though, is not a place of memory.
> Light tracks the Brecon Beacons,
> lies in pewter pools
> or flashes silver, sudden
> blinding falls along the Usk.
>
> The very air is quicker for his breath.

These are the last lines of 'St Bride's, Llansantffraed', and of the sequence 'God's Houses', as it appears in *Scattered Light*. 'Spirit' and 'quick' are keywords in the poem, the latter echoing Henry Vaughan's great poem, 'Quickness':

> But life is, what none can express,
> *A quickness, which my God hath kissed.*[15]

I cannot claim faith such as Henry Vaughan shared with his brother, but, reading my poem inspired by their words, I saw that it was a confession of faith, at least, as far as poetry was concerned. For me, too, life is sacred. There is a 'sacredness in nature', and, both in this sense and in the ground of our spiritual being, 'life' exists beyond our capability to wholly express it. I had said what I believe but did not know I was so sure of: that a sacred poet, like Henry Vaughan, inspires us with spiritual life. The church at Llansantffraed, with old stones remembering the building Henry and Thomas Vaughan knew, is a site of 'dust and clay'. But it is not just 'a place of memory'; it is where

> The very air is quicker for his breath.

In this last line of 'God's Houses' I recognize a truth that I discovered in the process of writing the sequence, or, to speak both literally and metaphorically, of opening the doors of ancient buildings that, for me, remain open, and which I shall revisit.

Notes

[1] Jones, *The Anathemata*, p. 10
[2] Quoted by A. C. Graham as epigraph to *Poems of the Late T'Ang*, Penguin Books, 1965.
[3] Burton Hatlen, 'A Poetics of Marginality and Resistance: The Objectivist Poets in Context', in *The Objectivist Nexus: Essays in Cultural Poetics*, ed. Rachel Blau DuPlessis and Peter Quartermain, University of Alabama Press, 1999, p. 48.
[4] In Anthony Conran (ed.), *The Penguin Book of Welsh Verse*, 1967, pp. 254–5.
[5] Stephen Fredman, '"And All Now Is War": George Oppen, Charles Olson, and the Problem of Literary Generations', in *The Objectivist Nexus*, p. 291. Fredman is quoting Olson's 'The Kingfishers'.
[6] George Oppen, *New Collected Poems*, ed. Michael Davidson, New Directions, 2002, p. 159.
[7] Hatlen, 'A Poetics of Marginality and Resistance', p. 45.
[8] Paul Evans, *Field Notes From The Edge*, Rider, 2015, pp. 9–10.
[9] Philip Larkin, *Collected Poems*, Faber & Faber, 1988, p. 98.
[10] Geoffrey Hill, 'Conversation with John Haffenden', in *Viewpoints: Poets in Conversation with John Haffenden*, ed. John Haffenden, Faber & Faber, 1981, p. 93.
[11] Interview with David Tress, in Andrew Lambirth, *David Tress*, Studio, 2015, p. 204.
[12] David Jones, *Epoch and Artist*, Faber & Faber, 1959, p. 86.
[13] This is a variant translation from Berdyaev, *The Divine and the Human*, p. 183.
[14] Hooker and Grandjean, *Their Silence a Language*, p. 75.
[15] Emphasis in the original.

Mystery at the Heart of Things:
An Interview with Jeremy Hooker

Fiona Owen

1. Let's begin by considering where, when, and how your affinity with landscape began. Perhaps, too, you could tell us a little about how you began to write and what you feel you were doing in those early experiments.

Well, Fiona, to begin at the beginning (but what is the beginning?) … When I was a boy, eleven or twelve years of age, I wrote atmospheric nature sketches, responding to the seasons and the wildlife I saw about me. These reflected the activities I loved, such as fishing and watching birds and exploring the fields and commons and hopelessly chasing rabbits with a dog. And they were influenced by Richard Jefferies, by essays in the selection *Jefferies' England*, which my parents owned. On reflection much later, it seemed to me that I first really saw the life in things, in trees for example, at the same time that I was responding to Jefferies' evocative prose. I suppose it had something to do with puberty too, coming awake to being alive in the world!

As one gets older, I find, the 'beginning' becomes harder to pin down. With time, I have learned how much I owe to my parents and, through them, to ancestors. My father began working life – he was then not much more than a boy – as a gardener, following his father, who was head gardener at different times on a number of large estates. Much later, my father became Horticultural Advisory Officer in the New Forest area, but he remained lifelong a wonderful gardener. He was also a passionate and accomplished landscape painter. My mother also came from an agricultural background – her father began by working as a boy on the land in Wiltshire and Hampshire, scaring crows from cornfields – and she too loved gardening, and had a special interest in flowers and birds, as well as poetry. 'In the blood' is a strange expression, but I feel strongly that I received my love of nature from my parents, and that they connected me to a history of life on the land, to the experience of men and women for whom nature was an ever-present reality and represented hard toil as well as material and spiritual sustenance.

I don't claim that I realized this all at once. Awareness has grown with time, and both in periods when I have suffered the consequences of being out of touch with nature, and from writing, from that making 'a shape out of the very things of which one is oneself made', that is also a process of discovery. I was rarely not writing, or trying to write, something after those early nature sketches, but I wrote what I feel were my first real poems in my twenties, and, with increasing confidence, in my late twenties and early thirties. By then I was teaching English literature in a university and living in rural mid-west Wales. Here I had the dual experience of both responding to the strangeness (to me) of Welsh landscape and culture and seeing my native country in the south of England with a new eye.

It was both in and out of books that I first 'discovered' nature, and so it will always be. One of the things I have always dwelt on as a teacher is the 'place' of nature in literary works, not nature as 'background' only, but as integral to the writer's shaping vision of the non-human and human world.

In my first book of poems, *Soliloquies of a Chalk Giant*, in 1974 I was thinking of my subject as a 'ground'. This meant the total environment of the Cerne Abbas Giant: the geology and natural history of the chalk landscape, the long human occupation of southern chalklands, as well as the mythology and history (much of it speculative) of the figure. Study of these things is a conscious process, but I had come to think of poetry too as a channelling of energies. It is to me an 'art of seeing', but also a way of working in the dark. Ground is something I seek to see in its totality, but it also involves seeking connection with energies beyond consciousness, with the life one is part of and cannot see. I thought of *Soliloquies* as constituting a sequence or network of poems – something like a whole ecology! It is how, in the main, I have thought of my work as a poet ever since.

2. *You speak of waking up to 'the life in things' through both contact with living nature and through the written word (e.g. the 'evocative prose' of Richard Jefferies). Would you like to say more about the way the written word has deepened your experience of the natural world? Do you find any affinity with, for example, Snyder's view of language as a 'wild system' that unites us with, rather than separates us from, the natural world?*

From early on, I was fascinated by the presence of nature in Thomas Hardy's novels, where it inspires a sense of awe, but also, according to Hardy's Darwinian perspective, contributes to tragic outcomes. I am equally interested in conceptions of nature in Romantic and modern literature, and the differences between ideas of nature in British and American poetry. I acknowledge in particular the influence on my own writing of the 'art of seeing' which we find in, for example, the journals of Dorothy Wordsworth, in Ruskin and Jefferies and Gerard Manley Hopkins, and also in Thoreau and William Carlos Williams. In my essay 'Ditch Vision', I argue that while Americans are fascinated by wilderness and what they call 'naked Nature', British writers have, for the most part, found the life of nature in hedges and ditches and field corners. Yet there are affinities as well as differences. Only the other day I learned from Linda Lear's biography of Rachel Carson that Jefferies was one of Carson's favourite writers and influenced her writings. In *Under the Sea-Wind*, for example, she draws on 'The Pageant of Summer' and Jefferies' description of how 'the whole office of Matter is to feed life'. As for Carson, science and poetry, and matter and spirit, are closely related in the kind of 'seeing' that I value most.

Diverse traditions and different literary forms – poetry, novel, journal, essay – come together in the writing that sustains me. And 'sustain' is the right word. At one time or another I have found different writers life-enhancing, quickening, as I did the Powys brothers during a period when my spirits were especially low. You also mention Gary Snyder. Over many years I've delighted in Snyder's poetry and prose. It's also been, for me, work that marks the differences between the sense of possibility in America and Britain. It isn't only, as I've already indicated, that the scope of the 'wild' is larger in America. 'The American Indian', Snyder says, 'is the vengeful ghost lurking in the back of the troubled American mind.'[1] If we in Britain have a 'vengeful ghost' haunting the land it's likely to be the agricultural labourer. Some American ecocritics (Max Oelschlaeger for instance) speak admiringly of 'the Palaeolithic mind' and disparage 'the Neolithic revolution', the advent of settled farming which displaced hunter-gatherer culture. This, it seems to me, is something a British writer could never do. Our debt to those who have shaped our landscapes is too great, and they are an integral part of our living history. I can appreciate how an American writer may feel about the American Indian, but when we in Britain sense a presence in the landscape it will probably be what John Clare represents: both the history of toil and deprivation and the love of the local fields and commons and their wild-life. None of this means that I do not accept Snyder's sense of connection to the natural world. It means that in Britain the language connecting us to the natural world also carries a history to which, in a sense, we are bound.

3. You mention having 'suffered the consequences of being out of touch with nature, and from writing'. Would you be prepared to develop this a little more fully? If you have read Richard Mabey's book Nature Cure *you will know that he writes about his 'disconnection' from self/nature and his subsequent 'return' in which what reoriented him was the act of writing. Would you share his view that language and imagination, 'far from alienating us from nature' are 'our most powerful and natural tools for re-engaging with it'?*

I've yet to read Richard Mabey's *Nature Cure*. I can certainly say, however, that a sense of reconnection to nature, of coming back into touch, has been deeply restorative to me at certain periods of my life. From boyhood I experienced recurrent bouts of depression and acute anxiety, times of solipsistic self-entrapment and mental stasis, release from which, when it came, was like coming back to life. Such experiences are no doubt one of the reasons why Wordsworthian poetry of relationship means so much to me, and why I value Martin Buber's philosophy of 'I and Thou', with its belief that

'All real living is meeting', so highly. To give one example: in the late summer and early autumn of 1969 I was able, with my first wife, to spend several weeks living in Dorset, in a village not far from Hambledon Hill. At the time, I was ill in the way mentioned above – frozen in a state of depression and anxiety. The hill drew me out of myself; I wanted to climb it at all hours. This was a health-giving activity in any case, but one day, lying down on the grassy summit, I looked down at a wheatfield, which suddenly seemed to 'unfreeze', and appeared to me like a weir of gold. The earth moved! But, of course, it always does: mental stasis and self-enclosure is a wretched human condition; we are always connected with our bodily rhythms and our language to the great rhythmic life of nature. I think a lot of my poetry has occurred in the space 'between', when I recognize, as I did in the wheatfield, the greater world beyond me, which, in some sense, I'm part of.

4. How to do you feel your experience of living in Wales has helped to shape your poetry?

Coming to live in Wales in 1965 was for me a culture shock. I had no idea that a whole other culture rooted in another language existed within a two-hour drive from the English border. The idea of poetry I brought with me was emotional, coloured by Beat generation romanticism, but drawing also on traditional English lyricism. Reading modern Welsh poetry in translation, at that time especially Tony Conran's translations from Gwenallt (who was then an impressive, familiar figure on the campus at Aberystwyth), I found a poetry engaged with the historical experience of a people. Gwenallt's involvement in the life of his people, flesh of their flesh, spirit of their spirit, was quite different from the English poetry of the 1930s I had studied and admired. It gave a new meaning to the imagination as agent of political and social experience. The newness, to me, of the modern Welsh poets expanded my sense of the possibility of poetry, and made me more aware of my own subject, which was larger than emotional states and states of mind.

'Poetry of place' became my preoccupation in the years after coming to live in Wales, both my native places in the south of England and the area in which I settled. This was also the period in which I discovered the work of David Jones and John Cowper Powys, which had a further liberating effect on my imagination. I came into contact also with writers of great integrity, such as Roland Mathias and Emyr Humphreys, who in different ways reflected the experience of their Welsh culture. The contrast in each instance was with the attitudes I had brought with me which defined the poet as an isolated individual concerned exclusively with his or her own experience. My subsequent detachment from the fashion for 'confessional' verse reflected my conviction that poetry could be drawn from deep within common human experience, from personal depths that are shared.

I spoke just now of having 'settled' in Wales. In one sense, I never settled, and my love of a particular area in Ceredigion was coloured always by my sense of being a stranger, even an intruder, in a country where my Welsh neighbours belonged. The experience made me more aware of my own Englishness and enhanced my awareness of native 'ground'. At the same time, it made me feel an alien presence where I was. In both respects, it was quickening, and helped to shape the poetry I wrote. I suppose I could say that knowing myself a stranger in Wales enhanced my sense of the strangeness in all things that is for me, first and last, the source of poetry.

5. You mentioned above, as elsewhere, your relationship with 'ground' as something you 'seek' – is this something both material and metaphysical or ontological in the 'total' sense of 'ground of being'? What also interests me is that, lately, you have 'become more conscious of a certain groundlessness'. I'd be very interested to hear more about the connotations of this shift in emphasis.

To revisit the subject of ground/groundlessness, I'm aware that, from the outset, growing up during and after the Second World War, there was an element of defensiveness – or protectiveness – in my primary attachments to people and place. My first landscape – the shore at Warsash, between the bombed towns of Southampton and Portsmouth – was unstable, with sea-eroded concrete paths and wartime flotsam. Like many people maturing in the 1950s and 1960s, I had an acute sense of the nuclear threat – against its shadow the things I loved and valued shone with a dazzling intensity. Out of this came a politics, passionate about post-war socialist reconstruction, and at the same time anti-centralist, hostile to the language and images of consumerist uniformity, and committed to the human and creative potential of the local and particular. The sense of 'ground', and therefore 'home', in my earlier poetry was shaped in part by the threat to essential human attachments.

This was enhanced by my experience of living in rural Wales, and by contact with Welsh nationalist cultural politics and the socialist communitarian tradition in Wales. As a critic, I have written about writing that I love, in order the better to understand it. And in Wales I found a cause in important writing neglected by the metropolitan and Oxbridge coteries that dominate literary life in England. My sense of 'ground' became connected to the belief that everywhere is a 'centre' – a belief reinforced by reading Welsh poets as well as by the thinking of William Carlos Williams and Patrick Kavanagh.

So much is a rehearsal, in general terms, of a personal history. From the beginning, my sensibility was, I suppose, religious, drawn to a sense of mystery at the heart of things. Language, I found, provoked questions, and answers led to new questions. Words were unstable, with shifting meanings, and no fixed foundations. With time this sense has increased, until it seems to me that in our time everything is in question – human relationships, the relationship between the human and the non-human, and between matter and spirit, sexual and personal identity, the very image of 'man'. This, I suppose, is what I mean by 'groundlessness', which is both abyssal and a source of imaginative possibility. It isn't only fear of sounding pretentious that makes me shy away from talking about it – poets shouldn't be afraid of ideas! It's rather that the experience – the very groundlessness – is a creative matrix. As in 'Seven Songs', it's the 'place' I start from, the area of exploration. I was aware of the theological meaning of 'Ground of Being', but ground/groundlessness came to mean all it has for me through this personal history, from the first sense of material reality to the radical question of who and what we are and what sustains us. Poetry is perhaps the only way in which I can speak of it.

6. *I notice that in 'Seven Songs' you seem to explore a more feminine personal/voice, 'characterized', as you write in the journal* Scintilla, *'by fluidity'. Is this an attempt to integrate masculine and feminine energies within the psyche? You speak in that article of 'imaginative energy' and 'a sense of wonder at the strangeness of existence'.*[2]

This returns us to the subject of identity. It's true that during the 1990s, when I was writing poems subsequently published in *Adamah*, I became interested in ideas of 'the androgynous mind', as expressed by Coleridge and Virginia Woolf, for example. This in turn reflected my desire to escape from narrow egoistic confines and from what I conceived as masculine forms of possessiveness and 'mastery'. I am aware of the risk in talking about 'masculine and feminine energies' that one will deal in gender stereotypes. I would argue that it is precisely such stereotypes that writers such as David Jones and John Cowper Powys transcend, with a corresponding enlargement of imaginative possibility. There are also, it seems to me, special qualities of intelligence in women's writing that arise in part from resistance to stereotypical gender models. I admire greatly the work of writers such as Dorothy Richardson and Lorine Niedecker, and the work of friends such as Anne Cluysenaar, Wendy Mulford, and Kim Taplin has inspired me. These are diverse writers indeed! What they may be said to have in common, however, are a sense of connection to a world beyond themselves, and the ability to draw upon natural and spiritual energies. And who wrote better about nature in the last century than Rachel Carson? Carson's 'sense of wonder' seems to me something every poet needs, whether man or woman. But let's beware of gender stereotypes. Who expresses tenderness – sometimes regarded as a feminine quality – more movingly than Thomas Hardy? It is connection to nature – to realms of matter and spirit – that releases us from narrow conceptions of individual and sexual identity. Are women naturally more prone to this because they are capable of carrying another life within them? I only know that some of the finest poetry of relationship in our time is by women poets.

7. *I have referred above to the journal* Scintilla *and, over the years, you have made many valuable contributions towards the study of poetry and the sacred. Do*

you want to say a little more about your 'sense of the sacred' and how this relates to poetry and nature?

Some years back, I made a radio programme, *Daring the Depths*, which discussed, partly through interviews with a number of poets, the problems of writing religious poetry in a largely secular society. Based on an earlier conference paper, this marked the beginning of my study of poetry and the sacred, which, in recent years, has been stimulated further by connection with *Scintilla* and other writers associated with it who share an interest in poetry in relation to science and religion. In *Scintilla*'s pages one finds a new nature poetry, which can be described, roughly, as exploring the connection between matter and spirit.

As far as my sense of the sacred is concerned, I had, from early on, an acute sense of reality as other, of the presence of individual beings and things, and of their unknowability. This is temperamental and probably helps as much as anything to account for the poetry I write. I felt a depth in the world around me, and experienced language as that which could partially illuminate it and point to what remained essentially mysterious. In time, I came to think of every image as provisional, and of poetry as both a making and breaking of images, in the approach to what the mind can never fully grasp, whether person, or bird, or tree. I repeat: this is not a philosophy or theology, but a way of experiencing the world and both the capabilities and limits of language. Both human beings and nature, I feel, are more than we can know. Are we part of nature? Certainly. Are we more? Possibly. But nature too is more than we can know.

I don't have a fixed position. My work, including the words I'm using now, is exploratory. Ruth Bidgood speaks, in her poem 'Little of Distinction', of 'the mystery that complements precision'.[3] Hence, perhaps, the paradox that a poet can value precision, clarity, concreteness, yet also espouse ways of unlearning, unknowing. In my own case, what I call 'ground' was initially the material world, in places that I knew and loved, and sought to know, as I said earlier, as a whole ecology. It retains this meaning for me, but has become, also, deeply mysterious – as we are, as nature is, whatever the laws science partially reveals. If this is naïve realism it isn't for want of reading Marx and Freud and Darwin (whom I greatly admire), or from ignorance of critical theory. I can't provide a watertight rational philosophy. I can only attempt to write poetry that is true to the spirit of this unknowing, yet seeing.

8. I very much appreciate your stress on poetry as exploratory. This opens up the sometimes closed concepts of 'nature' and 'human beings' – well, in a nutshell, 'life'. You have commented elsewhere that 'life is essentially metamorphic'. Is the role of poetry 'metamorphic' too?

I have in mind evolutionary theory – the idea of life itself as fundamentally 'metamorphic', in the sense that living forms evolve and dead matter feeds the continuing cycle. No doubt the word appeals to me because of the power over me of the sea and the seashore, and my awareness, from childhood, of the sea as moulder both of life forms and of geological formations such as the chalk. Given this awareness, my sense of language was metamorphic. Metaphor connects, and language is endlessly generative. As I try to tell my students when they become tongue-tied or unable to begin an essay, words breed words. Look, I have started this sentence and I don't know where it will lead!

We learn from language as well as with it. I have learned from my own poems, finding, after the event, that they have said something I was unaware of saying, or shown me something I hadn't seen before. Poetry can be exploratory because language is creative, leading us from one image to another, and from surfaces to depths. It can be used for surrealistic purposes, but its fluidity and malleability make it also our way to approach the real. Language changes historically and retains its history within it. It connects us to the living, but it relates us also to the dead. We repeat words, but because language is metamorphic we can say new things, too.

9. According to Laurence Coupe, for 'ecocritical' writers 'the point is not to merely speak about nature but also to speak for nature'. 'Speaking for nature' is thus, arguably, a political orientation, especially now that the natural world is so imperilled. Do you feel that you are in any way a political writer?

Politics? I'd invoke Keats's letter of 19 February 1818 to Reynolds in which he speaks of 'a grand democracy of Forest Trees'. I harbour ideas that are radical, ideas that are conservative, which have to do with patience, attentiveness, opposition to destructive forms of human mastery, including misuse of our power over nature. I value the particular, in persons and places; my criticism has been political in that I have sought recognition for the unjustly neglected, in opposition to the metropolitan 'centre'. Often, my aim as a teacher has been to encourage those who doubt themselves to have confidence in their voice and ideas. A poem says this person, this place, this thing matters. The 'political', as generally understood, seems to me to leave out a great deal of what concerns our common depths and what lies between us and the world around us.

10. In your autobiographical work Welsh Journal, *you say, 'It is what I have remembered and forgotten over and over again: neither self nor world exists separately; each is discovered in the other.' This view strikes me, in the context of your work, as utterly 'green' in orientation. It speaks of a symbiotic relationship where 'self' is fluid and not confined by boundaries that are arbitrarily defined. Does seeing the world as profoundly interconnected have implications for action – for example, adopting an attitude of care and taking pragmatic steps, as well as poetic ones, to save what is left of the non-human world? Or need this not necessarily follow?*

I think this follows from the question about politics. I accept that my belief in interrelationship is 'green'. It has several sources, the primary one of which is my need as a human being for relationship, and my recognition that, in the words of Jacques Maritain, used by George Oppen as an epigraph to *The Materials*, 'We awake in the same moment to ourselves and to things.' In a literary context, I could invoke Wordsworth. I found in the American Objectivists, and especially in Oppen, a profoundly sympathetic orientation. This echoes the communitarian spirit prevalent in Wales. It is to do with valuing each and every one: care of people, care of nature, care of words – a poet can't separate one from another. I live now virtually in sight of Aberfan and Senghenydd; the valleys are green again – how speak of such places without recognizing that human history and nature are inextricably bound up with one another? Whitman's spear of grass was a symbol of democracy. More even than Whitman knew, perhaps, we must now see that every actual spear of grass matters. The shadow of the atom bomb was a great equalizer. Everything that has happened since August 1945 should make us more aware of our common predicament, and that our responsibility to the natural world cannot be separated from our responsibility to one another, and vice versa.

11. As we draw towards the end of the interview, can I ask why you chose 'The Cut of the Light' as the title poem in your new book?

I chose *The Cut of the Light* as the title for my collection drawing on work done over forty years not because the poem of that name is the most central, but because the words connect the metaphor of light with the idea of shaping. The image has behind it a physical sensation – that of light seeming to strike through forest trees – but it refers also to the sculptural idea of cutting a form in wood or stone or some other material. It contains, then, a covert reference to my collaborations with the sculptor Lee Grandjean, which have been so important to me in recent years. More broadly, it refers to the shaping of images intended to reveal and illuminate. I like its sharpness! It suggests to me a shining edge.

12. Yes, I like it too. In The Song of the Earth, *Jonathan Bate ends his final chapter 'What Are Poets for?' with the following: 'if poetry is the original admission of dwelling, then poetry is the place where we save the earth'. For, according to Bate, poetry may be able to 'restore us to the earth, which is our home'.[4] I wonder if you share this view?*

I admire Jonathan Bate's book. It may be that, writing as a literary critic, he is able to be more forthright about certain things than I, speaking here as a poet, should be. One of the things that inhibits me in speaking about politics is the wish to avoid preaching. Another is the sense that poetry alone is not enough. I don't believe with W. H. Auden that poetry makes nothing happen. But can poetry be 'the place where we save the earth'? No individual poet could claim that of his or her poetry! To my mind it's a question of orientation. Jonathan Bate in that book is more Heideggarian than I am. However, I could agree that if all poets had treated their place as John Clare did his, the world wouldn't have needed saving. Except, of course, power politics would have rooted them out. Which brings us back to politics! But all I personally can do is try to take care of the ground given to me.

Notes

[1] Gary Snyder, 'Passage to More than India', in *Earth House Hold*, Jonathan Cape, 1970, p. 112.
[2] Jeremy Hooker, 'A Note on the "Groundwork Poems"', *Scintilla*, Vol. 2, 1998, p. 157.
[3] Ruth Bidgood, 'Little of Distinction', in *The Given Time*, Christopher Davies, 1972, p. 18.
[4] Jonathan Bate, *The Song of the Earth*, Picador, London, 2000.

Land and Sea and Sky

In some places, land and sea and sky form together a peculiar intimacy. This was the case in the two areas of the south coast where I was brought up. At Warsash the Hamble River flows into Southampton Water, which opens into the Solent, with the Isle of Wight beyond. On the southern edge of the New Forest the sea is close, and the chalk of West Wight and the Needles gestures across Christchurch Bay towards the Isle of Purbeck. Here, between the opposite ends of a broken geological bridge, the sea is contained, gathering the sky's many changing colours, which are also reflected in waves breaking on the shore.

The shingle formed a marginal world, which drew me from the first. It was a place that brought things together – pebbles and shells, corks, feathers, driftwood, dogfish egg sacs, dry bladderwrack with 'bubbles' that I loved to burst. Gleaming, pure white cuttlebones lay among globs of tar. The sound of small waves breaking mingled with the cries of black-headed gulls. A salt smell pervaded all.

It was a fascinating world, and, in wartime, a dangerous one. Attractive things the tide brought in, such as biscuit tins, might be booby-trapped. A marine's helmet bobbed up and down in the line of scum. Someone picked up a glove with the hand still in it. As the concrete sea wall was treacherously eroded, so Southampton was cratered with bombsites, with bits of bedroom walls, wallpaper hanging from them, leaning over pits of gravel and clay. My earliest memory was of being carried down into the dark, smelling damp earth and the utility blanket I was wrapped in, and hearing the whine of mosquitoes and the crump of distant bombs.

Sky and sea seemed close within the waterways and the sheltering Island. Sunderland flying-boats, drawing their graceful hulls overhead, brought sea and sky closer. But the drone of aircraft might mean enemy bombers. At night, among the fingering searchlights, a raider hit by gunfire fell like a flaming star.

The land too, when I first saw it, revealed its underside. Chalk cliffs at roadsides held, I was told, remnants of an earlier creation. There were fossil fish in the dark under the field. Barrows on the downs housed the crouching dead. What I also knew from early on, from the life-experience of forebears on both sides of the family, is that the land is a work vaster than the pyramids. The fields speak of the unknown labourer.

> No monument
> For time to smear;
> No statue
> That a man conceives
> To trap himself in stone.
>
> Only earth
> Where a night's rain
> Washed out his prints,
> Chalk where his life
> Was moulded;
> Fields like hands after work,
> Rough palms spread.

Sea and river were marked with stories of wrecks, some mythical, most true. Skeletal timbers half sunk in mud were said to be the remains of Viking longboats. The ghost of Henry V's *Grace Dieu*, greatest warship built in England at that time, was a shadowy presence in the mud above Bursledon Bridge. Boldre Church, secluded on a hill among oak trees in the New Forest, is charged with memories of HMS *Hood* and the ship's company that died with her. And in every house in some Southampton streets dreams and memories of family members lost in RMS *Titanic* continued long into the twentieth century.

Thomas Hardy heard a cold music in the loss of the great liner, as he imagined her lying on the floor of the Atlantic:

> Steel chambers, late the pyres
> Of her salamandrine fires,
> Cold currents thrid, and turn to rhythmic lyres.
>
> Over the mirrors meant
> To glass the opulent
> The sea-worm crawls – grotesque, slimed, dumb, indifferent.
> ('The Convergence of the Twain')

The poem betrays a romantic relish that islanders find hard to keep out of their poems about disasters at sea and that may affect their use of the sea as metaphor or symbol. One hears it in Matthew Arnold's evocation of waves bringing 'The eternal note of sadness in'. 'Dover Beach' was a poem I could never take quite in the spirit in which it was intended, largely because I love shingle, both the thing and the word. To me there is something exhilarating, rather than drear, about the 'naked shingles of the world'.

There is, though, a spirit of melancholy in the great poetry of my native region, which I learnt to love as a boy. It's present in Thomas Hardy, and in Isaac Watts:

> Time, like an ever-rolling stream
>   Bears all its sons away;
> They flie forgotten, as a dream
>   Dies at the opening day.

All my life, Watts's water of time, which bears all its sons away, has clashed in my mind with the phenomenon of living water, which forms a channel connecting the quick and the dead, and flows out into the world, restoring and making new. But our greatest poet was the most melancholy: Tennyson, whose memorial on the downs at West Wight can be seen from the mainland. As a boy, I loved, as I still do, his 'Crossing the Bar'. When I was a student, working one summer as a deckhand on the Lymington to Yarmouth ferry, the sight of the evening star, as we crept back across the Solent and up the Lymington River on the last crossing of the day, would have me repeating the poem to myself:

> Sunset and evening star,
>   And one clear call for me!
> And may there be no moaning of the bar,
>   When I put out to sea,
>
> But such a tide as moving seems asleep,
>   Too full for sound and foam,
> When that which drew from out the boundless deep
>   Turns again home.

'Crossing the Bar' is a poem of Christian hope. But it carries in verbal music and image, like a horn moaning in fog, a peculiarly Victorian melancholy, which virtually rhymes the word 'home' with death. Much of our English sea poetry from 'The Seafarer' to Shakespeare and later deals with shipwreck and the elemental cold. But it has, too, a resilience, which is lost in Victorian melancholy and the morbid spirit of a post-imperial, shrinking island. Growing up, I felt the melancholy in my bones and was drawn to resist it. When in the 1970s, in my collection *Solent Shore*, I came to write a poetry of my home ground, I was aware of powerful crosscurrents. I felt the pressure of the past in conflict with the desire for newness. One night, fishing off the shingle-spit below Hurst Castle, my friend and I frightened ourselves with an imagined ghost. Charles I had been imprisoned in the castle before being taken to London and executed. Now, we heard his ghost rustling over the stones behind us. But the cold night air was fresh, a ship with lit portholes passed by the dark shape of the Island, like a greater ship at anchor, and the tide turning moved with an enormous surge of power. In land and sea and sky the presence of the past bears down, yet also, in every crumb of soil and wave and ray of light, and in every individual life, the moment is new.

Following my move to Wales in 1965, distance gave me the perspective upon home ground that enabled me to write the poems in *Solent Shore*. At first, when I was living on the seafront in Aberystwyth, the waters of Cardigan Bay seemed to me peculiarly empty. The broken-off pier, where shags held their wings out to dry like broken umbrellas, was a poor substitute for the docks where great ocean liners had awed me as a boy. Above all, there was no island to check the sight, only an expanse of blue or slate-grey water. When the Welsh sea came alive for me, it was with the loud voices of herring gulls and in storm. Rough seas would throw pebbles from the beach against the boarded-up house fronts and send shocks through the road that made the buildings tremble. I woke one night to find the wardrobe inching across the room towards me, and in the morning found a strand of red algae clinging to a third-storey window at the back of the house, facing away from the sea. But still, looking out across Cardigan Bay, I felt an emptiness, even in the sun-tracks that lay golden blades on the water. Then, one evening, as if by magic, a chain of islands, like the peaks of volcanoes, appeared far out. It was as if an Otherworld had manifested itself. In fact, there was no mystery – these were the mountains of the Llŷn Peninsula, which can be seen from the Ceredigion coast in a certain light.

But mystery is part of the reality of Wales. Strange appearances and disappearances characterize Celtic poetry of land and sea and sky. They come with ancient stories of an Otherworld existing alongside this world, and are born of imagination working upon the history of bloody conflict, and with the natural magic of light and darkness, and mist hiding and revealing mountains and sea. Poems and stories contain rumours of actual events and geological processes. Cardigan Bay has its sunken lands. 'It may be remembered Seithenin and the desolated cantrefs, the sixteen fortified places, the great cry of the sea.' So Lance Corporal Aneirin Merddyn Lewis reflects in David Jones's *In Parenthesis* as he looks around him at the waterlogged landscape of the Western Front. Like David Jones himself, Lewis is a Welshman for whom the present calls up the past, the desolate watery trenches reminding him of the tradition of the dyke-warden whose drunken carelessness resulted in the inundation of the land he was meant to guard. And indeed there is evidence of lost lands in Cardigan Bay, in the stumps of a primeval forest disclosed by the receding tide on the coast above Aberystwyth.

The emptiness I first saw in Wales, in wilder hills than any I had known before, as well as in the sea, was an effect of ignorance. What I learnt to know was a rich cultural landscape, in which the two languages, in tension with one another, make a world with its own distinct identity. Living in Wales, in hill country in view of the sea, renewed my sense of the natural elements and at the same time quickened my sense of cultural differences. I came to understand poetry in David Jones's terms: 'one is trying to make a shape out of the very things of which one is oneself made'.[1] In *Solent Shore* I turned back imaginatively to the south coast. Not to personal experience alone, but to the making of place itself:

From a Pill-Box on the Solent

On a day of ripped cloud,
Angled light, wind against tide,
I am tempted to begin
The story of my life.

Waves come from far off,
Through the gap they have made,
Between Purbeck and Wight.

Surf booms in the pill-box,
Rattles the shingle,
Folds over it, unfolds,
Laying it bare.

Let it blow sand or salt.
Here at least I tread without fear
Of unsettling dust.

Rather than telling a narrow life story, the poem was a grounding of self upon historical and geological elements of place. It embodied a resistance to the spirit of melancholy, to that 'unsettling dust' which in so much English poetry attaches to the word 'home'. It acknowledges conflict – 'wind against tide' – which, in my poem 'Gull on a Post', at first opposes, and finally relates, rootedness to freedom:

Gull on a post firm
In the tideway – how I desire
The gifts of both!

Land and Sea and Sky

Desire against the diktat
Of intellect: be single,
You who are neither.

As the useful one
That marks a channel, marks
Degrees of neap and spring;
Apt to bear jetties
Or serve as a mooring;
Common, staked with its like.

Standing ever
Still in one place,
It has a look of permanence.

Riddled with shipworm,
Bored by the gribble,
In a few years it rots.

Desire which tears at the body
Would fly unconstrained
Inland or seaward; settle
At will – but voicing
Always in her cry
Essence of wind and wave,
Bringing to city, moorish
Pool and ploughland,
Reminders of storm and sea.

Those who likened the soul
To a bird, did they ever
Catch the eye of a gull?

Driven to snatch,
Fight for slops in our wake.

Or voice a desolation
Not meant for us,
Not even desolate,
But which we christen.

Folk accustomed to sin,
Violent, significant death,
Who saw even in harbour
Signs terrible and just,
Heard in their cries
Lost souls of the drowned.

Gull stands on a post
In the tideway; I see

No resolution; only
The necessity of flight
Beyond me, firm
Standing only then.

It has been said that 'life in the depths is war'. And that, perhaps, is a requirement for lyric poetry, the tension that generates it. I think also of Sir Thomas Browne's image of Man as an amphibian who lives between the visible and invisible worlds. At any rate, I feel sure that having been brought up by the marginal sea strongly influenced my sense of life as a liminal situation, tidal in its rhythmic movements, and existing between contraries. I found a distinctive poetry in breakwaters:

> The posts are vaguely human in shape and they stand for a massive effort that is only temporarily effective and has to be renewed over and over again; and at the same time they are completely non-human, insensate, and like a strange thing emerging from the sea. They belong and do not belong, they become part of the sea against which they are a defence, the waters they are meant to break.

Belonging and not belonging: that, perhaps, was what I derived from living by the marginal sea.

Shortly before she died, my mother told me that when she wanted to get to sleep at night she imagined herself walking along the shore, counting the different things she saw there. She too was a child of Solent shore, who had walked on the same shingle – if shifting shingle can ever be said to be the same – as I had walked on. Following her death, the poem I wrote for her – 'Walking to Sleep' – began with a reminiscence of one of the poems she had read to me as a child and which we both loved: Matthew Arnold's 'The Forsaken Merman':

> Hours before you died,
> I read you once more the poem
> you first read to me
> in which the merman mourns
> for his human wife
> who has left the sea
> and will not come away,
> down, down, who will not come away.
>
> Then you, whose life
> had been to care and comfort,
> were walking to sleep –
>   walking
> counting the stones the shells
> dog whelk cuttle bone
> shepherd's crown
> fairy loaves anything
> of interest on the shore
> in sight of the Island
> in sound of the sea.
>
> Walking, walking down
> where, hours before,
> you heard a voice that said
> 'Start again, Start again'.

Words may name but cannot hold what we love, 'any more than shingle keeps/the water that sluices it'. The sea is a good discipline for a poet. The impressions it makes, breaking on shingle, mirroring the sky, dissolve, as language itself breaks, and dissolves, in attempting to hold the real. But the elemental rhythms, though they vary, do not change. The shore is an ancient place where land and sea and sky meet, but its very elusiveness means that it has too, at each moment, a sense of possibility, of new beginning.

Note

[1] Jones, *The Anathemata*, p. 10.

Acknowledgements

Earlier versions of 'Ditch Vision', 'Versions of Freedom', and 'Three "Powys Poems" with a Commentary on Each' first appeared in the *Powys Journal*. 'Richard Jefferies: A Personal Discovery' was published in the *Richard Jefferies Society Journal*. 'Alone in Life: The Friendship of Robert Frost and Edward Thomas' was published in *Dymock Poets and Friends*. 'Reflections on "Ground"', 'Reflections on the Lyric "I"', and 'Revisiting "God's Houses"' appeared in *Scintilla*. 'Reflections on "Ground"' is an expanded version of an essay published in a chapbook, *Free Poetry* (2005), published in the USA by Martin Corless-Smith. 'Alun Lewis: "The Tragic Condition"' was published in *Poetry Wales*. The interview Fiona Owen conducted with me, 'Mystery at the Heart of Things', appeared in *Green Letters*. 'Land and Sea and Sky' was commissioned by and broadcast on BBC Radio 3. With the exception of 'Song of the Ashes', all my poetry quoted in this book appears in two volumes published by Enitharmon Press: *The Cut of the Light: Poems 1965–2005* (2006) and *Scattered Light* (2015). I am grateful to all who encouraged me with the publication or commission of these writings, and especially to Stephen Stuart-Smith of Enitharmon Press, and the late Anne Cluysenaar and the late Peter Thomas, who made *Scintilla*, for me and others, an intellectual lifeline in recent years; and I am grateful to David Tress for permission to use a detail from his beautiful painting as the image on the book cover. My special thanks are due also to Anthony Nanson, whose detailed suggestions enabled me to make improvements to the text. Any remaining error or infelicity is solely my responsibility.

Index

Aberystwyth, 210
Abram, David, 148–9
Ackland, Valentine, 108
Ackroyd, Freda, 83–4, 86
Aldington, Richard, 125
Alexander the Great, 98
aloneness, 55–6, 62
Alpers, Svetlana, 170
America, 3, 53, 65–6, 68, 197
Anglo-Catholicism, 100
animism, 20, 93
anti-Semitism, 101
Aquarian New Age, 45
Arnold, Les, 154–62
　'The Brassrubbing', 155
　'Entries from Mother Ann's Journal', 159
　'The Fell Runner', 156, 158
　'Her Head Turns', 157
　Joy Riding, 156, 161
　'Moving in', 161–2
　'A Poem Like a Lemon', 156, 158
　'Running', 154
　'Sandstone', 156, 158
　Shaker City, 156, 158; 'Shaker City', 158–61
　'Snow', 157
Arnold, Matthew, 150
　'Dover Beach', 209
　'The Forsaken Merman', 215
art of seeing, 9, 126, 138, 167, 180–2, 191, 195–6
Auden, W. H., 5, 10, 85, 107, 129, 150, 205
Austen, Jane, 123

Badbury Rings, 90, 101
Baker, J. A., 78–80
Ballard, J. G., 13
Barle, River, 25–7
Barnes, William, 5, 164
Bate, Jonathan, 205–6

Beat generation, 72, 144, 155, 198
Bellerby, Frances, 107–15
　'Brother and Sister', 113
　'The First-Known', 110–11, 114
　The First-Known and Other Poems, 107–8, 111, 114
　Hath the Rain a Father?, 109, 112
　'The Heron', 112, 114–15
　'In Place', 127–8
　'The Little Lamps', 113
　'On the Third Evening', 108
　Selected Poems, 110–11
　'Soft and Fair', 113
　'Strange Return', 112
　'The Valley', 113
Berdyaev, Nicolas, 36–41, 46–50
　The Divine and the Human, 50, 190
　Slavery and Freedom, 36–9, 46
　Solitude and Society, 47
Berlin, 38
Betjeman, John, 186
Bidgood, Ruth, 202
Black Hawk Island, 139
Black Mountain poetics, 159
Blake, William, 43, 45, 80, 93, 99, 104, 124, 128
Blaser, Robin, 90
Blondel, Natalie, 89, 102
Boehme, Jacob, 40, 181
Bohm, David, 149
Boldre, 208
Brahman, 148
Britain, 66, 197
Brontë, Charlotte, 5
Brownjohn, Alan, 107
Buber, Martin, 167, 174, 197
Buddhism, 143, 145
Bull, Wesson, 90
Bunting, Basil, 107
Bunyan, John, 123
Burlesden Bridge, 208
Butts, Mary, viii, 88–105, 109

Index

Armed with Madness, 97–8, 103–4
Ashe of Rings, 92, 96
'Corfe', 102–3
The Crystal Cabinet, 91, 96, 101
The Death of Felicity Taverner, 99–100
'From Altar to Chimney-Piece', 100
Imaginary Letters, 90
The Macedonian, 98
Scenes from the Life of Cleopatra, 98
Butts, Thomas, 93

California, 69, 72
Canada, 155, 158
Cardigan Bay, 210–11
Carson, Rachel, 201
  Silent Spring, 74
  Under the Sea-Wind, 196
Casey, Gerard, 116, 118, 121, 123, 181
Casey, Mary, 108, 116, 123, 124
Causley, Charles, 107–8, 111
Cerne Abbas, 120, 168, 195
Cézanne, Paul, 140
Channing, Ellery, 19
Chaucer, Geoffrey, 93
Chesil Beach, 117–18
Charles I, 210
Child Okeford, 120
Christ, 43–4, 49–50, 80, 101, 143
Christianity, 44, 46, 49, 143, 150, 186, 190
Chuang Tzu, 143–4, 173
Clare, John, 2, 10, 11, 66–8, 72, 74, 197, 206
  'Emmonsails Heath in Winter', 66–7
  'The Nightingale's Nest', 5–6
Clarke, Gillian, 74–6
  'Birth', 74–5
  'Calf', 76
  'Fox', 75
  'Making the Beds for the Dead', 75
Clodd, Alan, 107–8, 114
Cluysenaar, Anne, 170, 175, 201
Coate, 7, 20, 23–4
Cobbett, William, 2–3
Cocteau, Jean, 88, 90
Cold War, 183
Coleridge, Samuel Taylor, 3–4, 65, 129, 131, 157, 189, 201, 173, 177
Commoner, Barry, 9
Coniston Fells, 4
Conrad, Joseph, 56
Conran, Tony, 198

Constable, John, 17
Conte, Joseph M., 148
Coomaraswamy, Ananda, 41
Corfe, 102
Cotswold, 131, 155, 157–8
Coupe, Lawrence, 203
Cowper, William, 45
Creation, 40, 138–9
Creeley, Robert, 125
Crimean War, 89
Crowley, Aleister, 88–9

daffodils, 68–9, 124
Darbishire, Helen, 4
Darwin, Charles, 80, 180, 190
Darwish, Mahmoud, 175
Davie, Donald, 165
de la Mare, Walter, 59
Delphi, 92, 102
De Quincey, Thomas, 4, 68
Derbyshire, 12
Derry (New Hampshire), 58, 61
Devon, 78
Dickinson, Emily, 134–6, 140, 151, 168
ditch vision, viii, 1, 6, 9, 14, 66, 80, 190, 196
Dogen, 146
Dorset, 5, 9, 88, 99, 102, 104, 116, 120, 122, 164, 197
Dostoievsky, Fyodor, 38, 46
'The Dream of the Rood', 101
Duncan, Robert, 90
Dungeness, 13
Dunkirk, 83

earthworm, 180
Edwards, Colin, 160
Egypt, 99
Eleusis, 92
Elijah, 143
Eliot, George, 3
Eliot, T. S., 89, 97, 103, 145, 150, 176, 183
  Four Quartets, 105
  The Waste Land, 97, 164
Emerson, Ralph Waldo, 58, 60, 64–6, 71
Emmonsails Heath, 66–7, 76
Enclosures, 67
England, 1–3, 53, 64–5, 68, 71, 76, 95, 99, 104, 200; southern, 116, 158, 163, 173–5, 182, 195; wild, 6–7, 24, 30, 78–9, 190

Enitharmon Press, 107
Essex, 78
Evans, Paul, 185
'extremity', 33–4

Farjeon, Eleanor, 54, 69
Fitzgerald, F. Scott, 65–6
First World War, 71, 88, 96–7
Fisher, Roy, 107, 129
Ford, Ford Madox, 88
Forster, E. M., 105
Franciscan poetry, 137–8, 180–1
Francis of Assisi, St, 119, 137
Frazer, Sir James, 93, 97
Fredman, Stephen, 184
Frost, Robert, vii, 52–62, 135
   'After Apple-Picking', 58
   'Bereft', 55
   A Boy's Will, 58, 61
   'The Fear', 58
   'Home Burial', 55, 57
   'The Mountain', 58
   Mountain Interval, 58
   'Mowing', 61
   New Hampshire, 54
   North of Boston, 52, 56–8, 61
   'To E. T.', 54

Gill, Eric, 41
Ginsberg, Allen, 144
Gittings, Robert, 110–11
Gloucestershire, 132, 155
God, 39–40, 42–5, 47, 80, 109, 143, 146–50, 176, 187
Golden Age, 5
Grace Dieu, 208
Grail Quest, 97
Grandjean, Lee, 168–9, 205
Green, Bernard, 149
Grigson, Geoffrey, 10–11
   'To Wystan Auden', 5
   The Freedom of the Parish, 11
'ground', viii, 163–6, 171, 182, 195, 199–200, 202
'groundlessness', 40, 171, 199–200
gull, 212–14
Gurney, Ivor, 130, 157, 167, 131–2
Gwenallt, 165, 198, 184

Hambledon Hill, 120, 197
Hampshire, 18, 60, 69, 82, 164, 195
Hardy, Thomas, 27, 45, 59, 78, 88, 104, 108, 116, 137, 139, 144, 164, 167, 181, 183, 185–6, 196, 201
   'An August Midnight', 137–8
   'The Convergence of the Twain', 208–9
   Jude the Obscure, 138
   The Mayor of Casterbridge, 3
   The Return of the Native, 9, 67, 104
   'The Self-Seeing', 111
Harrison, Jane Ellen, 93
Hatlen, Burton, 184
Hay, David, 176
hawkmoth, 77–8
Hawthorne, Nathaniel, 1–2, 14, 65
Hazlitt, William, 69, 80
Hepworth, Barbara, 168
Herbert, George, 155
Higginson, Thomas Wentworth, 134
Hill, Geoffrey, 129, 186
Hitler, Adolf, 10, 46, 129
hiraeth, 175, 182
Hobson, J. A., 104
Hood, HMS, 189, 208
Hooker, Jeremy
   Adamah, 171, 201
   'And Shall the Spring Be Desolate?', 183
   'At the Edge', 126, 171
   'Boldre Church Revisited', 189
   'Brother Worm', 180, 190
   'Cathedral', 187, 190
   'At Coate Water', 17
   The Cut of the Light, 205
   Daring the Depths, 180, 202
   'Easter at White Noise', 119–20
   'Eglwys Hywen Sant, Aberdaron', 187
   The Elements, 118
   father of, 17, 25, 167, 169, 189, 194
   'From a Pill-Box on the Solent', 212
   'God's Houses', 123, 180, 182, 187–9, 192
   'Groundless She Walks', 150–1
   Groundwork, 168
   'Gull on a Post', 212–14
   'Kilpeck', 188–9
   'Like Thistledown', 181
   Master of the Leaping Figures, 166
   mother of, 17, 163, 182, 195, 215
   'Nobbut Dick Jefferies', 32–3
   'A Poem Like a Place', 166
   Poetry of Place, vii

Index

'Salisbury Cathedral', 190–1
'Saltgrass Lane', 178–9
Scattered Light, 123, 180, 182, 192
'Seven Songs', 171, 200–1
Solent Shore, 165, 178, 210, 212
Soliloquies of a Chalk Giant, 120, 195
'Song of the Ashes', 117–18
'St Bride's, Llansantffraed', 191–2
'St Faith's, Little Witchingham', 188
'St Mark's, Pennington', 185
'St Peter and St Paul, Mappowder', 121–3
Their Silence a Language, 126, 168, 171
'An Unfinished Portrait', 181
'Walking to Sleep', 215
Welsh Journal, 168, 204
Writers in a Landscape, vii, 30, 34
Hooker, Joseph Llewelyn, 120
Hopkins, Gerard Manley, 5, 9, 11, 27, 78, 80, 147, 196
Hudson, W. H., 20–1
Hughes, Ted, 71, 76, 78, 80, 107, 157
Hulme, T. E., 21
Humphreys, Emyr, 199
Hurst Castle, 210

Imagism, 27, 125, 139, 167, 176, 181, 183
Inanimate, 44
Incarnation, 109, 143
India, 83–4
inhumanism, 1, 71
inscape, 11, 142

Japan, 144
Jarman, Derek, 13–14
Jefferies, Richard, vii–viii, 1, 5, 9–10, 12, 14–5, 17–35, 60, 77, 79, 130, 148, 150, 164, 166–7, 176, 190–1, 196
  After London, 6
  The Amateur Poacher, 8, 21
  Bevis, 29–32
  The Dewy Morn, 31
  'Hours of Spring', 17, 23
  Jefferies' England, 18, 194
  'Meadow Thoughts', 18–25
  'Nature and Books', 173
  'Nature in the Louvre', 18
  The Old House at Coate, 24, 29
  'Out of Doors in February', 31
  'The Pageant of Summer', 6–8, 24, 66, 190, 196
  The Story of My Heart, 8, 21–2, 28, 31, 33–5
  'Summer in Somerset', 25–6
  'The Sun and the Brook', 29
  'Wild Flowers', 27–8, 33
  Wild Life in a Southern County, 20–1, 183
Jeffers, Robinson, vii, 1, 68–9, 71–2, 76–7, 79–80
  'Birds and Fishes', 72
  'Subjected Earth', 64
Jennings, Elizabeth, 108, 150
Job, 72
John, St, 44, 47
Johnson, Samuel, 1
Jones, David, 41, 101, 135, 140, 145, 150, 170, 189, 199, 201, 212
  The Anathemata, 138–9, 165, 176, 182
  In Parenthesis, 211
Julian of Norwich, 142

Kavanagh, Patrick, 200
Keats, John, 74, 80, 123, 133, 150, 175–6, 204
Keith, W. J., 19
Kenya, 116
Kerouac, Jack, 144
Kierkegaard, Søren, 147
Kiev, 36
Kilpeck, 188–9
Kipling, Rudyard, 59
Klimek, Ray, 173
Knight, Wilson, 118
Kopland, Rutger, 169–70
Krasner, James, 25
Ktaadn, Mount, 145

Lake District, 1
Lame Deer, 151
landscape painting, 17, 167
Larkin, Philip, 186
Laureata, 163–4
Lawrence, D. H., 71, 103, 177
Lear, Linda, 196
Lee, Ann, 158–9
Leopold, Aldo, 66
Lewis, Alun, 82–7
  'All Day It Has Rained', 82
  'The Jungle', 84–6
  'Last Pages of a Long Journal', 86
  'The Orange Grove', 84–6

'The Soldier', 83
'They Came', 83
'To Edward Thomas', 85
Lewis, C. S., 49
Lewis, Wyndham, 88, 133
liminal ontology, 135
Llŷn Peninsula, 211
logos spermatikos, 133
London, 12, 19, 23, 88–9, 165
Longmor, 82
Looker, Samuel J., 18–19
Lymington River, 209
Lyrical Ballads, 3, 7, 129, 131, 133, 138, 167, 180

Mabey, Richard, 12
   Country Matters, 13
   Nature Cure, 197
   The Unofficial Countryside, 12–13
Maitland, Cecil, 89
mana, 93
Mandelstam, Osip, 125
Mappowder, 116, 121–3
Maritain, Jacques, 41, 49, 140–1, 176, 204
Marxism, 37
Mary, Virgin, 143
'mastery', 170, 201
Mathias, Roland, 199
Matthias, John, 165
McFague, Sallie, 136
McKibben, Bill, 1, 15
Merleau-Ponty, Maurice, 34–5
Merton, Thomas, 143–4
Metaphysical poetry, 126
Milosz, Czeslaw, 174, 176
modernism, 27, 125, 164, 167
Moore, Henry, 105, 168
'mosaic', 167
Moses, 143
Muir, John, 73
Mulford, Wendy, 142–3, 201
Myrddin Wyllt, 45, 49

Nash, Paul, 105
Native Americans, 73, 145, 197
negative capability, 123, 150, 176
The Netherlands, 169–70
New Forest, 194, 207–8
New Hampshire, 69
Newman, Cardinal, 186
Niebuhr, Reinhold, 49

Niedecker, Lorine, 124, 147–8, 201
   'Darwin', 139
   'My Life by Water', 139
   'Paean to Place', 148
   'Traces of Living Things, 139–40
Nietzsche, Friedrich, 48, 98
Nodens, 99

Objectivism, 139–40, 167, 176–7, 180, 184–5, 204
Oelschlaeger, Max, 197
Olson, Charles, 66, 125, 184–5
Ong, Walter, J., 134, 137, 149
Oppen, George, 159, 167, 177, 184
   The Materials, 141, 204
   'Sara in Her Father's Arms', 141
   'World, World –', 185
organic community, 10
Original Sin, 47
Orthodox Church, 37, 125
Orwell, George, 85
otherness, 174
Otherworld, 211
Ovid Press, 89
Owen, Wilfred, 60
Oxfordshire, 64, 67, 76–7

Pacific Ocean, 66, 72
Palmer, Samuel, 10
Paris, 38, 88
Parkstone, 88–9
Pascal, Blaise, 147
Pasternak, Boris, 150
Paul, St, 43–4, 47, 112
Pelagius, 45
Pelynt, 10
peregrine, 78–9
'perfection', 111–13, 127–8
Perrin, Jim, 11–12
personalism, 38
Peter, St, 133
Plath, Sylvia, 107
Plush, 116
Pollock, Jackson, 178
Poole Harbour, 91
Pope, Alexander, 163
Pound, Ezra, 88–9, 125, 133, 183
   The Cantos, 164
   'In a Station of the Metro', 176
Powys, C. F., 41
Powys, John Cowper, viii, 36, 40–50, 104, 116–20, 123, 199, 201

Index

Autobiography, 9, 118
The Complex Vision, 42–3
Dostoievsky, 46
A Glastonbury Romance, 42–3, 46, 49
The Meaning of Culture, 44
The Menace of German Culture, 42
Mortal Strife, 39, 43–6
A Philosophy of Solitude, 44, 50
The Pleasures of Literature, 43
Porius, 36, 45, 49
Rabelais, 46, 49
Wolf Solent, 45
Wood and Stone, 42
Powys, Llewelyn, 119–20
   Advice to a Young Poet, 116
Powys, Theodore, 116, 121–3
   Soliloquies of a Hermit, 123
praise poetry, 139
prana, 148, 150
Prickett, Stephen, 143
primitivism, 72
prose poetry, 19, 22, 27

Rabelais, François, 49
Rackham, Oliver, 2
Raine, Kathleen, 107–8, 150
religious poetry, 128, 202
resistance, poetics of, 184
Reznikoff, Charles, 167
Richardson, Dorothy, 89, 201
Ridler, Anne, 108
Riley, John, 125–6
Rilke, Rainer Maria, 85
Roberts, Richard Ellis, 101
Rodker, John, 89
Romanticism, 21–2, 29, 56, 69, 80, 145, 167
Rossabi, Andrew, 31
Rueckert, William, 9
Ruskin, John, 27, 130, 139, 167, 196
   Modern Painters, 9, 129
   The Queen of the Air, 148

Salt, H. S., 19
Salterns, 89, 91–3, 95–6, 99
San Francisco, 90
Scintilla, 201–2
Scovell, E. J., 108
'The Sea Farer', 210
Second World War, 45, 183, 199
Selborne, 2, 11, 66, 82
self-consciousness, 54–5, 82–3, 87

Sennen Cove, 90
Shakers, 156, 158–9
Shakespeare, William, 80, 210
   King Lear, 67
   The Merchant of Venice, 72
Sicily, 89
Silesius, Angelus, 40
Simms, Colin, 11–12
Snyder, Gary, 68, 72–4, 76, 144–7, 157, 196–7
   'Burning the Small Dead', 72–3
   'Front Lines', 74
   'Piute Creek', 144–5
   The Practice of the Wild, 144
   Turtle Island, 74
social mysticism, 10, 12
Solent, 164, 207, 209, 215
Sooley, Howard, 13
Southampton, 207–8
South Country, 60–1, 95, 121
Southey, Robert, 186
Soviet Union, 37
speaking for nature, 203
'spirit', 47, 134
Stalin, Joseph, 47, 129
Steep, 82
Stein, Gertrude, 100

Tao, 25; Taoism, 143
Taplin, Kim, 201
   The Harbour Wall, 76
   'This year, next year', 76–8
Tarlo, Harriet, 11
Tchehov, Anton, 113
temenos, 92
Tennyson, Alfred Lord, 164, 209
   'Break, Break, Break', 163, 186
   'Crossing the Bar', 209–10
   'The Brook', 163
   'The Two Voices', 21
Thomas, Edward, vii–viii, 4, 5, 9–10, 12, 52–7, 59–62, 82–3, 87, 105, 108, 130, 164, 167, 183
   'Aspens', 61–2, 69–70
   'As the team's head brass', 60
   'But These Things Also', 130–1
   The Country, 56
   'Lights Out', 55
   'March', 62
   'March the Third', 62
   'The Other', 55
   'A Private', 60

Richard Jefferies, 54
The South Country, 10, 55
'This England', 52
'Two Houses', 59, 61
'The Unknown Bird', 61
Walter Pater, 56
'Wind and Mist', 53
'The Word', 62
'Words', 61
Thomas, Ivor, 161
Thomas, R. S., 137, 149, 168, 187
   'The Bright Field', 128
   'Tell Us', 146–7
'Thomas the Rhymer', 93
Thomson, Virgil, 89
Thoreau, Henry David, 19, 65–6, 73, 145, 196
Titanic, RMS, 208
Tolstoy, Leo, 38, 85
Traherne, Thomas, 10, 126–8, 170
Transcendentalism, 58, 65, 180
Tress, David, 187
Trilling, Lionel, 135
Triskel Poets, 118

Ungrund, 40
United States, 73–4. *See also* America
Upanishads, 148

Van Gogh, Vincent, 34
Vaughan, Henry, 108–9, 126, 169–70, 191–2
Vaughan, Thomas, 191–2
veery, 140
Vermeer, Johannes, 170
Victorian poetry, 19, 27, 164
'vision', 124–31

Wales, 165, 182, 195, 198–200, 204, 210–11; North, 11; South, 85, 173, 175
Warner, Sylvia Townsend, 108
Warsash, 199, 207
Waste Land, 97, 104
Watts, Alan, 25
Watts, Isaac, 186, 209
Weaver, Mike, 156
Wei T'ai, 182
Welsh, Andrew, 176
Welsh poetry, 75, 166, 184; in translation, 165, 198
Wessex, 9, 88, 104, 116

West Coast (America), 73, 145
West Country, 108
Weston, Jesse L., 97
Wheelwright, Philip, 135, 170
White, Gilbert, 1–2, 7, 10–12, 66, 78, 80, 82
Whitman, Walt, 10, 71, 128, 205
White, Lynn, Jr, 137
White Nose, 120
Wight, Isle of, 164, 207, 209–10
wilderness, 1, 3, 14, 65–6, 68–9, 73–4, 145
wildness, 3–4, 65, 78
Williams, Charles, 100
Williams, Rowan, 143
Williams, Waldo, 165, 184
Williams, William Carlos, 155–6, 158, 167, 179, 181, 196, 200
Williamson, Henry, 9, 79
Williamson, Hugh Ross, 103
Wiltshire, 60, 164, 195
Winchester Downs, 60; School of Art, 168
windhover, 80
women poets, 74–5, 107, 141, 150
Wood, Christopher, 95, 99, 105
Woolf, Virginia, 105, 201
Wordsworth, Andrew, 120
Wordsworth, Dorothy, 3–4, 7, 12, 27, 68–9, 77–8, 80, 167, 196
   Alfoxden Journal, 4
   The Grasmere Journals, 4
Wordsworth, William, 3–4, 22, 58, 65, 68–9, 124–5, 135, 149–50, 157, 167, 175–7, 204
   'Essay on Epitaphs', 183
   The Excursion, 69
   'Lines Written a Few Miles Above Tintern Abbey', 4
   poems in *Lyrical Ballads*, 129, 131
   preface to *Lyrical Ballads*, 133
Wright, Patrick, 101
writing in pictures, 27, 34
Wuthering Heights, 5

Yeats, W. B., 85, 128–9
Yorkshire, 78

Zaehner, R. C., 148, 150
Zen Buddhism, 72, 124–5, 144
Zola, Émile, 86

www.awenpublications.co.uk

Also available from Awen Publications:

A Dance with Hermes
Lindsay Clarke

In a verse sequence that swoops between wit and ancient wisdom, between the mystical and the mischievous, award-winning novelist Lindsay Clarke elucidates the trickster nature of Hermes, the messenger god of imagination, language, dreams, travel, theft, tweets, and trading floors, who is also the presiding deity of alchemy and the guide of souls into the otherworld. Taking a fresh look at some classical myths, this vivacious dance with Hermes choreographs ways in which, as an archetype of the poetic basis of mind, the sometimes disreputable god remains as provocative as ever in a world that worries – among other things – about losing its iPhone, what happens after death, online scams, and the perplexing condition of its soul.

'Lindsay Clarke's poems wonderfully embody what they describe: the god Hermes, who is comprehensively shown to be just as revelatory and double-dealing in the digital age as he ever was in antiquity.' *Patrick Harpur*

Poetry/Mythology ISBN 978-1906900-43-4 £10.00

Crackle of Almonds: selected poems
Gabriel Bradford Millar

In these renegade poems ranging from 1958 to 2011 Gabriel Bradford Millar presents a spectrum of life, in all its piquant poignancy, with unfaltering precision, defiance, and finesse. From the very first to the very last, the breathtaking skill of this consummate wordsmith does not waver. Many of the poems linger in the air – not least because Millar performs them orally with such verve. She believes 'that poems, like love-talk, should go from mouth to ear without any paper in between'. On the page their orality and aurality fragrance their presence without diminishing their literary elegance. Continually astonishing, these epicurean poems not only offer a lasting testimony to a 'life well-lived', but inspire the reader to live well too

'She does not just write *about* the world; she dips her syllables in the bitter sweet of its "gazpacho". She thinks melodically.' *Paul Matthews*

Poetry ISBN 978-1-906900-29-8 £9.99

Places of Truth: journeys into sacred wilderness
Jay Ramsay

Poet and psychotherapist Jay Ramsay has been drawn to wild places all his writing life, in search of a particular deep listening experience. 'Trwyn Meditations', a sequence set in Snowdonia, begins this 24-year odyssey. 'By the Shores of Loch Awe' takes us to the fecund wilds of Scotland. 'The Oak' celebrates an ancient tree in the heart of the Cotswolds. 'The Sacred Way' is an evocation of Pilgrim Britain. 'Culbone' records the hidden history of the smallest parish church in England in a steep North Somerset valley near where Coleridge wrote 'Kubla Khan'. The final sequences, 'The Mountain' and 'Sinai', takes us beyond, in all senses, touching the places where we find I and Self.

'Here is a poet who dares the big picture, writing unequivocally from the soul to the soul.' Alan Rycroft, *Caduceus*

Poetry ISBN 978-1-906900-40-3 £12.00 Spirit of Place Volume 4

Soul of the Earth: the Awen anthology of eco-spiritual poetry
edited by Jay Ramsay

Beautifully crafted, yet challenging received wisdom and pushing boundaries, these are cutting-edge poems from a new generation of writers who share a love of the Earth and haven't given up on humans either. In poems as light as a butterfly and as wild as a storm you'll find vivid, contemporary voices that dare to explore a spiritual dimension to life on Earth and, in doing so, imply that a way out of our global crisis of ecological catastrophe, financial meltdown, and bankruptcy of the spirit is to look beyond the impasse of materialism. With contributions from poets in the USA, Canada, UK, Australia, and New Zealand, this anthology reaches out across the planet to embrace the challenges and blessings of being alive on the Earth in the twenty-first century.

'All real poetry seeks to "renew the face of the earth" – and so to resist the exploiting, banalization or defacing of what lies around us. I hope this collection will serve the renewal of vision we so badly need.'
Most Revd Dr Rowan Williams

Poetry ISBN 978-1-906900-17-5 £12.00

Glossing the Spoils
Charlotte Hussey

Each poem in *Glossing the Spoils* works like an intricate time-travel machine, carrying the reader back to the beginnings of Western European literature. Like an ancient clapper bridge with its unmortared slabs of flat sandstone, these poems step us across the choppy currents of the past 1500 years. Anchored at one end in the deep past and at the other in the turbulent present, they explore interconnections between historical, personal, psychological, and mythic states. Plundering their opening passages from such early texts as *Beowulf*, *The Mabinogion*, and *The Tain*, these glosas address eternal themes of love and war and give voice to the surreal potency of the Western European imagination.

'The author is not only a gifted poet, but also well versed in Celtic mythology. She writes from a spiritual perspective that brings these ancient stories alive and relevant to our world today.' *Abena*

Poetry ISBN 978-1-906900-52-6 £8.99

Words of Re-enchantment: writings on storytelling, myth, and ecological desire
Anthony Nanson

The time-honoured art of storytelling – ancestor of all narrative media – is finding new pathways of relevance in education, consciousness-raising, and the journey of transformation. Storytellers are reinterpreting ancient myths and communicating the new stories we need in our challenging times. This book brings together the best of Anthony Nanson's incisive writings about the ways that story can re-enchant our lives and the world we live in. Grounded in his practice as a storyteller, the essays range from the myths of Arthur, Arcadia, and the voyage west, to true tales of the past, science-fiction visions of the future, and the big questions of politics and spirituality such stories raise. The book contains full texts of exemplar stories and will stimulate the thinking of anyone interested in storytelling or in the use of myth in fiction and film.

'This excellent book is written with a storyteller's cadence and understanding of language. Passionate, fascinating and wise.' *Hamish Fyfe*

Storytelling/Mythology/Environment ISBN 978-1-906900-15-1 £9.99

The Long Woman
Kevan Manwaring

An antiquarian's widow discovers her husband's lost journals and sets out on a journey of remembrance across 1920s England and France, retracing his steps in search of healing and independence. Along alignments of place and memory she meets mystic Dion Fortune, ley-line pioneer Alfred Watkins, and a Sir Arthur Conan Doyle obsessed with the Cottingley Fairies. From Glastonbury to Carnac, she visits the ancient sites that obsessed her husband and, tested by both earthly and unearthly forces, she discovers a power within herself.

Fiction ISBN 978-1-906900-44-1 £9.99
The Windsmith Elegy Volume 1

Iona
Mary Palmer

What do you do when you are torn apart by your 'selves'? The pilgrim poet, rebel Mordec and tweedy Aelia set sail for Iona – a thin place, an island on the edge. It's a journey between worlds, back to the roots of their culture. On the Height of Storm they relive a Viking massacre, at Port of the Coracle encounter vipers. They meet Morrighan, a bloodthirsty goddess, and Abbot Dominic with his concubine nuns. There are omens, chants, curses ... During her stay Mordec learns that words can heal or destroy, and the poet writes her way out of darkness. A powerful story, celebrating a journey to wholeness, from an accomplished poet.

Poetry ISBN 978-0-9546137-8-5 £6.99
Spirit of Place Volume 1

The Fifth Quarter
Richard Selby

The Fifth Quarter is Romney Marsh, as defined by the Revd Richard Harris Barham in *The Ingoldsby Legends*: 'The World, according to the best geographers, is divided into Europe, Asia, Africa, America and Romney Marsh.' It is a place apart, almost another world. This collection of stories and poems explores its ancient and modern landscapes, wonders at its past, and reflects upon its present. Richard Selby has known Romney Marsh all his life. His writing reflects the uniqueness of The Marsh through prose, poetry, and written versions of stories he performs as a storyteller.

Fiction/Poetry ISBN 978-0-9546137-9-2 £9.99 Spirit of Place Volume 2